In the SMALL KITCHEN

In the SMALL KITCHEN

100 Recipes from Our Year of Cooking in the Real World

Cara Eisenpress and Phoebe Lapine

Photography by Josh Shaub with images by
Allison Badea, Alexander Solounias,
Jonathan Meter, and the Quarter-Life Cooks

WM
WILLIAM MORROW
An Imprint of HarperCollinsPublishers

HarperCollins books may be purchased for educational, business, or sales promotional use. For information please write: Special Markets Department, HarperCollins Publishers, 10 East 53rd Street, New York, NY 10022.

Designed by Ashley Halsey

Library of Congress Cataloging-in-Publication Data

Eisenpress, Cara.
  In the small kitchen: 100 recipes from our year of cooking in the real world / Cara Eisenpress, Phoebe Lapine.—1st ed.
    p.   cm.
  ISBN 978-0-06-199824-9 (pbk.)
  1. Cooking. 2. Cookbooks. I. Lapine, Phoebe. II. Title.
TX714.E375 2011
641.5—dc22   2010049642

11   12   13   14   15   ID/QGT   10   9   8   7   6   5   4   3   2

To our families, who fed us at their tables long before we invited anyone to sit at ours

CONTENTS

FOREWORD

Forget the small kitchen—I want to work my way through this wonderful cookbook. I've adored Phoebe Lapine for her entire life, and through her, I've come to know the fabulous Cara Eisenpress. Of course, I knew they were smart and beautiful, but I would never have imagined that two young women fresh out of college could emerge from their shells as fully formed cookbook writers. They cook and write with an ease and a voice that took me a decade of writing cookbooks to develop.

I love *In the Small Kitchen* so much. It's packed with brilliant advice and delicious recipes for anyone who wants to cook and entertain—no matter what size your kitchen. If you think you don't have the time, the kitchen space, or the budget to entertain, think again. Cara and Phoebe show you how to do it. This book is for young people trying to make good food for themselves, or for anyone trying to get a special dinner on the table for friends. It's such fun to read and is filled with Phoebe's and Cara's personal experiences, from their disasters—why no one needs to make Manchurian Cauliflower ever again—to their triumphs—I loved their oatmeal chocolate chip cookie competition. They've written a book filled with outstanding recipes, dating anecdotes, and great entertaining advice that all of us can relate to, no matter how small our kitchen.

In the Small Kitchen is organized by reasons to cook—home alone and hungry, a romantic dinner for two, a weekend brunch, and easy dinner parties. Dishes range from earthy to elegant and everything in between. But most of all, Phoebe and Cara are absolutely right when it comes to their cooking philosophy: getting into the habit of cooking makes your kitchen a place that everyone wants to be. And that alone is the reason everyone needs this book, including me!

Ina Garten
Barefoot Contessa

INTRODUCTION

veto power

In November 2009, we fried our last batch of Manchurian Cauliflower.

Jordana is our best friend from high school, and Manchurian Cauliflower is one of her favorite things to eat. It is a transcendent dish: light, crispy cauliflower coated in a spicy and tangy tomato sauce, which gets stuck in the crevices of every last crunchy floret. Though it's immensely lovable, we've come to regret its position as one of our signature dishes and wish our friends would forget its existence completely. For a crowd of fifty, making Manchurian Cauliflower involves mincing whole heads of garlic. Worse, it involves deep-frying cups and cups of cauliflower florets to order.

We made it for the first time at Jordana's twenty-fourth birthday party because we didn't know about the hassle. We didn't yet have the experience to envision how long we'd be standing in the kitchen, chopping, frying, and plating the goddamn cauliflower. We also didn't know it would be such a hit. So when we cooked for Jordana's twenty-fifth birthday, it ended up on the finger food menu again. But as we were halfway through frying the third batch that night, guests began to arrive, and we abandoned all unfried cauliflower in a colander, turned off the burner under the oil, and called it a day. By that point, we understood that there were more important things than slaving away at the stove to achieve restaurant-quality food. It was our best friend's birthday, there were piles of summer rolls and saucy meatballs to be eaten, and we no longer wanted to be behind the scenes in the kitchen.

It's within the window of that year, between those two batches of cauliflower, that most of this book takes place.

As time has passed and we've logged more hours in the kitchen, we've gotten better at knowing what kinds of dishes aren't so conducive to feeding crowds of fifty. We've gained enough authority to choose what gets set down on the table. We will not be making Manchurian Cauliflower for Jordana's twenty-sixth birthday. We will refer to it a lot, but there will be no recipe for Manchurian Cauliflower in this book. The dish may mark the beginning and end of our story here, but we say no to Manchurian Cauliflower. After all, a party is only as fun as its least happy guests, and we will continue to say no to all fussy dishes that make those least happy, frizzy-haired, sauce-covered guests *us.*

from entry-level grown-ups to "big girls"

It took us a long time to earn enough veto power to say no to a vegetable. Like most kids, we started out with menial kitchen jobs, setting the table for dinner or adding chocolate chips to cookie dough. Despite this early training, we pursued non-food-related corporate careers when we graduated from college in 2007 and moved back to New York City, our hometown. Cara got the editorial assistant position she thought she had always wanted at a great publishing house; Phoebe accepted a job she was pretty sure she had never wanted, doing marketing for a beauty company. Jobs led to apartments and to our very own kitchens. In September 2007, Cara moved into an East Village converted three bedroom with Lisa, her college roommate, and Jordana, of birthday fame. Five months later, Phoebe moved out of her parents' place into a two-bedroom walk-up near Union Square with her friend from college, Caitlyn. That fall, Cara moved to her second apartment, a studio in Brooklyn, which she vastly preferred. In our new places, we really felt like adults. Even though we missed the daily proximity to friends we'd had in college and mourned the loss of summer vacation, we were happy to be on our own.

However, jobs and apartments don't make a life. We also had to eat. Using those kitchens for feeding ourselves and cooking for our friends rounded out our post-college existence. On Monday mornings, while the rest of the world slept off their dread of work, Cara could be found making Spinach Pie Quesadilla (page 30) in utter silence, so as not to wake up her roommates. On Tuesday nights, Phoebe was probably running home to scramble together a fish taco buffet (page 194) dinner for ten college friends. On Wednesdays, Cara sometimes made late-night Saucy Tomato Orecchiette (page 56) when she and her roommates needed food to absorb the few drinks they'd enjoyed earlier. On Thursdays, Phoebe might be transforming leftover dip into Black Bean Bites (page 266). On Fridays, Cara packed Soy-Honey Baked Tofu (page 76) and Phoebe loaded Roasted Butternut Squash (page 102) into plastic containers to bring to a potluck with high school friends.

Whatever the ritual, it became clear that feeding ourselves and others was important. We started our blog, *Big Girls, Small Kitchen*, to figure out exactly *how* food was important to us. Our first post was published in November 2008, with a photo gallery of Jordana's twenty-fourth birthday party, including the cauliflower. We posted more blog entries, and we cooked and hosted more parties. We read food blogs and wrote new recipes and ate. A year passed. And somewhere in the passing days and nights we honed a cooking philosophy that we now believe in like dogma.

the dogma

As cooks of limited resources, we constantly perform balancing acts. Whether we're pressed for space, time, or money, or challenged by dietary preference or perceived skill, we find ourselves carefully weighing demands against desires, the reality of our pantries against the whims of our taste buds. Of course, recipes and menus exist in conjunction with the rest of our lives—the hours we spend outside of the kitchen, the market, and our "dining room"—and we have to balance all that, too.

Equilibrium is the most important term for approaching your kitchen. Assess how much attention, skill, or money you're willing to invest in one dish, and then rely on simplicity to fill in the rest of the meal. When we go to potlucks, we weigh novelty against portability and shelf life. When we cook for a friend's birthday party, we obsess over the deliciousness of a dish but still factor in the number of guests, apartment layout, and host's preferences. When we cook for just ourselves, we mix inexpensive staples and fresh, healthy produce from the organic bin or the farmers' market. When time runs low, we open a can of beans. When money runs low, we buy 33-cents-per-pound dried beans and cook them from scratch. When all seems lost, we hope friends will arrive with many bottles of wine. And when we need a break from everything, we let our bodies rest and turn off our phones—if only, perhaps, to turn them on again and order Chinese takeout.

a cookie rivalry

As for us, we go back a long way, and everything in this book is a product of our friendship. Though countless cloves of garlic have been peeled and minced for our dishes, and many pots and pans have been purchased and subsequently scorched beyond recognition, what unifies the output of our kitchens more than any ingredient or technique is thirteen years of cooking and eating together. We did not meet in cooking school or while salivating over foie gras at a restaurant table, and there was no one moment when we looked at each other and knew for certain that our future held a food blog. We just ended up at the same middle school in 1997 and, against the backdrop of Hanson, 'N Sync, the Spice Girls, and kids wearing cargo pants and platform sneakers, we became friends.

But that doesn't mean that our relationship didn't touch on food from the beginning. We played field hockey together in high school, along with several of our best friends, and, especially after games, we were girls who could eat. We held celebratory potlucks on the field after victories, all of us inhaling hummus, baked tofu, and cookie cake. The cookie cake, made by Cara's sister Kate, was usually decorated with chocolate chips spelling out phrases like "Go Fieldston" or "Happy Birthday Phoebe!"

As city kids, we also ate out a lot, but our favorite food-related sessions were when we cooked together. We did this during free periods from school and after classes, instead of going to the park and smoking cigarettes like normal teenagers. If it was the evening, we'd gab away with Cara's sisters around the kitchen island while her mother's electric mixer creamed the butter and sugar—a fact Phoebe, who'd grown up without a mixer, found borderline appalling.

Oatmeal chocolate chip cookies eventually became our friendship's major point of contention and connection. Cara's recipe used more oats than flour, plus some cinnamon, and of course it was made with the mixer. Phoebe simply added oats to an existing chocolate chip cookie recipe, and she creamed her butter by hand. We used to make our friends taste-test, but beneath the competition, these cookies brought us together.

After graduating college, as we adjusted to our sort-of grown-up lives, we began relying on each other more and more for cooking advice. Even when we weren't making meals in the same small space, we found ourselves with cell phone in one hand, spatula in the other, discussing what the heck to do with celeriac, if three pounds of chicken could be stretched to feed ten mouths, and who would be joining us around our table. We started the blog when we realized that these joint food-life conversations were some of the most fun ones we had ever had.

Even though the East River may separate our kitchens, the memories of the cookies that started it all remind us that we continue to share the love of chocolate, cooking, and each other, for thirteen years and counting.

a year in our kitchens

This book is a collection of kitchen tools, useful tricks we've picked up, recipes, dating anecdotes, nostalgia for childhood, and the recounting of many, many meals. If you read it straight through, you'll discover a trajectory as we grow from the newbies we were even a year out of college to the slightly more able humans we are today. We hope you will find our struggles, setbacks, and small victories encouraging, entertaining, and in large part endearing.

The book takes you through our "sophomore year" in the real world, from fall 2008 to fall 2009. Since the events that played out over the course of this year had their beginnings long before, we couldn't resist reminiscing about the past too, from childhood birthday cakes to college dining hall woes.

In addition to our stories, this cookbook contains over a hundred recipes, intended both for quarter-lifers making first meals in first kitchens and for those, like us, with slightly more experience. Organized by reasons to cook—for one person, for brunch, for dinner parties, and for fun—it is full of good food for the hungry reader to feast on. The dishes go from humble to refined, and we've devoted our days and nights to making sure that these recipes, unlike the Manchurian Cauliflower, are the most useful, tasty, fulfilling, and stress-free ones we have to offer. There are meals for all occasions, and at the end of the book, there's a year's worth of menu suggestions, for real and made-up holidays alike.

Last but not least, this is a guide to getting in the habit of cooking for yourself and for others; of making your kitchen a place where you want to be; of making your apartment, no matter how small, conducive to dinner parties. We like to think that us giving advice to you is not exactly the blind leading the blind—more like someone with really thick glasses cheering you on for what is likely to be a bumpy, thoroughly enjoyable journey in your kitchen.

From our kitchens, albeit small, to yours,

—*Cara and Phoebe, the Quarter-Life Cooks*

GETTING STARTED

Let's start with the basics: how to stock your cabinets, pantry, and fridge with useful equipment, utensils, and ingredients, even when space and money are scarce resources. City life is hectic and expensive and, worst of all, requires us to carry all our groceries all of the blocks home. Follow our tips for creating a well-stocked pantry, and over-shopping will no longer take its toll on your biceps or your wallet. Understanding some principles about seasoning your food will help you make the most of the tools available, whatever that well-stocked pantry has to offer.

the ladle and other avoidable equipment

Our kitchen tool sets were born out of a series of haphazard hand-me-downs, determined bargain shopping at thrift stores and web warehouses, and equally determined improvisation. For the first year in her apartment, Cara had no baking dish and was forced to chisel slices of cornbread from the grooves of her cast-iron grill pan, resulting in crimped delicacies and delicious crumbs. Phoebe cooked most of her early meals entirely out of a 5-quart Dutch oven—everything from frittatas to pan-fried fish to brownies—and she made them all without the help of measuring spoons until she received a set as a gift from her boss, Stephanie.

As resourceful quarter-lifers, we trust you will find cheap ways to procure the essentials below, and with these tools on hand, you will be able to cook all the recipes in this book. Where we can, we give suggestions for substitutions and pose provocative questions like, why buy a rolling pin when you have plenty of wine bottles lying around?

on the stove and in the oven

medium enameled-cast-iron dutch oven (5- to 7-quart)

When people refer to one-pot-wonders, they are talking about this bad boy: the Dutch oven. Le Creuset makes top-of-the-line versions of these lidded pots that will likely outlive you (Phoebe uses her grandmother's). Lodge is a good cheaper option. Regardless of price, this item is a worthy investment, as you may otherwise find yourself buying a handful of other dinky pots and pans to compensate for the Dutch oven's many functions—it can double as a pasta pot, can be used in the oven in place of a baking dish, and has sufficient surface area for simmering a sauce or sautéing veggies.

large ovenproof skillet (12- to 15-inch)

Cast-iron skillets are our favorite type of ovenproof pan. They are multipurpose and make for a beautiful, rustic presentation if plopped down in the middle of a table. Use the cast-iron ovenproof skillet for items that need to be cooked stovetop and then baked in the oven. Make sure not to use soap when cleaning cast iron, or to go overboard with a Brillo pad—you want the pan to stay seasoned and well greased (new cast-iron pans come with seasoning instructions).

medium nonstick skillet (8-inch)

If you're using the Dutch oven for boiling pasta or simmering a stew, it's not a bad idea to have a shallow pan on hand. This nonstick skillet is also a great item to have when cooking for one. It is perfectly sized for single-serving eggs (like those found on page 28) and for quick sautés and sauces.

cookie sheet

This is the pan for both sweet and savory items (chocolate chip cookies, page 180; roasted veggies, pages 59, 102). It can also be a great item to help in the ever tiresome small-kitchen balancing act: most sheets will sit comfortably across your sink or on top of other pots and pans for use as an extra surface for prepped food. Keep a roll of parchment paper on hand to cover the sheet and cleanup will be easy. Be sure to measure the interior of your oven before you buy; we've owned cookie sheets that were tragically too large for our ovens. Two sheets would be ideal even if you only have one oven rack, so one sheet of cookies can be cooling while the other is baking.

9 × 13-inch baking pan

If you're not prone to baking blondies or large quantities of mac 'n cheese, you can get away with just using a cookie sheet for most of your baked meals. Otherwise, you'll want a metal or ceramic version of this pan. You can also use this as a vehicle for roasting meats or veggies. Pyrex is great too, but be careful when adding cool liquid to a hot Pyrex; it can cause the glass to shatter.

for the counter

cutting board

Make sure you get a large, sturdy cutting board. Store it vertically to save the most space, and balance it across your sink to gain more surface area. Don't buy floppy, soft cutting boards; these are an accident waiting to happen and will only add to your mess. A thick plastic or wooden board, and perhaps an extra small one for menial tasks that you can dole out to your roommates and/or guests, is all you need. Wood makes for a beautiful presentation, but it is not good for when handling raw meat.

cuisinart mini prep

Cara didn't believe Phoebe when she claimed that this $30 food processor was a necessary item for any small kitchen. That is, until she received one for her birthday (courtesy of an "anonymous" tip). Soon she was whipping up homemade butter in the time it takes to toast bread and venturing down Phoebe's path of endless herb dressing creations (see page 237). Now we both endorse this sucker in place of a blender or any other pureeing device. Trust us: it will change your life.

large good-looking mixing bowl
medium not-necessarily-so-good-looking mixing bowl

Mixing bowls are incredibly handy. We recommend you get a good set of glass, plastic, or ceramic bowls (metal means no microwave). At the bare minimum, you want at least one large and one medium, and preferably ones that are attractive enough to present to company (as in, not pink plastic) if you want them to double as salad or fruit bowls. If you don't have any smaller prep bowls, you can always use a mug or measuring cup instead.

utensils and tools

chef's knife (around 8 inches)

Invest in a decent knife. Don't go crazy, but we do recommend doing some research before you buy anything super-cheap. Dull knives are more likely to slip and cause injury. If you cut yourself badly, you will likely never want to (or, god forbid, be able to) cook again. And can you really put a price on safety? In this case, we say no.

serrated knife

We find that one serrated knife, either small or large, can accomplish a lot. We use our chef's knife for almost everything, but it really sucks for cutting bread, and when you make as much crostini as Phoebe does, that is a major deal breaker. Serrated edges excel at cutting tomatoes, bread, and chocolate.

paring knife

This knife is definitely third in line, so if you are investing piece by piece, get the other two first. Paring knives are helpful for smaller tasks such as peeling apples and deveining shrimp.

flat metal spatula

One sturdy metal spatula is really all you need for sautéing onions, flipping chicken breasts, and removing brownies from the pan.

silicone spatula/spoonula

Our moms ingrained in us at an early age that plastic + heat = death. We're always wary of using plastic spatulas for scrambling eggs (news flash: we don't use anything metal in our nonsticks—it ruins the pan and scrapes small pieces of it into the food). It's best to buy one all-purpose silicone spatula (or spoonula) to take the place of any plastic stirring utensil that might be used on the stove in a moment of crisis. We sometimes use wooden spoons, but if you're going minimal, go silicone. Be forewarned: heavily spiced dishes like our Smoky Chipotle Vegetarian Chili (page 200) can cause this utensil to smell like the spice for weeks.

peeler

Get a really hard-core peeler that can handle even the pesky tough skins on vegetables like butternut squash. Forking over $7 to $8 for a nicer peeler will be worthwhile—the $1 to $2 versions are not worth owning.

sturdy grater

This item was a point of debate: Cara has one big, badass box grater, and Phoebe has one large-holed handheld grater and one small zester. We concluded that if space is not an issue, it's best to invest in a really good box grater that has a zester on one side. If you have no drawers and need to hang your utensils or place them upright in an old pitcher as Phoebe does, get the two smaller items.

pastry brush

A cheap brush makes buttering and greasing a pan as easy as it should be. You can also use a brush to sweep olive oil across the surface of a piece of eggplant before you hurl it onto the hot grill (or cast-iron pan). Silicone brushes are nice if you'll be brushing oil onto hot pans.

colander

If you are purchasing one of these, make sure it stands on its own. Some of the collapsible, space-saving varieties are very flimsy. Others don't have much of a stand on the bottom and can easily fall, mixing your draining pasta with the gunk in your sink. To prevent this in any case, balance your colander on top of an upside-down bowl set on the sink floor.

oven mitts and dish towels

Don't burn yourself, or burn through your wallet, by buying roll upon roll of Bounty. Oven mitts and dish towels will be your savior.

can and wine openers

If you don't cook often, these two tools can still allow for a meal of fine wine and canned beans in front of the television. And if you do, well, more power to you.

measuring cups and spoons

Besides allowing you to follow our recipes and those of other cooks, measuring cups can serve a variety of different purposes: prep bowls, serving spoons, and, yes, the 1-cup can allow you to avoid buying a ladle. Supplement your regular set with a 4-cup liquid measuring cup as well.

baking

pans

Loaf pan

12-cup muffin pan

8×8-inch baking pan

9-inch round springform cake pan

9-inch fluted tart pan with removable
   bottom

If you love to bake and plan to make cupcakes, quick breads, muffins, tarts, or cakes frequently, purchase some or all of these pans in nonstick versions—all are inexpensive. If you bake only rarely, or space is at a premium, disposable aluminum pans can be picked up at the grocery store along with your confectioners' sugar when the occasion arises.

To remove a cooled cake from a springform pan, run a butter knife around the edge, then loosen the spring and remove the sides. To serve a tart made in a pan with a removable bottom, hold the cooled tart from the bottom with one hand and let the sides drop down your arm.

handheld electric mixer

If you whip a lot of cream, this will prove to be priceless; it's also pretty awesome to have around when making cookies or cakes, or even for mashing potatoes (the mini prep tends to make them gluey). Cara uses a Sunbeam mixer that cost about $30 and has threatened to fail her only once. We beat with either this or two forks clamped together in one hand like chopsticks. If you've got counter space and a gift certificate to a kitchenware store, by all means get yourself a stand mixer instead. We'll be really jealous.

rolling pin

Though bottles of wine work fine, we'll admit to owning rolling pins (they were gifts!). Get a heavy one, store it out of the way, and take it down when making an onion tart, a blueberry tart, or Christmas cookies.

serving

We're not going to tell you to go out and buy a 10-person dinnerware set to serve your every dinner party need. Quarter-lifers can get away with mismatched plates, bowls, and cutlery. We think this shabby chic vibe actually adds to the charm of the meal. Rather, we recommend that you own at least eight large dinner plates—if you are having more than eight people over for dinner, our rule is to always use disposable (preferably a sustainable brand; we like VerTerra, which is bamboo). It's also nice to have another eight or so smaller salad plates or bowls, just in case you decide to host a meal with a salad course or dessert.

It's great to have one or two large serving or salad spoons on hand as well, and one large platter if you serve a lot of finger food or like to present meals family-style at the table. If you have a large cast-iron skillet, this can serve as a nice platter or serving dish. For more tips, see How to Set the Coffee Table (page 192).

stocking the quarter-life pantry

One of the biggest deterrents to getting started in the kitchen has to be the initial stocking of the pantry. However, keeping cabinets filled with necessities means there's always the possibility of dinner without having to resort to (a) leaving the apartment, (b) takeout, or (c) a bowl of cereal with stale rice crackers on the side.

We both go through pantry phases. Cara's cupboards once contained four varieties of dried beans, Phoebe's five boxes of pasta shapes—a killer arts and crafts selection, but not enough of any one type to make a four-person entrée. And there will always be occasions when we've polished off the last can of diced tomatoes and, alas, that ever-ready dinner of Saucy Tomato Orecchiette (page 56) is totally unattainable. For days like these, make our Saddest Pantry Pasta (page 57) instead. Otherwise, try to restock at least once a month using the items below as your checklist, and a home-cooked meal will always be there should you wind up in massive gambling debt, locked inside your apartment, or with two hungry friends on your couch in need of nourishment.

on the shelves

staples

Extra virgin olive oil

Vegetable, safflower, or canola oil

Stock (chicken or vegetable)

White flour (or whole-wheat pastry flour)

Two types of rice (Arborio, white, and/or brown)

Two types of pasta (one long, one short)

Two types of canned beans (cannellini, chickpea)

One type of dried beans (lentils, black beans)

Miscellaneous grains (quinoa, barley)

Canned whole, diced, or crushed tomatoes (Muir Glen or San Marzano)

Two types of nuts (almonds, pecans, and pine nuts are best kept in the fridge)

Raisins (golden or regular)

Two types of vinegar (balsamic, rice, white wine)

Soy sauce

Honey

White sugar

Brown sugar

on the counter (in a basket)

Onions or shallots

Garlic

baking specific

Confectioners' sugar

Chocolate chips

Unsweetened chocolate squares

Baking soda and baking powder

Vanilla extract

Rolled oats (also good for breakfast)

in the fridge and freezer

You'll be surprised at how long main meal-making ingredients—winter vegetables, cheese, and even bread—can last in a cold environment. With eggs on hand as well, you will have an infinite number of dinner possibilities from the humble contents of your fridge.

staples

Butter

Eggs (seriously, at least a dozen)

Lemons

2 types of cheese (ungrated Parmesan
    is a mainstay)

Bread*

Two types of fresh vegetables (carrots,
    cabbage, celery, potatoes)

One type of fresh fruit (apples,
    oranges)

Two types of frozen vegetables
    (spinach, peas, corn)

Bacon and/or precooked sausages
    (turkey or pork)

Toast refrigerated bread before eating it, and when it's too dry for that, pulverize it into breadcrumbs.

condiments

Ketchup

Mustard (Dijon and whole-grain)

Hot sauce (Sriracha, Tabasco)

Mayonnaise

Half-empty (or -full?) bottle of white wine

Worcestershire sauce

Tahini

Sun-dried tomatoes (packed in oil
or dry)

on the spice rack

The spices below cover all those used in this book, and you will find infinite possibilities beyond our pages if you have them on hand. For spices that are more specific to particular ethnic cuisines, see The Global Kitchen (page 259).

basic seasoning and heat

Salt (kosher or sea)

Whole peppercorns (in a mill)

Crushed red pepper flakes

Cayenne pepper

Chili powder (try experimenting with
different varieties, like ground ancho
or chipotle chile powder)

ground spices

Cinnamon

Coriander

Cumin

Turmeric

Ginger

Nutmeg

Paprika (hot, smoked, or sweet)

dried herbs

Oregano

Thyme

Bay leaves

at the market

It all starts at the store. Shopping well is the first step to cooking well. Here are our grocery guidelines for planning, budgeting, and picking out the best fresh ingredients.

the shopping list

Make a shopping list and try to remember to bring it to the store. Make sure to organize your items by category (produce, dried goods, dairy, meat). We cannot tell you how many times we've forgotten to pick up frozen spinach because it was written alongside fresh herbs on our shopping list. Once you are familiar with the grocery store where you do most of your shopping, you can group items by specific aisle.

budget

When you go into the grocery store, have a figure in mind that is your maximum spending amount. If you see the items in your basket adding up to more than you expected, take out any extras. It's the little things that can get expensive, and part of being a practiced grocery shopper is knowing when you can afford the extra $1.50 for fancy organic baby carrots and when you'd be better off buying them from the conventional bulk bin. In general, organic items are more expensive. Decide what's important to you. We try to eat local produce from the farmers' market whenever possible and are willing to pay inflated prices for those perfectly imperfect potatoes. We buy cage-free eggs and organic strawberries. But canned beans? If we're running over budget, we'll grab the generic variety or cook dried beans from scratch. It always costs more to buy pita chips or bakery bread than to make them yourself. Determine what you have time for, and see where you need to cut corners and what can be prepared at home. Make sure to compare prices. When we are not in a rush, we painstakingly pick up a block of every type of cheddar in the cheese aisle, smell it, and take note for the future.

transportation

If you're shopping for a big party and you don't have a car or delivery service, remember that you'll have to carry everything you buy. If you bring your own bags with shoulder or messenger straps, or even a backpack, you'll be able to haul home more than if you rely on flimsy supermarket bags with their easily broken handles.

choosing fruits and vegetables

Pay attention to what you are grabbing from the bins. You want to inspect your produce with all five senses. Don't be afraid to fondle the fruit, making sure that there are no mushy areas that could mean bruising under the surface. Look for worm holes in vegetables, and any signs of wilting or discoloration. Choose fruits and vegetables that look and feel beautiful.

avocados

These should be soft to the touch but not mushy. Most avocados darken as they ripen. Keep in mind when you plan to use them. If you are buying these a few days in advance, you can afford to choose a firmer vegetable. To speed up the ripening process, place avocados in a paper bag and stash it in a dark corner of your kitchen (not in the fridge).

lettuce

Check the expiration date—pre-packaged salad sits on the shelf for a while. Pay attention to how fresh the leaves look within the package. If you see any overly wilted or gross discolored leaves, don't buy that bag. The more moisture you see on the inside of the package, the more likely the lettuce is to have already spoiled.

lemons and limes

The firmer these are to the touch, the less juice they will generate. If the skin has some give to it, it is going to be easier to squeeze, and ultimately a juicier fruit. This goes for other citrus fruits, like oranges and grapefruits, as well.

butternut squash

The more orange in color, the riper, drier, and sweeter the squash will be. Make sure to weigh the squash before you buy it. They can be deceptively heavy, and you don't want to walk away with five pounds of squash when you only need two.

chile peppers

The hot pepper section of the produce aisle is notoriously disorganized. Sometimes it's hard to tell which signs go with which peppers, and the last thing you want is to add three habaneros (these are small, round, usually red, and will burn your face off) to your enchilada sauce. In general, the smaller the pepper, the hotter it will be. Serrano peppers and jalapeño peppers are both green and the same shape, but the serrano is the smaller and hotter of the two.

fresh herbs

Buy a bunch that still has its roots intact. You can place the roots in a glass or pitcher filled with a little bit of water, and the herbs will last longer. If a bunch with its roots is not available, make sure to wash the herbs when you get home, dry them thoroughly, wrap them in a paper or dish towel, and store them in an airtight plastic bag in the fridge.

melons and pineapples

You want to choose both of these by their scent. Sniff each piece of fruit. The more it smells like melon or pineapple, the more it will taste like it, too.

mangos

Like most other fruits, the softer the mango, the riper it will be. Though mangos come in different colors and shades, most are green when first picked and turn red or orange as they ripen.

dairy

cheese

Bags of pre-shredded cheddar will always be more expensive and less flavorful than a block from Wisconsin. If you have the time (and the muscle power) to do all the shredding yourself, your wallet and your meals will be all the better for it. This is especially true of Parmesan and pecorino. To get the consistency of pre-grated Parmesan, simply cut a block into chunks and place it in your mini food processor.

The longer a cheese has aged, the sharper, harder, and more pungent it will be. If you are looking for a good melting cheese, choose a younger block. If you want great sharp flavor in addition to gooeyness, get a small block of each. If you'd like a smaller block, simply ask the people at the cheese counter to cut something in half for you. They are usually more than willing to do so. On the other hand, cheese keeps for a remarkably long time in the fridge. If your cheese begins to develop green mold, do not throw it out. The cheese beneath is still perfectly good to use. Simply cut off the moldy edges, discard them, and shred away.

butter, milk, and cream

Always buy sticks of unsalted butter, never whipped. You can store the excess in the freezer, so stock up. Most of our recipes specify whole milk, but if low-fat is what you have on hand, you can always substitute that. To make whipped cream, make sure you buy heavy whipping cream.

fish and meat

Picking out fish and meat can be daunting. Find fishmongers and butchers you trust, and ask their advice. If we specify a certain type of fish or cut of meat that's unavailable, or if there is a better, cheaper substitute, the person behind the counter will be able to help you. As for freshness, use your nose at the store. Fish should not smell overly fishy. Meat should have little to no scent.

storing

Onions, garlic, potatoes, bananas, and tomatoes generally do not need to be kept in the fridge. Lemons, limes, and other fruit can go either way. They'll last a little longer in the fridge, but they are fine if left on the counter. Think about what you see where in the grocery aisle and try to mimic that at home. Herbs and green vegetables are generally kept in the crisper box in the fridge. Of course, sometimes we keep the vegetables and fruits mentioned above in the fridge simply to save on space—they won't be harmed if you do. But people don't paint still-lifes of fruit bowls for naught—in larger kitchens, these items are often kept in a bowl on the counter.

COOKING
FOR ONE

There's something so grown-up about eating alone when you frame it right. Eating alone is freedom when it's done in the comfort of your first apartment. It's pleasure-reading time when done in front of a computer at work. It's a chance to indulge in the strange foods you would never serve to another human being. It's also an opportunity to grow more adept in the kitchen. Cooking for one allows you to play around without pressure. It's a time to practice. We've made some of our best (and worst) dishes by ourselves in our tiny kitchens and enjoyed every last bite in our own company.

peas for one

I didn't really learn how to feed myself until the summer before my senior year of high school. Up until then, I had been mainly a baker, focusing my energies on one-upping Cara's oatmeal chocolate chip cookie recipe rather than trying my hand at sautéing onions. I could boil water and chop tomatoes, but it wasn't until that summer that I learned how to fry an egg, to scrape together a meal from a box of frozen vegetables, and to figure out what I would possibly put in my body without any adult there to dictate my choice.

My parents spent that summer away from the city, and I stayed behind to do an unpaid internship—which, at the time, was actually something I was excited about. Some might have worried about leaving a sixteen-year-old unchaperoned for three months (and given their prior strictness, I would have counted my parents among them). But really, I had so little funds that it was difficult for me to get up to too much trouble. They had left me with twelve weeks' worth of my regular allowance, which was good for pizza after school, a dinner out on weekends, maybe a taxi, but not quite enough to provide me with three meals a day. To keep my budget in check, I ate Tasti D-Lite for lunch with the waiflike editorial assistants at the fashion magazine where I was working. At night, I turned to my mother's pantry.

At first, there was a bounty to choose from. I'd defrost salmon and turkey burgers, call my mom on the phone to ask how best to cook them, then curse as hot oil splattered up my forearms and curse some more as I transferred disorderly chunks of overcooked, pinkish-gray protein to my plate. One night I burned a turkey burger so badly, a less desperate person would have deemed it inedible. I covered it in ketchup and dug in.

When the frozen fish and burgers were gone, I turned to the cabinets for sustenance. Because of her wheat allergy, my mother's pantry contained millet, quinoa, and brown rice but lacked penne and macaroni, items that might have made for carbo-centric, remedial meals fit for a high schooler. I chose to try my hand at the rice, waiting patiently by the stove, gnawing my lip as it cooked for what felt like forever. When I pulled off the lid, the grains were soupy and burned at the same time. I was hungry. So I stirred in some hot French mustard and ate it anyway.

Soon I discovered cheese inside a small vegetable drawer. A moment later, I realized that the slices were soy singles. Luckily, the one thing my mother had stocked the fridge with was a surplus of eggs. I fried them up in olive oil in abundance, scrambled them, and used them as a way to hide soy cheese inside crispy omelets. The eggs were all I had for a little while. And then there were just peas.

Somewhere on the cookbook shelf, I found a recipe for peas and spinach in a buttery sauce, and since I had the frozen produce on hand, this became the answer to my pantry woes, seven nights a week. It reminded me of my mom's home-alone meal of choice: Peas-from-a-Mug, filled nearly to the brim with olive oil, the perfect dinner of flash-frozen vegetables and monounsaturated fatty acids. My version required white wine instead. I pilfered from my parents' wine rack. By law I was too young to drink it, but no one said I couldn't mix it with my peas.

I ate a lot of frozen peas in white wine and butter that summer. And still I feared what I would do when they ran out. My allowance was dwindling, but worse, I was getting skinnier. For a late bloomer like myself, this was not an attractive development. I slipped more generous pats of butter into the bowls of peas, and I added toppings to my Tasti D orders. Eventually my far-away parents mandated a doctor's appointment.

As it turned out, I had been living with mono, undetected, for months. With this news, it made sense that an eater like myself had been able to live on lo-cal soft-serve and bowls of green vegetables for weeks. The peas were so delicious, I hadn't minded that my plate lacked a main dish. But I also might not have been hungry enough to care.

Now I've gotten a little more practiced at financial independence, feeding myself, and hiking up the four narrow flights of stairs to my own apartment. In doing so, my pantry has come to resemble my mother's, quinoa and all. But in moments of desperation (when my bank account is overdrawn), exhaustion (after hiking up the stairs), or impatience (at the thought of waiting for brown rice to cook), it is the peas I continue to rely on, just as I did back in high school. And since there is usually a bottle of white wine already open in the fridge, when my roommate, Caitlyn, is working late I'll find myself reaching for that square green package, melting a few pats of butter on the stove, and curling up on the couch with two mugs—one of wine, the other of just peas.

peas with white wine and butter

Makes 1 to 2 servings

{
2 tablespoons butter

1 small shallot or 1 clove garlic, thinly sliced

⅓ cup dry white wine

One 10-ounce bag or box of frozen peas

Salt and freshly ground black pepper
}

1. In a small saucepan, melt the butter over medium heat. Add the shallot or garlic (whichever you have on hand), and sauté for 1 to 2 minutes, until aromatic. Pour in the wine and bring to a simmer. Cook until the alcohol has burned off and the liquid has reduced by half and become opaque, about 3 minutes.
2. Stir in the peas and reduce the heat to medium-low. Cook, stirring occasionally, until the peas are just cooked through, about 3 minutes.
3. Season with salt and pepper, pour the peas into a mug, and enjoy.

the single-serving egg

Cara, Winter 2008

Everyone laughed at me when I told them I lived on East 13th Street, worked on East 45th, and set my alarm for 6:45 a.m. when I didn't have to be at work until 9:00 a.m. Why, they asked, did I get up so early?

The answer was, for my hair, for my meals, and for my sanity.

Like most entry-level employees, especially those in publishing who take home hours of reading homework each night, I was perpetually exhausted. That didn't stop me from scheduling activities almost every night after work. Running from yoga to spur-of-the-moment drinks to potlucks to dinners at my sister Jill's apartment, I drove myself a little insane. After work was my time to see people. But before work, that was alone time.

One morning my alarm went off at the usual hour and I leaped out of bed, somehow energetic, and headed for the shower. Unlike most, I don't shower in the morning to wake up; I shower to appease my hair. If fifty percent of the reason I get out of bed so early is to have time to myself, twenty-five percent is to let my curly hair dry shiny and frizz-free. That morning, post-shower, I layered on my curl-inducing gel and went about figuring out how to dawdle away the remaining hour and a half before my hair was dry and I had to catch the subway.

First, I shopped online for socks and books. Whereas my internet browsing later in the day tends to be filled with many-tabbed windows and abandoned shopping carts, in the morning I am focused. I probably spent more money before 7:30 a.m. than I'd make that day. Realizing this—though I'd bought necessities (mostly)—and remembering that I was going out to dinner, I felt guilty enough to fixate on making a frugal lunch. I scrounged through the fridge, finding things to pack. There were leftover mashed potatoes and a block of smoked tofu that Jordana and I loved to share (this was in my most strict vegetarian days). I packed servings of each, plus some carrot sticks and a cookie. Then, going in reverse order, it was time for breakfast. The remaining twenty-five percent of my reason for getting up so early is to cook—and eat.

Since then, when I've made this Spinach Pie Quesadilla, I've eaten it for dinner, lunch, or brunch, but that morning I must have been in a savory-breakfast mood. I started sautéing garlic, onions, and spinach around 7:40 a.m. My roommates must have wondered if it was dinnertime already as they sleepily sniffed, then pressed *Snooze* yet again. I beat an egg white with some Greek yogurt and feta and added the spinach mixture before pressing it all inside a folded tortilla. As the fusion filling cooked and the tortilla pocket crisped, my mind wandered. I was thinking about what it would be like to live without my roommates, much as I loved them, in a quiet corner of a borough so far removed from Manhattan that I'd have to start waking up at 6:15 a.m. Over breakfast, I started browsing Craigslist for studios in Brooklyn.

Afterwards, I finished washing the dishes and looked up at the clock. It was 8:45 a.m. I brushed my teeth, packed up the manuscripts I was reading, and grabbed my bag: 8:48 a.m. In spite of the sweeping hours of time I'd left myself, I was still—as usual—going to be late for work.

spinach pie quesadilla

Makes 1 serving

I have my superhuman early morning powers to thank for the simplicity and deliciousness of this Spinach Pie Quesadilla. I also have to give credit to eggs, though. Eggs allow me to feed myself even when there's not much else in the fridge, and I always keep them handy—then, in the East Village apartment, and now, in the dream-to-reality Brooklyn one. In the egg recipes that follow, I add eggs to vegetables and to pasta, and as with the quesadilla, they transform these simple staples into a satisfying meal. Of course eggs this good can and should feed more than one, if it's an hour removed enough from breakfast that friends might actually want to join in.

1 teaspoon olive oil	Pinch of cayenne pepper
¼ small onion, finely diced	1 ½ cups fresh spinach
2 scallions (white and light green parts), sliced	1 large egg white
1 clove garlic, minced	1 tablespoon plain Greek yogurt
¼ teaspoon salt	2 tablespoons crumbled feta cheese
Freshly ground black pepper	¼ to ½ teaspoon olive oil, or cooking spray
Pinch of dried thyme	1 small wrap or flour tortilla (8-inch diameter)
Pinch of dried oregano	

1. In a small nonstick pan, heat the oil. Add the onion and scallions and cook until soft, 3 to 4 minutes. Stir in the garlic and cook for a minute or two, until soft. Sprinkle with the salt, black pepper, herbs, and cayenne.
2. Mix in the spinach and cook until wilted, about 2 minutes. Transfer to a bowl and cool slightly. Use a wooden spoon to press out some of the liquid from the cooked spinach, and drain.
3. In a small bowl, whisk together the egg white, yogurt, and 1 tablespoon of the feta. Add this to the cooled spinach and mix until combined.

4. Wipe out the pan, and then brush it with the olive oil or spray with cooking spray. Over low heat, put the wrap or tortilla in the pan. Sprinkle the remaining 1 tablespoon feta over one side of the wrap and heat until the wrap softens slightly. Raise the heat to medium and pour the egg-spinach mixture over the same half of the wrap. Fold the other half over, and cook on one side until the egg white begins to firm up, 3 to 4 minutes. Flip, and cook on the other side for 2 to 3 minutes. Then cut into wedges and serve immediately.

swiss chard frittata

Makes 2 servings

I remember my mom making frittatas for Saturday lunches. She used leftover pasta and mixed in eggs and probably some veggies and cheese. I didn't eat them then, but once I was cooking in my own kitchen, I came to love frittatas because, made in my little nonstick skillet, they were perfectly sized for one.

When I came into a larger cast-iron pan in the spring, and in the summer went on several dates with a software developer from Baltimore named Alex, I realized the full potential of a frittata shared: you can coax out a surprising elegance from its apparent humbleness. For one of my first meals with Alex, I decorated a Swiss chard frittata with grilled slices of eggplant. This frittata is wonderful even without the eggplant because the chard leaves give a lovely spongy, ricotta-like texture to the baked egg. But if company calls, try the eggplant-topped or (veggie) sausage-flecked variation.

{
4 large eggs

2 large egg whites (see Note)

½ teaspoon salt

Freshly ground black pepper

½ bunch Swiss chard

2 tablespoons olive oil

2 cloves garlic, minced

4 sun-dried tomatoes, slivered (optional)

2 tablespoons grated Parmesan cheese (optional)
}

Note: Frittatas and omelets benefit from a mix of whole eggs and egg whites. If you don't feel like discarding the yolks, though, you can make this with 6 whole eggs.

1. Preheat the broiler.
2. In a bowl, whisk the whole eggs and egg whites with the salt and ¼ teaspoon pepper. Set aside.
3. Remove the Swiss chard leaves from their stems. Rinse both thoroughly under running water until all grit and dirt is removed. Cut the stems into ½-inch-thick slices

and reserve. Roughly chop the leaves into bite-size pieces or ribbons (you should have about 2 cups).

4. In a medium-size ovenproof sauté pan or skillet, warm the oil over medium heat. Add the garlic and sauté until it is golden, 2 to 3 minutes. Then add the sun-dried tomatoes if you're using them. Raise the heat to medium-high and add the sliced chard stems. Stir constantly for about 2 minutes, until the stems are tender. Add the chopped chard leaves and toss with tongs to coat them with the oil. Sauté for 5 minutes, or until tender. If the mixture starts to stick, you can add a little water.

5. Pour in the eggs and stir with a silicone spatula, pulling the entire mixture towards you every 30 seconds, in order to create large curds. When the eggs have nearly set, sprinkle the top with the cheese (if using) and some more pepper.

6. Place the pan under the broiler and cook for about 2 minutes, until the top of the frittata is golden and the cheese is melted. Let rest in the pan for 5 minutes.

7. Serve the frittata in wedges, warm or at room temperature.

Eggplant–Swiss Chard Frittata: Cut 1 medium eggplant into ⅓-inch-thick slices. Toss the slices in a colander with 1 tablespoon kosher salt, and allow to sit for 1 hour. Pat the slices dry, then toss them with 2 tablespoons olive oil to coat. Heat a cast-iron pan over medium-high heat for 5 minutes. Add a single layer of eggplant and cook for about 5 minutes per side, until cooked through. Repeat until you've cooked all the slices. Press them onto the top of the frittata before you stick it under the broiler.

Swiss Chard and Sausage Frittata: Crumble 1 link of your favorite cooked chicken, pork, or veggie sausage (for veggie, try Field Roast; it's legitimately delicious). Add it to the pan just after adding the garlic, and let it get crispy and golden before adding the chard. You may want to decrease the salt slightly, since sausages can be really salty.

yogurt "carbonara"

Makes 1 serving

I came within inches of overdosing on this very pasta while I was living with a host family in Paris during my junior year in college. As per our agreement, I ate with the family three nights a week and was on my own for four. On the weekends this was great—I'd go out to bistros with my American friends. But during the week, it could be downright awkward. I would try to use the kitchen before my host family came home to eat. Their dinner times were unpredictable, so my method was to zip in and out as quickly as possible.

This is what I cooked many of those nights. The reason this dish is so fast is that you use the heat of the pasta to warm the sauce, cook the egg, and melt the cheese. By the time the noodles were drained I was done with the kitchen completely, and only one pot was used; I didn't even have to dirty measuring cups, since the yogurt in France comes in perfect-size containers for one serving. All in all, it was a very good arrangement. And then, as now, it was a very good meal.

1 cup (3 ounces) short pasta
(my favorite is penne)
⅓ cup plain Greek yogurt
1 egg
3 tablespoons freshly grated
Parmesan cheese

¼ teaspoon salt
Pinch of ground cinnamon
Pinch of cayenne pepper
Freshly ground black pepper

1. Bring a medium pot of salted water to a boil. Cook the pasta, following the package directions, until al dente.
2. Meanwhile, in a small mixing bowl, beat together the yogurt, egg, 2 tablespoons of the Parmesan, and the salt, cinnamon, and cayenne.
3. Drain the pasta and immediately add it to the yogurt mixture. Toss to combine. Top with the remaining 1 tablespoon Parmesan and a few grinds of black pepper.

eggs from our mothers' kitchens

When we were kids, our moms taught us how to make our first egg dishes. Now, though we modify recipes and mess around in the kitchen, we turn back to those early techniques time and time again.

sarah's olive oil fried egg

Makes 1 serving

My mother loves to coat her food in really good olive oil, and she ingests a crazy amount of it on a daily basis. It's because of this that I never thought the idea of frying a single egg in a huge pool of olive oil was an insane thing to do. In fact, I would say that this egg is the best kitchen gift my mother ever gave me.

Though olive oil is usually too expensive to squander these days, I haven't found an apt substitute in the fat department for creating this perfect egg. You get the oil really smoking hot before you begin. Then when you introduce the egg to it, it actually does go insane: the whites begin bubbling wildly, the oil splatters over your stovetop, and the pan produces very loud and alarming sputtering noises. Within less than a minute, the egg whites begin forming crispy brown edges and the top of the egg, covered in a light stream of hot olive oil, cooks through while remaining perfectly fluffy. Best of all, the yolk is barely harmed by the cooking process, and when you take the egg off the stove, it is in perfect condition to ooze all over your plate.

{
2 to 3 tablespoons olive oil
1 egg
Pinch of salt
}

1. Coat a small nonstick pan or cast-iron skillet with a generous layer of olive oil and allow it to get hot. You want to make sure it's really, really hot. To test this, my mom always used to spit in the pan and see if it caused the oil to spatter and sizzle. If cooking for yourself, go for it. If not, you might want to just flick some water.

2. Crack the egg in the pan and immediately turn the pan from side to side so the white spreads evenly across the surface. Allow the egg whites to fry in the oil (beware, this may splatter). When the edges have begun to crisp up and brown but the top is still slightly undercooked, tilt the pan, and with a spoon, collect some of the hot oil. Use this to douse the top of the egg. Collect more hot oil and repeat. Once the whole egg is cooked and crispy, slide it onto a plate, leaving most of the oil in the pan.

joanne's soft scrambled eggs

Makes 1 serving

My mom showed my sisters, Jill and Kate, and me the best way to scramble eggs: over the lowest possible flame. We'd melt a pat of butter in the pan and stand there with forks in hand, scribbling away. It felt like a lifetime before the eggs would morph into solid curds, but once they did you had to be especially careful to scramble, lest the end result taste like a chopped-up omelet. That is the kind of egg that some people like, but not us. On weekends, we'd pull out the insides of fresh croissants and fill up the empty crust with the finished eggs; but on regular days we'd just eat them with toast.

When paired with bread or salad, soft scrambled eggs are acceptable to offer to others. I'd even consider them classy when served with chives and creamy mushrooms as part of a tartine (see page 154).

{
2 teaspoons butter

2 eggs

Pinch of salt

Freshly ground black pepper
}

1. Heat the butter in a small nonstick pan over the lowest possible heat.
2. Beat the eggs thoroughly in a mixing bowl and season with the salt and pepper.
3. Add the eggs to the pan and cook, stirring constantly with a spatula, until small curds begin to form on the bottom of the pan. Continue to cook and stir until there is no liquid left. This will take at least 10 minutes. When the eggs are soft but set, scrape onto a plate and serve immediately.

grilled cheese, plain and fancy

Grilled cheese is one of the most comforting, satisfying meals we feed ourselves. We've often found our fridges containing nothing more than drying bread and miscellaneous molding cheese—together, a blessing in disguise. Cara's perfect grilled cheese requires just those two sad objects (mold removed, bread toasted), while Phoebe's version re-envisions the ingredients as a meal refined enough to serve to company.

phoebe's pesto panino

Makes 4 sandwiches

I spent the fall semester of my junior year of college abroad in Rome. After two years of dining hall cuisine, the Italian markets were a dream. There were perfectly purple eggplants, cases of cured meats, and the silkiest mozzarella to choose from. But the one item that always made it into my basket was a big loaf of ciabatta. With the other fresh ingredients beside it, my bread became the centerpiece of the most bare-boned of cooking practices.

My lunches consisted of alternating bites of juicy tomatoes, fontina cheese, smoky speck, and bread dipped in store-bought pesto. A sandwich rarely came together in the traditional sense, but the meal was influential. Once I returned home, I found myself unable to return to everyday sandwich fixings. Now ciabatta still finds a place in my apartment, giving me a mission: to eat it all before it goes stale. I'll make a whole loaf of this fancy grilled cheese and invite my roommate, Caitlyn, and a few friends to join me for a meal that is as comforting as the childhood classic—especially when Workweek Tomato Soup (page 52) is served alongside—and as elegant as anything from a Roman holiday.

1 loaf ciabatta, sliced in half horizontally

2 tablespoons extra virgin olive oil

½ cup Basil Pesto (page 255)

¾ pound fontina or whole-milk mozzarella, sliced

1. Turn on the broiler.
2. Lay both pieces of ciabatta, cut side up, on a baking sheet, and drizzle the olive oil over the the bread. Broil for a few minutes, until the bread is slightly crispy on the top but not yet beginning to brown. Remove from the broiler.
3. Slather the pesto over both pieces of bread (be as generous as you like). On the bottom piece, lay the cheese slices over the pesto in one even layer. Replace the top piece of ciabatta and press down so the sandwich sticks together slightly.
4. Return to the broiler for 3 minutes, until the cheese has melted and the loaf is nice and crusty. Slice into 4 sandwiches and serve.

cara's classic gooey grilled cheese

Makes 1 sandwich

When I was growing up, grilled cheese was two pieces of bread or an English muffin that had been covered with cheddar and toasted—in the toaster oven, not in a frying pan—a technique similar to Phoebe's panino. For special treats, we made "fried grilled cheese," which was like the version you got in a diner: a sandwich pan-seared in lots of melted butter.

In the college dining hall, I figured out how to make a grilled cheese that meshed the two. I couldn't mimic the open-faced sandwiches of my youth since the exposed cheese would stick to the top of the cafeteria's George Foreman. So I toasted and buttered multigrain bread before filling it with Swiss and putting it on the grill, and the result was so gooey and crispy that I was sure I'd one-upped the white bread American cheese sandwiches the dining hall served.

Now I make grilled cheese in the frying pan, since my small kitchen doesn't have room for a George Foreman. My technique is not unlike the way we made "fried grilled cheese," though I think it's most influenced by those college lunches; the sandwich is made crispy by toasted, buttered bread, though not so heavily buttered that I couldn't, in theory, eat it almost every day.

{
2 slices sandwich bread

1 tablespoon butter, at room temperature

2 ounces cheese (4 slices or ½ cup

shredded), preferably a mix of sharp cheddar and Jarlsberg

Salt and freshly ground black pepper
}

1. Lightly toast the bread in a toaster or under the broiler.
2. Slather one side of each slice of toast with the butter. Cover one unbuttered side with the cheese, and season the cheese with salt and pepper. Cover with the second slice of toast, buttered side facing out.
3. Cook in a frying pan over medium-low heat, flipping once, until the toast is golden and the cheese is melted. Serve immediately—and fill out your plate with veggies and chips.

me and the microwave

Cara, Winter 2008

When I got home from my trip to Spain, I walked into my studio apartment wearing grubby sweats. Though I was tired, jetlagged, and bloated from too many servings of *churros con chocolate* and *patatas bravas*, I managed to slip on a dress an hour or two later and head into Manhattan for one of my favorite events of the year, my old friend Kate's holiday party. I arrived just in time to grab a serving of her mother's corn pudding. The rest of the party is a blur. Afterwards, I slept for eighteen hours. It wasn't until after work on Monday that I turned on my stove.

Or, I tried to. In my dream world that winter evening, stockpots were steaming broccoli and sautéing kale, but in my real closet kitchen, the gas had been turned off. Absolutely nothing was stewing.

I am not a delinquent. I don't have that many bills, and I pay the ones I owe on time. Rather, under the impression that Con Ed took care of both gas and electric, as it had at my previous rental, I had never officially activated the gas. (I'd been living in the apartment for more than two months at this point.) When I say "under the impression," I suppose I mean delusional: my landlords had told me I'd have to switch the gas to my name. Yet when the burners and oven worked immediately after I moved in and then continued to, I ignored them. I guess I thought the gods were smiling down on me.

With my head bowed low, I called National Grid and said, "I'd like to open an account. I *recently* moved."

There were seven days between my call and the first available appointment, and I still had to eat. After dining in restaurants all through my trip, there was nothing I wanted more than healthful home-cooked meals. But my negligence had made pipe dreams of steamed broccoli and sautéed kale, and I had to turn to cans and to the freezer, to my slow cooker, and to my blender. It was December, and I craved hot food, too. So I turned to my microwave and I started to nuke. I made mashed potatoes, and you would never know they weren't cooked in a pot. I cooked an egg in the microwave, but I'm not sure I'd recommend this. Other triumphs? Angel hair pasta with butter and cheese, corn and bean salad, hummus, bananas Foster.

The low point came when I had to bring cookie dough to a holiday party for which I'd volunteered to bake gingersnaps (or, rather, for which Phoebe had volunteered me). I went early, carrying a Tupperware filled with sixty preformed balls of dough, and I baked them in the host's oven.

Though I didn't realize it at the time, this entire experience brought me back to another culinarily challenged era of my life. I first noticed the comfort a microwave could provide a kitchen-less soul when I was a freshman in college. In the microwave in the dining hall, I pioneered a recipe for pasta primavera (see page 133), and for the bananas Foster that I had no suspicion I would return to years later. In the microwave back in our dorm (placed, grossly, in the bathroom), I made gourmet chocolate bark out of white chocolate with pistachios or dark chocolate with walnuts and raisins, which I brought to end-of-semester class parties or to any event where sweets were called for. I would melt the chocolate, stir in whatever nuts or fruit I'd picked up from the local specialty store, and then I'd spread the whole mess on a wax paper–lined baking sheet.

Limited resources often lead to moments of genius—as the small kitchen itself forces us to invent new techniques and dishes—and the lack of a stove, then and now, forced me to try experimental methods (slow-cooker frittata?) until, in the end, I found a way to feed myself.

chocolate bark

Makes 20 servings

It's been a while since I made this in my college dorm bathroom, but I discovered during that stove-less week that it's as good now as it ever was. You can use fancy chocolate for these recipes—substitute 1½ pounds of milk, semisweet, or bittersweet chocolate if that's more your bag. (I like Callebaut and Scharffen Berger.) For white chocolate, make sure the ingredient list contains cocoa butter. If you're using chips, go for Ghirardelli, which is a good-quality supermarket brand.

CHERRY-WALNUT CHOCOLATE BARK

4 cups milk chocolate chips

3 cups unsalted walnuts, coarsely chopped

1 cup dried cherries

PRETZEL-TOFFEE CHOCOLATE BARK

2 cups milk chocolate chips

2 cups semisweet chocolate chips

3½ cups broken salted pretzel pieces (see Notes)

2 cups toffee bits (see Notes)

Notes: To break up the pretzels, put a handful or two in a resealable plastic bag and pound with your fist until they're broken up. Measure after breaking. You may need to repeat this until you have 4 cups.

You can usually find Heath brand toffee bits in the baking aisle. If not, purchase Heath Bars and chop them up.

1. Melt the chocolate in a double boiler or in 20-second intervals in the microwave (see page 303). You want it to be just melted—don't let it bubble or burn. As it's melting, stir it occasionally with a heatproof spatula.
2. Remove the chocolate from the microwave or the heat, and add the nuts and cherries *or* the pretzels and toffee bits. Stir to distribute.
3. Pour the mixture onto two parchment-lined cookie sheets, and spread it evenly with a spatula. Put the sheets in the freezer and let the bark sit until hardened. This should

take about 1 hour. If you don't have room for both pans in the freezer, place them in the fridge—they will just take a bit longer to harden.

4. Using your hands or a knife, break the bark into bite-size pieces. Keep in the fridge until ready to serve.

Chocolate Bark with White Chocolate Drizzle: Before breaking up the bark, melt 4 ounces of white chocolate in the microwave or a double boiler until just melted. Remove the chocolate bark from the freezer. Dip a fork into the white chocolate, and flick your wrist to create streaks of white chocolate all over the bark. Return to the freezer and let harden. Then break up the bark as instructed above.

soup is what you make yourself

Phoebe, Winter 2008

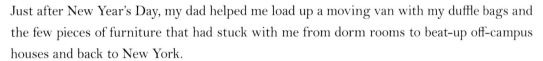

Just after New Year's Day, my dad helped me load up a moving van with my duffle bags and the few pieces of furniture that had stuck with me from dorm rooms to beat-up off-campus houses and back to New York.

Growing up on the Upper West Side, downtown always felt like a world away. Even without heavy bags to carry, my parents get in the car and drive if they have to go anywhere below 14th Street. So as my dad and I made our way through midtown down 9th Avenue to my new apartment, it felt like I was indeed moving a world away from my childhood bedroom, to an area unreachable by subway to a certain pair of parents. Don't get me wrong, I love them. But after six long post-college months living under their roof, it was very clear that we loved each other a lot more from afar.

It was winter, but we were drenched in sweat when we finished lugging all my belongings up the claustrophobic green-carpeted stairwell. Without much furniture, my new apartment seemed vast and inviting, though by any standards other than New York City's, it was a closet. Still, its exposed brick walls, run-down appliances, and poor lighting stood for a new kind of freedom, perhaps even maturity. It felt this way for a little while. That is, until three weeks into the new living arrangement, when I got sick.

Caitlyn was away in Seattle for work, and at first I was relieved, figuring she'd fear that she had unknowingly moved in with the *Outbreak* monkey. But this also meant I had no one to walk up and down the four flights of stairs to get me Pepto, Jell-O, and ginger ale. So, no sooner had I left my mom's uptown world than I begged her to come down to mine. An hour later, my mother was huffing and puffing on my doorstep, bearing love, attention, and a thermometer.

Luckily, she also brought the only cure-all not to be found within a ten-block radius: garlic soup. While most kids may recall being fed traditional chicken noodle, my memories of sick days home from school include two very important remedies: garlic soup and *The Price Is Right*. On this particular afternoon, the latter was replaced with eight hours of *Lost* reruns, with my mom tucked in bed beside me and a computer balanced on a pillow between us. Even with mysterious island monsters replacing Bob Barker on the screen, the first sip of soup brought back all the comfort of my days being doted on in front of the TV.

Over the course of that first year in my apartment, I got sick a few too many times—a lack, perhaps, of the maturity I thought I'd developed. For most bouts, Caitlyn was indeed there to pick up my antibiotics, watch bad TV with me, and disinfect the remote control immediately after I'd touched it. Once I learned to take care of myself, though, I found the strength to do what any mature, home-cooking individual would think to do. I made this soup.

Whether or not my health warrants the intake of a whole head of garlic, a humble soup offers the kind of comfort that transports me from my fourth-floor walk-up to my mother's kitchen. It is the first thing I think to make when I am run-down, home alone, or in the mood for regression to childhood and resuscitation from adult life—soup is my favorite meal to eat all by myself.

my mother's garlic soup

Makes 1 serving

{
1 whole head of garlic (about 15 cloves)
1 quart chicken stock
¼ cup brown rice

¼ teaspoon salt
Pinch of cayenne pepper
1 egg yolk
1 tablespoon lemon juice
}

1. In a medium Dutch oven, bring 2 cups of water to a boil. With the flat side of your knife, crush the head of garlic so the cloves separate from the base. Discard any loose skins. Add the cloves to the boiling water, and blanch for 2 minutes. Using a slotted spoon or a fork, remove the garlic cloves and any wayward skins from the pot, and let them rest on a cutting board until cool enough to handle. Pick the skins off with your fingers—they will come off extremely easily.

2. Add the chicken stock to the water in the pot, cover, and bring it to a boil. Add the brown rice, peeled garlic cloves, salt, and cayenne. Cover, and simmer over medium-low heat for 35 to 40 minutes, or until the rice is cooked. Remove the pot from the heat.

3. In a shallow bowl, beat the egg yolk. Temper the egg: slowly whisk ¼ cup of the hot broth into the bowl, adding a very small amount at a time so as not to scramble the egg. Once the broth is fully incorporated, stir the mixture into the soup and add the lemon juice. The egg yolk will give the soup a subtle, silky quality, while the lemon adds brightness to the rich, sweet garlic.

green goddess soup

Makes 2 servings

When I was little, my mother exposed me to *haute* baby food by asking the waiter to run leftover veal scaloppine through a blender to bring home to me. In this sense, my first exposure to soup came from savory dishes reduced to an unidentifiable mush and packed with unexpected flavor. Though I may have occasionally needed the airplane-to-the-mouth enactment to swallow buttery vegetables, I've always enjoyed my mother's cooking, be it in liquid or solid form. But for a while, there was one limit to my consumption: green soup. I assumed that this concoction served some mysterious medicinal purpose, and I avoided the crusty-rimmed Saran-wrapped mugs of it she left in the fridge at all costs.

It wasn't until one Sunday night, a few months after I stopped sharing a kitchen with my mom, that I finally sampled it. I had happily returned uptown to visit my parents after a long workweek and a short but intense weekend of partying, in need of some pampering and detoxing. My mother prescribed this soup, and I gratefully accepted the dose. It turned out that like the veal scaloppine puree, the soup was more delicious than appearances let on. Now it's what I make myself when I need to get back on my feet for Monday morning, or when I plan to spend a quiet weekend night alone with no plans to re-tox.

If you're not the type of person who shies away from green food, you'll find this soup incredibly healthy and satisfying. If you're sharing it with skeptics, try adding a splash of heavy cream to lighten the soup's complexion, and top it with a dollop of sour cream and some lemon zest.

2 large Swiss chard leaves with stems

2 cups chicken stock

2 cups coarsely chopped zucchini (about 1 large zucchni)

1/2 teaspoon salt

1 cup fresh cilantro leaves

2 tablespoons heavy cream (optional)

1 tablespoon lemon juice

Pinch of cayenne

1. Remove the Swiss chard leaves from their stems. Rinse both thoroughly under running water until all grit and dirt is removed. Coarsely chop the stems (you should have 1 cup). Chop the leaves (you should have 2 cups, tightly packed).

2. In a medium Dutch oven, bring the stock and the chard stems to a boil over high heat. Reduce the heat, and simmer for 4 minutes. Then add the chard leaves, zucchini, and salt. Cover, and simmer for another 5 minutes. When the vegetables begin to soften, but are not completely cooked through, add the cilantro and cook for an additional minute. You want the cilantro to just wilt slightly.

3. Transfer the entire contents of the pot to a food processor or blender. (You can also use a handheld emulsifier.) Add the cream, if using, and puree until the mixture is completely smooth.

4. Add the lemon juice and cayenne, and taste for seasoning. This soup is best enjoyed in a large mug.

workweek tomato soup

When I first started my job, I was assigned to a position in my company's office on Hudson Street. Three of us from the same training program shared a row of neighboring desks, where we sat from morning until night. Every afternoon, my friend Lauren and I would lament our lunchtime splurges on $13 West Village salads as we watched our third member eating a hand-packed lunch her mother had made her. I had just moved into my new apartment at this point, but even if I were back at my parents' I wouldn't have pushed it by asking my mother to bag a lunch. By the end of the month, when Lauren and I had blown through our paychecks and were sustaining ourselves on ramen noodles and free wine and cheese from Chelsea art gallery openings (maybe that was just me), I began to notice how we both renounced our salads and went for the same bottom desk drawer at lunchtime. In it was a $2 can of soup, bought during more prosperous times.

Soon we came to embrace the soup lunch and integrated it into our menus at the beginning of the month so that by the end, Lauren didn't have to go home to Cup-o-Noodles and I could stop gorging myself on stale Carr's crackers and bad art. Once I got used to my kitchen and gained enough culinary maturity to try my mother's healthy Green Goddess Soup (page 50), I started to make my own versions of workweek soups, to be consumed in place of the sad supermarket can.

{

1 yellow onion, coarsely chopped

2 carrots, peeled and coarsely chopped

1 fennel bulb, trimmed, outer layer removed, and coarsely chopped

1 tablespoon olive oil

2 cloves garlic, finely chopped

One 28-ounce can crushed tomatoes

1 quart chicken or vegetable stock

¼ cup red wine

1½ teaspoons salt

¼ teaspoon crushed red pepper flakes

¼ cup heavy cream (optional)

½ cup fresh basil leaves, roughly chopped

Freshly grated Parmesan cheese

}

1. In a small food processor, pulse the onion, carrots, and fennel until finely minced and almost pastelike. (If you don't have a food processor, just mince them as fine as possible by hand.)

2. Heat the olive oil in a large stockpot or Dutch oven over medium heat. Add the minced vegetables and sauté until they are tender and beginning to brown, 8 to 10 minutes. Add the garlic and sauté for another 2 minutes, or until softened but not browned.

3. Stir in the tomatoes, stock, wine, salt, and red pepper flakes, and bring the soup to a boil over high heat. Reduce the heat to medium-low and simmer, uncovered, for 30 to 40 minutes, until the flavors taste balanced and earthy. For creamy soup, add the heavy cream and simmer for another 5 minutes. Add half the basil and simmer 5 minutes more.

4. To serve, ladle the soup into bowls and garnish with the remaining basil and grated Parmesan to taste. (The soup can also be cooked and then poured into plastic containers and stored in the freezer for future workweek lunches.)

the quarter-life lunchbox

Cara, Spring 2009

After I started working, I was good about bringing my lunch, and once Phoebe got over paying for deli salads, she was too. At my office, we ate lunch in our individual cubicles, surrounded by scores of manuscripts and constantly full e-mail inboxes. A couple times a month, our band of editorial assistants would take over one of the small windowed conference rooms and eat together, some of us from our own Tupperware, others from midtown takeout containers. Regularly, conversation would turn to the contents of our lunches, with those of us who were brown-baggers having to explain what we were eating. I'd happily discuss what I had brought, though I rarely mentioned that I'd been up at 6:30 a.m. in the morning to make it.

I would sometimes bring in leftovers, but it was Christina, my cubemate, whose meal would most often reflect what she and her husband had eaten the night before. I especially envied the leftover sausage, peppers, and onions she would microwave and stuff into a whole-wheat roll.

Sometimes I'd eat salads for days, having invested in a big box of greens. Sometimes I'd make strange and whimsical pasta dishes. Other times, lunch was more of a mismatched affair, bits of this and that mixed together or piled inside a sandwich. It was on these occasions that it could be a little embarrassing to face the other assistants. Once in a while I worried that even my computer would judge me.

If for whatever reason you're compelled to display the contents of your fridge (via lunchbox) in front of your coworkers, here are four big considerations a lunch-packer should keep in mind. Or rather five, if we consider rule #1: never bring tuna, ever.

budget

Reason: As long as you've already convinced yourself to forgo that tempting-but-disappointing sandwich, salad, or pasta from the deli downstairs, you may as well save yourself some money.

In the Brown Bag: Workweek Tomato Soup (page 52) costs little more than a can of tomatoes.

appearance

Reason: These are the "wish-list" lunches that are as beautiful as they are aromatic. Though you may be required to add some items to the grocery list, if you're the type of person who enjoys making coworkers near and down the hall salivate with envy, you'll want to try to bring in a lunch like this at least on occasion.

In the Brown Bag: Baby Arugula Salad with Radish, Mango, and Creamy Ginger Dressing (page 236) topped with Soy-Honey Baked Tofu (page 76) is a real aesthetic pleaser.

leftovers

Reason: If you've got a plan for the week that involves cooking dinner, you're well positioned to pack a lunch full of delicious leftovers. If dinners or other meals have parts that are prepped in advance, it's also totally possible to save some to use in your lunch. This can be part of a larger strategic plan where you make extra Basil Pesto (page 255) and, say, toss it together with leftover roasted chicken to create a Pesto Chicken Salad Sandwich (page 64).

In the Brown Bag: Even when what you already own is decidedly less exciting than pesto and is more along the lines of dried pasta, you can still come up with a decent lunch. This Saddest Pantry Pasta (page 57)—which is the rather depressing version of the already minimal Saucy Tomato Orecchiette (page 56)—received more coworker mmmmmms than normal.

the afternoon snoozes

Reason: The nutritional components of lunch seem to be impossibly tricky and somewhat unpredictable—the same meal that will leave me bright and productive one day might leave me groggy and grouchy on another. Until after-lunch napping becomes accepted, it's worth trying to put together a balanced meal, slightly on the lighter side, if only for the sake of keeping one's eyes open during important afternoon activities.

In the Brown Bag: Roasted Cauliflower and Quinoa Salad (page 59) is packed with protein and filling enough to prevent any sugary snack cravings later in the day.

saucy tomato orecchiette

Makes 1 serving

The classic at-home dinner, pasta with tomato sauce, gets a twist in technique here. This pasta is great for mornings because the labor-intensive steps are condensed into a few minutes. Then you've got ten minutes to run to your room and pack your bag, dry your hair, and apply makeup. At work, you can eat it at room temperature or reheated. It also works really well for any meal for one, since it makes such a compact single serving. If you own a tea kettle or if you heat the water in the bowl you're going to eat from, you'll have only one dish to clean at the end. The tomato paste is optional, but we think it ramps up the flavor.

1 tablespoon olive oil

1 clove garlic, minced

3 ounces orecchiette pasta

1 teaspoon tomato paste
(optional)

½ teaspoon dried oregano

Pinch of crushed red pepper flakes

½ cup canned crushed tomatoes

½ teaspoon salt

¼ teaspoon sugar

2 tablespoons freshly grated
Parmesan cheese

1. Bring 1¼ cups of water to a boil in the microwave, a teakettle, or a small saucepan. Set aside.
2. In a small Dutch oven or saucepan with a lid, combine the olive oil and the garlic. Cook over medium heat for 1 to 2 minutes, just until the garlic starts to sizzle but not brown. Add the pasta and cook for 2 minutes, stirring constantly. Some sides of the orecchiette will start to lighten in color. If the garlic starts to brown as the pasta is cooking, proceed to the next step immediately.
3. Add the tomato paste (if using), oregano, and red pepper flakes and stir to coat the pasta with it.
4. Add the tomatoes, hot water, salt, and sugar, and turn the heat to high. Stir well. Bring the liquid to a boil, then lower the heat slightly (you still want a pretty rolling

boil—not so low as a simmer), and cover. Cook, stirring every minute, for 10 minutes. The pasta may stick to the bottom of the pan, but it will loosen as you stir it.

5. Check the pasta for doneness. If it's still hard, cover and cook for another 2 to 5 minutes, checking often. At this point, if there isn't enough liquid in the pot, add a little more. If there's too much liquid when the pasta is al dente, simmer for a minute with the lid off to make sure the sauce has thickened.

6. Add half the Parmesan and toss well. Cool slightly before filling up your lunch container and topping with the remaining Parmesan.

Springy Asparagus Pasta: Omit the tomato paste, dried oregano, and crushed tomatoes. Add ¼ teaspoon dried tarragon or thyme with the red pepper flakes. Then add ⅓ cup ¼-inch-thick slices of asparagus (from 5 spears) after the first 10 minutes of cooking. Mix in 1 teaspoon butter at the end.

Saddest Pantry Pasta: Omit the tomato paste and the canned tomatoes. Add an extra clove of garlic and lots of cheese.

roasted cauliflower and quinoa salad

Makes 2 servings

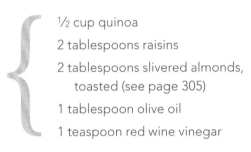

½ cup quinoa

2 tablespoons raisins

2 tablespoons slivered almonds, toasted (see page 305)

1 tablespoon olive oil

1 teaspoon red wine vinegar

¼ teaspoon ground coriander

Salt and freshly ground black pepper

1½ cups Roasted Cauliflower (recipe follows)

8 cherry tomatoes, halved (optional)

1. In a small lidded saucepan, bring 1 cup of water and the quinoa to a boil. Cover, and turn the heat to the lowest possible setting. Cook for 10 minutes. Then remove from the heat and leave covered for another 10 minutes.
2. Fluff the quinoa with a fork. Mix in the raisins, all but a few almonds, the olive oil, vinegar, coriander, and a pinch of salt and a grind of pepper. Arrange in your lunch container, top with the roasted cauliflower, and garnish with the remaining almonds and the tomatoes, if using.

{roasted cauliflower}

Makes 3 to 4 cups

1 head cauliflower, trimmed and divided into florets

2 tablespoons olive oil

Salt

1. Preheat the oven to 375°F.
2. Toss the cauliflower with the olive oil and ½ teaspoon salt, and arrange it in one layer on a baking sheet lined with parchment paper. Bake for about 40 minutes, flipping the cauliflower partway through. You want each floret to be quite brown and tender.
3. Remove from the oven, season to taste, and enjoy hot or at room temperature.

POTLUCKING

Potlucks are amazing. They are such a great kind of party—a democratic way to enjoy food with your best friends. The potluck eases the responsibility and financial burden from one person's shoulders at the same time that it spreads the glory of creation among all invited. We're actually kind of obsessed with potlucks, to the point where we make up all kinds of weird excuses to hold them. Starting a magazine club may be our most far-fetched reason yet.

packing a picnic

In September 2008, just weeks after Lehman Brothers collapsed, a promotion moved me to my company's midtown office. The cafeteria there, "Le Café," as it was called, was a social place, not unlike a high school lunchroom; even though the VPs were, for the most part, French alpha males, they possessed the terrifying aura of mean girls and could choose whether to acknowledge your presence in the sandwich line or to ignore the sea of empty seats at your table in favor of a chair by the posh women over in Skincare.

In December, with the recession upon us, the cafeteria closed and we were left to fend for ourselves in the wasteland of mediocre midtown delis. At first, my boss, Stephanie, and I would stroll to restaurants and take-out joints in a few-block radius, admiring all the handsome men in suits who also, apparently, went out at lunchtime. But soon it all got a little tired, and we stopped being stimulated by the East 40s, the cobb salads, and the $10 we spent on them. After a few unfortunate run-ins with past flings, we started to dread the men, too.

The next week we started picnicking. I brought in an extra-large portion of leftover salad and Stephanie added a helping of the delicious pasta she had made the night before. Soon we got into a good meal rhythm together. We hit the first speed bump when I contributed Green Goddess Soup (page 50)—Stephanie took one look, then ran out for pizza. The next came in the form of her mushroom risotto.

As we sat in her office reading aloud the *New York* magazine *Gossip Girl* recap, Stephanie paused and grimaced. I thought she was going to make a comment about Jenny Humphrey's eye makeup. Instead she asked, "Does this taste weird to you?" motioning to my container, where I had been politely pushing around the tangy grains to look like I had eaten more than half my portion.

"I guess it's a little tart," I said.

Stephanie made a comment about perhaps using a bad bottle of wine in the cooking process. When she got home that night, she discovered it was indeed a bad bottle, because it wasn't wine—it was champagne vinegar.

As our office lunches progressed, we began sharing much more than just an occasional sandwich. I learned a lot about feeding men from Stephanie, mainly about pork tenderloin as a go-to first date meal. It was also Stephanie who taught me the art of real outdoor picnicking. For her July birthday, she asked me to help micromanage a picnic dinner in Central Park. Of course when I arrived at her apartment, she had already thought of everything. As we packed the makings for Pimm's Cup into tiny plastic baggies, Stephanie confessed, "Sometimes I wish I could carry my entire life's contents inside a Ziploc bag."

The two of us arrived on the Great Lawn with a huge blanket, pasta salad, hummus, baby carrots, and bags of chips. As people showed up, Stephanie poured them cups of Pimm's. Other friends came bearing panzanella and wine, and as we drank and ate, the New York Philharmonic played in the background. It was a magical evening, a night that felt utterly New York. Then, as the orchestra performed its final crescendo, the sky opened up with *Fantasia*-esque fury, and Mother Nature poured rain on the half-eaten hummus, the blanket, the birthday girl, and all her guests.

Moments later, we fought through the soggy crowds, lugging home a very heavy, very wet blanket (unfortunately too big for a Ziploc). Stephanie wrung out the bottom of her blue silk birthday dress and lamented the flaws in her picnic planning: she had remembered the corkscrew but had forgotten all about an umbrella.

picnic checklist

You can't control the weather, but you can control most everything else about your picnic, outdoors or at work. Here is our checklist for a hassle-free, over-prepared picnic, enriched by Stephanie's wisdom:

- ☐ paper or plastic plates
- ☐ plastic forks
- ☐ plastic cups
- ☐ napkins
- ☐ serving spoons
- ☐ salt and pepper
- ☐ corkscrew/bottle opener
- ☐ booze
- ☐ blanket
- ☐ plastic bags for trash
- ☐ cooler (optional)
- ☐ umbrella (optional)
- ☐ food!

pesto chicken salad sandwiches with arugula and sun-dried tomatoes

Makes 8 sandwiches

Stephanie's biggest foodie fear is a soggy sandwich. Chicken salad sandwiches have great portability because they allow you to avoid having to put condiments directly on the bread. We add two elements of flavor—pesto and a light, subtle hit of mayo—to give these non-soggy sandwiches some moisture. Instead of regular plum tomatoes, which release a lot of liquid as they sit, we use sliced sun-dried tomatoes. A healthy handful of arugula helps protect the bread even more. You can use the meat from a whole rotisserie chicken or roast your own (see page 305).

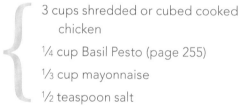

3 cups shredded or cubed cooked chicken

¼ cup Basil Pesto (page 255)

⅓ cup mayonnaise

½ teaspoon salt

1 baguette, cut in half horizontally

½ cup sun-dried tomatoes (about 10 tomatoes), thinly sliced

1 cup tightly packed fresh baby arugula leaves

1. In a large mixing bowl, combine the chicken, pesto, mayo, and salt. Taste for seasoning. (This can be done 1 or 2 days ahead.)
2. Preheat the broiler.
3. Place the bread, cut side up, on a baking sheet and toast under the broiler until crusty but not browned, about 2 minutes.
4. Spread the chicken salad evenly over the bottom half of the bread. Add a layer of the sun-dried tomatoes and then the arugula. Top with the remaining bread, and cut into 8 even sandwiches.
5. Wrap each sandwich tightly in plastic wrap, and then in aluminum foil. Keep shaded or in a cool spot until time to eat.

pimm's cup

Pimm's is a classic British cocktail especially perfect for daytime outdoor drinking.

{
1 large cucumber, cut into
 ¼-inch-thick slices

1 pound strawberries, hulled
 and halved

2 small lemons, cut into
 ¼-inch-thick rounds

1 cup fresh mint leaves, plus extra
 for garnish

3 cups lemonade or Sprite

3 cups Pimm's No. 1

Ice
}

If you are serving this at a party, combine all the ingredients in a large punch bowl, and scatter a few mint leaves on top.

   If you are packing a picnic, load the cucumber slices, strawberries, lemons, and mint leaves into separate sandwich bags. Play bartender and prepare each individual's cup with ice, cucumber, mint, and fruit, and use a 1:1 ratio of Pimm's to lemonade or Sprite when pouring. Garnish with a few extra mint leaves.

the simplest pasta salad: fusilli with pomodoro fresco

Makes 4 to 6 servings

This pasta salad gets better the longer it sits. Make it a day or two in advance, but reserve the basil to add just before serving (it will go limp in the tomato juices).

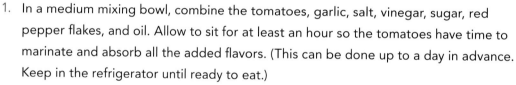

2 pounds tomatoes, seeded, cored, and finely diced

2 cloves garlic, minced or pushed through a press

1½ teaspoons salt

2 teaspoons balsamic vinegar

1 teaspoon sugar

½ teaspoon crushed red pepper flakes

¼ cup olive oil

1 pound fusilli, penne rigate, or other short pasta

½ cup chopped fresh basil leaves

1. In a medium mixing bowl, combine the tomatoes, garlic, salt, vinegar, sugar, red pepper flakes, and oil. Allow to sit for at least an hour so the tomatoes have time to marinate and absorb all the added flavors. (This can be done up to a day in advance. Keep in the refrigerator until ready to eat.)

2. Bring a large pot of salted water to a boil over high heat. Cook the pasta, following the package directions, until al dente. Drain, and add the pasta to the tomato mixture.

3. Stir in the chopped basil and toss everything together. It's best if served at room temperature—preferably on a picnic blanket.

magazine club: an idea with follow-through

Cara, Summer 2008

One day in late July 2008, Kate—my camp friend, Phoebe's doppelgänger, and the host of our favorite annual holiday party—had an idea.

It was a Sunday, and we were eating Mexican food outdoors in the insane noontime heat and talking about how people start book clubs but almost no one really has the time and follow-through to maintain one. Then, as she polished off the quesadilla we were sharing, Kate perked up with a look of pure cartoon-lightbulb genius.

"You know," she said, "what if we started a magazine club?"

I laughed, imagining us all sitting around discussing the meaning of the latest dating advice in *Cosmo* or trying to act out the calisthenics routines in *Shape*. But that wasn't exactly what Kate meant.

"We'll each bring our own article and talk about it," she went on.

"And eat?" I asked, immediately brainstorming ideas for how to make food a crucial element of our new group gathering.

"Exactly!"

Though I'm not a magazine aficionado, I saw the genius in Kate's plan. A magazine club would remove all the pressure of reading and thinking that makes book clubs boring. I had an inkling that if the monthly event were a potluck too, we would make a point of keeping it up.

On Monday morning, Kate sent an e-mail to ten friends with a date for our first meeting, as well as the club's four rules: (1) Arrive with a magazine article. (2) Bring a dish. (3) The article should inspire the dish brought. (4) At the meeting, each member should summarize her article and explain its connection to her dish.

Kate's e-mail examples went as follows:

(a) This past month's issue of *W* had a photo shoot about camp, therefore 'smores or anything that reminds you of camp would be appropriate.

(b) There was a purple dress on the cover of *InStyle*, and thus you made eggplant parm!

In other words, we left room for interpretation.

The group we invited was a mix of our high school friends, some of whom—like Leora, Julie, and Jordana—are themselves old friends from summer camp. The ten of us arrived that first week at Julie's new apartment on the Lower East Side, magazines in one hand and containers of food in the other. Phoebe came bearing an extremely large bowl of "Go Green!" pesto pasta salad. She claimed the dish's quantity and color were inspired by an extremely long Thomas Friedman article on sustainable living, but it may have been the wilting basil in her fridge that really compelled her to make it. I took a more visual approach, of the purple dress–eggplant school, bringing a rustic plate of crostini slathered with creamy ricotta and broccoli rabe, also known as an edible interpretation of the impressionistic landscape on the cover of the current *New Yorker*. Kate made spicy, sensual, Eva Mendes tostadas, accompanied by a profile of the actress. Jordana brought wine. And Leora, as she would

continue to do for Mag Club eternally, set down a huge caprese salad, inspired by her undying love of caprese salad.

It was a little awkward at first to try to discuss silly articles in such a formal way, but after the first meeting everyone but Kate stopped following rules #1, 3, and 4, and we were rid of that problem. Still, we religiously blocked off the second Tuesday of every month for our Mag Club potluck, rotating hosting duties. The more we met, the more we grew attuned to each other's food cravings, and by the fall, most of the potluck spreads were as bountiful and almost as well-rounded as if one cook, albeit a really hungry one, had prepared it all.

In November, we all converged on a seasonal theme. Arriving Mag Clubbers lined Phoebe's table with roasted butternut squash, pumpkin muffins, two types of spiced nuts, Brussels sprouts, and a root vegetable gratin. Even Leora conceded to the season, making caprese salad with *roasted* tomatoes. As usual, we sat around talking too loudly and eating too much, bringing everyone up to speed on work, travel, apartments, guys, and the ingredients in our potluck dish.

After more than a year, Magazine Club is an official tradition. Even during busy months, we know for certain we can count on eating Leora's mozzarella, talking about how Jordana wants to quit her job, listening to Kate's steadfast article summaries, and weighing in on Julie's dating stories. For though it was never written, our club's fifth rule decrees that cancellation is not an option. Yet like the other rules, this one too has grown irrelevant. The face-to-face time, the eating, and the chatting are, I assure you, valuable enough to ensure our devoted membership in what might seem, to outsiders, like just a silly club.

corn and barley salad with lemon-chive vinaigrette

Makes 4 to 6 servings

For Mag Club March, Phoebe made this salad, inspired by an image in *Teen Vogue*. Though she would not normally publicly admit to reading this magazine, at work she was paid to think like a fifteen-year-old girl. While she was casually browsing its pages, she was struck by a fashion spread of teenage hillbillies flirting in a barley field.

{
2 teaspoons salt

1 cup barley, thoroughly rinsed in cold water and drained

2 tablespoons finely chopped fresh chives

Juice of 1 lemon

2 teaspoons white wine vinegar

1 tablespoon Dijon mustard

2 teaspoons honey

¼ cup olive oil

½ teaspoon ground cumin

One 15-ounce can corn kernels, rinsed and drained, or 2 cups fresh or defrosted frozen kernels
}

1. In a medium stockpot or Dutch oven, bring 2½ cups of water and 1 teaspoon of the salt to a boil. Add the barley and reduce to low heat. Simmer, uncovered, for about 45 minutes, until the barley is al dente. If liquid remains, drain the barley in a colander or use the lid of the pot to strain off any excess moisture. Set aside.

2. In a salad bowl, whisk together the chives, lemon juice, vinegar, mustard, honey, olive oil, cumin, and the remaining 1 teaspoon salt.

3. Add the barley and corn, and toss to combine. Taste for seasoning, and serve at room temperature.

smoked mozzarella tartlettes

Makes 30 tartlettes

These are easy but impressive, and they work best if you bring the prepped ingredients and bake at the host's apartment, though they taste good at room temperature. Whatever variation you choose, everyone will love them, so customize them to go with your magazine article. Whatever quantity you make will disappear. We love them almost as much as we love Mag Club itself.

{

One 17-ounce package puff pastry sheets (we use Pepperidge Farm), thawed if frozen

¼ cup canned crushed tomatoes

1 clove garlic, minced

Salt

Crushed red pepper flakes

½ pound smoked mozzarella, coarsely grated

⅓ cup grated Parmesan cheese

1 handful fresh baby arugula leaves (optional)

}

1. Preheat the oven to 400°F.
2. Using a 3-inch round cookie cutter, cut the puff pastry into rounds (or just use a glass and cut circles around it). Line two baking sheets with parchment paper and arrange the rounds on them (15 rounds per sheet).
3. In a small bowl, combine the crushed tomatoes with the garlic, and season to taste with salt and crushed red pepper flakes.
4. Place a teaspoon of the tomato sauce on each pastry round, and use the back of the spoon to spread it out, leaving a ¼-inch border. Cover each with a sprinkling of the mozzarella and a bit of the Parmesan cheese.
5. Bake in the oven for 20 to 25 minutes, until the puff pastry is golden and cooked through the center, and the cheese is melted and becoming crusty. The rounds will be quite puffed up. Remove and let sit for 5 minutes (the pastry will de-puff in that time).
6. Top each tartlette with a few arugula leaves, if using, and serve.

Caramelized Onion Tartlettes: Top each tartlette with a spoonful of Spiced Caramelized Onions (page 137).

Mini Meatball Pizzas: Add a halved meatball (see page 281) to each.

White Tartlettes: Omit the tomato sauce, and replace it with ½ cup ricotta and thin slices of zucchini.

soy-honey baked tofu

Makes 2 to 4 servings

This is one of those tofu dishes that will win people over, even if they're not already as veggie-centric as some of our Mag Club members. It's also a great topping for Baby Arugula Salad with Radishes, Mango, and Creamy Ginger Vinaigrette (page 236).

One 1-pound package firm tofu, drained and cut into eight ½-inch-thick slices

One 2-inch piece of fresh ginger, peeled and minced (about 1 tablespoon)

2 cloves garlic, minced

2 tablespoons soy sauce

2 tablespoons mirin or white wine

2 tablespoons rice vinegar

1 tablespoon vegetable oil

1 tablespoon toasted sesame oil

1 tablespoon honey

1. Place the tofu slices in one layer on a platter lined with a clean dish towel. Cover the tofu with another towel, weight it with a book, and let it rest on the counter for 30 minutes.

2. Meanwhile, in a small bowl, whisk together all the remaining ingredients.

3. Preheat the oven to 350°F. (Or wait—see step 5.)

4. Arrange the tofu in an 8×8-inch baking pan (or in any other ovenproof pan in which the tofu fits snugly). Pour the marinade over the tofu. Turn the tofu over slices to make sure the marinade evenly coats each piece.

5. If you have time, let the tofu rest in the marinade for 1 hour.

6. Bake for 45 minutes, until the tofu is brown and mostly dry. Let it rest for 10 minutes on the counter so it firms up. Then serve or load into plastic containers for your potluck.

the new hosting democracy

Phoebe, Fall 2008

When Virginia went blue, we knew it had happened.

A few of my college friends and I were watching the election unfold at one of their apartments. Before the last few states were called, I quickly said my overjoyed good-byes and went home to be with Caitlyn for the pivotal moment. But I miscalculated the timing, and halfway down 6th Avenue the announcement was made on the radio that Barack Obama had become the 44th president of the United States.

My taxi driver stopped the cab, got out, and hugged me. New York seemed to have stopped for a moment, too. But then I heard the collective cheers coming from the apartment windows above, the faint sound of foghorns from Washington Square Park. I reached into my purse and handed the cabbie all the bills that my wallet had to offer. I think I also told him that I loved him. And then I started sprinting like a crazy person.

When I walked into my apartment, it was dark and empty, and Caitlyn was nowhere to be found. So I dropped my purse, grabbed my keys, and headed for Union Square. I high-fived a man walking his dog and accepted a blue streamer from a girl on a stoop. When I arrived at 14th Street, I grabbed an edge of the star-spangled parachute spread across the crowd, and with every ounce of me, started to shake the crap out of it.

In the months that followed, friends threw plenty of parties to celebrate the new president. The best one took place on January 20th, inauguration night. It was cohosted by our friend Carolyn, a New York version of the countless balls taking over Washington that evening. In our excitement, Cara and I had been discussing sparkly party dresses on the phone for weeks. But our outfits and accessories took on a new set of complications when Sarah announced that she was throwing a potluck party before the gala. We now had to carry both food and clothes to work that day.

Our high school friends, even those who are not Mag Clubbers like Sarah, are no strangers to potlucks. Eating this way became our tradition starting in the summer of 2008—a year after graduation—when Jocelyn wrote in an e-mail that we should all go out for dinner. I suggested that instead of choosing a restaurant, we stay in, and because I also offered my apartment as the venue, I took the liberty of assigning tasks: to the cooks, veggies, meat, or dessert; to the non-cooks, wine.

The food bringers kept with the eating habits that have defined our group dining since we came together for our first meal around age fourteen. Carolyn, whose vegetarianism introduced us early to hummus, baked eggplant, and zucchini fries, went out of her way to pick up some of her dad's amazing baked dill tofu. Jennie, who started roasting a Christmas goose for her family back in tenth grade and now works at a fancy French restaurant, was still in cooking school that summer. She made a huge dish (like, could have fed an entire restaurant) of peanut noodles. Cara brought a lemon layer cake, half of which was eaten and half of which endured a slow, painful death in my freezer. Those who'd been assigned wine that fateful summer evening, mainly Sarah, seemed to take it as both an affront and a challenge, and soon embarked on paths of cooking for others and throwing their own potluck parties to prove it.

Though I know we were all excited to step into our sparkly dresses for the inauguration ball, I think most of us were even more eager to add our own dishes to the shared potluck table. As we landed at Sarah's, Cara and I realized we had taken opposite approaches. Cara spent the night prior making a simple onion tart that could survive several trips on the subway and still taste delicious. I, on the other hand, arrived with a shopping bag full of packages, which were tossed together in minutes to create a Super Bowl–size dip to serve with blue tortilla chips. I may have gotten cream on my satin shoes as I stirred, and Sarah's pecan bars might have made our party attire a little more snug than we had intended, but we were happy we had eaten and hung out the way we had.

I can remember how fun the Inauguration Ball was, heightened by a sense of political promise—there was the same unifying exuberance in the air that I had felt rubbing shoulders with strangers in Union Square. But it's hard to claim that it was more fun than the potluck, immortalized by a series of Polaroids taken that night. At Sarah's, we had been energized by the same promise and the same exuberance, but they felt somehow more concentrated, not diffused by the clamor of a party but rather amplified by the closeness of our friends and the food from our collective homes. It was a start to the new presidency that was a little more intimate and relaxed—a party that was, well, maybe just a little more democratic.

dump and stir mexican dip

Makes 10 servings

I owe the ingenious simplicity of this dish to my college roommate, Jillian, who ensured that it was on the table at every festive gathering and helped me achieve the freshman fifteen by junior year.

One 10-ounce package frozen chopped spinach, defrosted and drained (see page 299)

One 8-ounce package shredded Mexican fiesta blend or Monterey Jack cheese

One 8-ounce package cream cheese, at room temperature

1 cup half-and-half

One 15-ounce jar medium salsa

1 teaspoon chili powder (optional)

Tortilla chips, for serving

1. Preheat the oven to 350°F.
2. In a large bowl (or in the skillet/dish itself), combine all the ingredients except the chips. Whisk together until the mixture is fully blended, eliminating any large chunks of spinach or cream cheese.
3. With a spatula, scrape the mixture into a large ovenproof skillet or casserole dish and bake for 20 to 30 minutes, until the cheese is fully melted and the top has begun to set. Raise the temperature to 400°F and bake for 5 to 10 more minutes, to create a slight crust.
4. Serve with tortilla chips. If, as in this case, the occasion calls for it, make them blue.

sexy-ugly onion tart

Makes 8 servings

"Sexy-ugly," a term we learned from the movie *Kissing Jessica Stein*, refers to people (or tarts) who are attractive without being conventionally beautiful. This pastry recipe makes a little more than is necessary for one tart. You can either save the extra for another tart or cut into small rounds and use them instead of puff pastry for tartlettes. Another option is to make the tart free-form—just roll out the dough to ⅛-inch thickness and arrange it on a parchment-lined baking sheet. In addition to being sexy-ugly, this tart is also delicious.

2 tablespoons unsalted butter

2 onions, halved and sliced into thin half-moons

1 teaspoon fresh thyme leaves, plus some extra for garnish

¼ teaspoon salt

1 cup whole-milk ricotta

1 egg yolk

Dough for 1 pie crust (recipe follows)

1. In a large cast-iron skillet or Dutch oven, melt the butter over low heat. Add the onions and cook, stirring occasionally, for about 45 minutes, until caramelized (see page 297). The onions should be deep brown and sweet. Add the thyme leaves and the salt, and let cool off the heat.
2. Whisk the ricotta and egg yolk together in a small bowl. Set aside.
3. Make sure your work surface is clean and cool. Lightly flour the surface and roll out the dough until it is large enough to cover a 9-inch fluted tart pan with a removable bottom.
4. Roll up the dough on your rolling pin and then slowly unroll it on top of the tart pan. Use your fingers to press the dough into the tart pan and a paring knife to trim off any excess. If the dough breaks, don't worry—just pull it together and patch it. Try to make the walls a bit thicker than the bottom.
5. Chill the tart shell in the fridge for 10 minutes so that the dough remains cold. Clump together any excess dough and store it in plastic wrap for another use.

6. Meanwhile, preheat the oven to 400°F.
7. Remove the tart shell from the fridge, and use a spatula to spread the ricotta mixture evenly across the surface. Arrange the onions on top.
8. Bake for 25 to 30 minutes, until the ricotta filling is firm and the crust is beautifully golden.
9. Let the tart cool in the pan. Garnish it with thyme leaves. Slice the tart into 8 pieces (if you're potlucking, wrap the tart pan and bring it with you to slice on-site).

{pie crust}

Makes more than enough dough for one 9-inch crust

2 cups all-purpose flour

1¾ teaspoons salt

1 cup (2 sticks) cold butter

1 egg yolk

3 to 5 tablespoons cold water

> *Note: If you don't have a food processor, you can do this in a bowl: Mix the flour and salt, then use your fingers to rub the butter into the dry ingredients, until it looks like crumbs, touching the dough as little as possible. Combine the egg yolk and 3 tablespoons of the cold water, and add this to the bowl. Mix together with a spatula until the dough comes together.*

1. In a food processor, combine the flour and salt. Cut the butter into roughly tablespoon-size pieces and add them to the flour. Then pulse until the butter pieces are the size of peas, about 20 pulses. Add the egg yolk and 3 tablespoons of the cold water, and run the processor until the dough starts to come together. It should clump into a big ball; if it doesn't, drizzle in another tablespoon or two of the water. You want to add as little liquid as possible.

2. Form the dough into a 7-inch disk on a lightly floured surface. Wrap it tightly in plastic wrap and chill it in the fridge for 1 to 2 hours. (You can store it for up to 4 days.)

3. Let the dough sit at room temperature for 15 to 20 minutes before trying to roll it out.

other great potluck portables

Roasted Cauliflower and Quinoa Salad (page 59)

Ratatouille (page 129)

Black Bean Dip (page 111)

Smoky Chipotle Vegetarian Chili (page 200)

Noodles with BGSK Peanut Sauce (page 91)

Pesto Chicken Salad Sandwiches (page 64)

Three-Onion Dip (page 275)

Thin and Snappy Ginger Cookies (page 176)

Banana Chocolate Chip Bread (page 185)

teaching the tenets of byob

Phoebe

As far as I am concerned, there are two types of potluckers: those who bring food, and those who bring wine.

When I am in charge of organizing these meals, I put someone in charge of beverages. Yet for regular dinner parties, assigning wine to guests can feel a little inappropriate, even downright bossy. That's where the beauty of BYOB comes into play. More often than not, my friends are polite and generous enough to understand that wine is part of the "entrance fee" into my apartment. I haven't had to teach them this at all. Instead, I've found that the steepest learning curve when it comes to the tenets of BYOB is my own.

Since I'm known to like food, some of my wine-loving friends with expensive tastes and generous spirits assume I'm able to detect and appreciate a fine grape and vintage. These friends are the ones I know will bring nice bottles of wine to my parties, but they usually alert me and my less appreciative guests anyway by saying, "Don't guzzle this one, guys— it's good." It's crucial that they tell me this, because at the dinner parties I throw, the bottles brought are almost always opened, rarely saved. I don't exactly have a wine cellar to draw from, should all the party wine be consumed, and in fact, when the bottles brought to the event run dry, the dinner usually comes to a halt since there is nothing else in the apartment to drink save for that quarter handle of cheap vodka in the freezer. On the other hand, I don't want to squander a special bottle meant for me on a group of rowdy friends.

At our housewarming, I awkwardly asked my friend Alix, upon receiving a bottle from him, "Should I hide it in my bedroom, or should we hide in my bedroom and drink it together?"

"It's up to you," he said casually. "I just want you to enjoy it."

Of course, hiding in my bedroom with guests outside the door is not an ideal scenario, nor is hoarding the bottle for the remainder of the night, sipping slowly, sharing none. In this case, I would have enjoyed the bottle most if Alix and I were sharing it over a bowl of risotto or, say, a good steak—depending on the wine. Instead, I awkwardly snuck into my bedroom to stow the bottle away, and I hoped that the opportunity would present itself for us to drink it together. In truth, though, I knew the next time I invited Alix to dinner he would likely arrive with another nice bottle for us to consume on the spot.

BYOB strategy for both host and guest really is contingent on the occasion. Here are some guidelines I've come to embrace from hosting and attending lots of rather boozy parties.

party gifts

As a partygoer, if your ultimate goal is for the recipient to enjoy the wine you've brought, don't contribute an expensive bottle on an occasion when he or she can't do so. If you want it to be enjoyed at a later date, and it deserves to be hidden underneath a bookshelf in the bedroom, make sure to let the host know this. Wrapping the bottle is a good way to signify that it is special. (If you wrap it in aluminum foil, as my friend Blake did at my twenty-third birthday party, your intention will be less clear. But for what it's worth, that bottle did successfully make it under the bookshelf.) Still, unless the host is a good friend and you know her taste, don't count on her to know enough about wine to recognize a great bottle when it's handed to her.

From the host's perspective, it's important to remember your friends' strategies. If Alix gives me a bottle of wine, I always hide it. If it's my friend Adrienne, I know the bag contains a delicious buttery chardonnay, nice enough that I wouldn't buy the bottle every day, but not so nice that I couldn't replace it on my own if it got downed at the party. I usually instruct Adrienne to open the bottle and pour herself a glass, as I know it's exactly what she wants to be drinking.

a bottle of bubbly

For big parties, cheap sparkling wine is always a good choice. It is festive enough for a special occasion, and even if it's the cheapest of the cheap, the bottle is still "fancy" enough to give as a gift. Champagne is also way better when consumed with a room full of friends, so even if someone brings a fancy bottle of Veuve, why not pop it open right then and there, even if it means you only get half a Dixie cup full? Here the gift giver will not be offended or upset if he only receives a scant portion—bubbly is meant for sharing.

the go-to bottle

Some people, like Adrienne and her La Crema chardonnay, pick a go-to bottle and stick with it. If you do not know a lot about wine in general, it's often more convenient to educate yourself on your local wine shop's selection than to embark on becoming an oenophile. This way you'll have red and white staple bottles that are both inexpensive and reliably delicious.

You'll avoid getting stuck staring blankly at the wine store's shelves, and you'll steer clear of the large-scale, low-quality importers when searching for something affordable and familiar.

quantity over quality

If the purpose of your wine contribution is to grease the wheels of forty or fifty party guests, bring a magnum. We're talking quantity over quality at this point, for, as a host, the biggest concern is running out of liquor altogether. To speak to this, sometimes it's better not to bring wine at all. Consider bringing beer or whiskey. You don't have to bring a whole handle of liquor, which is clearly more expensive than wine. But a smaller bottle of hard liquor will last the host longer than one bottle of decent wine, and if it is premium enough, it won't even need mixers, which is one more annoying thing the host has to worry about running out of.

karma counts

As a bringer of booze, your taste counts most of all. I always hope that the bottle chosen is decent enough that the giver would want to drink it him- or herself.

I never know which bottle might be the one left unopened at the end of the night, the one left for my own enjoyment when I'm alone in front of the TV with my mug of peas. Then, after all the pots and pans have been put away and the last bags of trash taken down to the Dumpster, I'll really be focused on its taste. Though I'm not a member of a demographic that easily turns down a glass of anything, I'll hope that if it was good enough for my guests' palates, it'll be good enough for mine.

COCKTAIL PARTIES

Sometimes all you need to make a party special are a few little things to nibble on. We'll rarely ever have people over for a drink without making some sort of snack, and usually, if the crowd is big enough, there will be enough to constitute a small meal. If you stick with room-temperature finger food like the dishes in this section, there's no last-minute cooking and you're free to entertain your guests, so long as they don't arrive while your hair is still in a towel.

the art of finger food

Cara, Fall 2008

In college, the professors who oversaw each dorm threw open houses once every few weeks for the three or four hundred students in their particular building. My senior year, I became co-chef for these events and took home a paycheck every month for the work I had done, menu planning, baking for hours, directing the student workers, and flinging baking pans around like a diva on her stage, work I'd have done for free.

I made nacho bites and mini grilled cheeses, sausage-filled crescents and crepes. I baked cookies upon cookies, all kinds of brownies, and loaves of zucchini bread. When I graduated, I missed this job a lot. My new apartment—and my new salary—were not of the caliber to support this kind of over-the-top party. But I soon discovered that there were other ways.

In November 2008, just after I'd moved to Brooklyn, Jordana was turning twenty-four. She and I had just come off a year of living together, and though we both preferred to forget the crappiness of the East Village tenement apartment, I missed our shared food rituals, like making sure we were always stocked with smoked tofu. I even missed opening the fridge to find that she had polished off all my leftovers, including the extra peanut noodles I'd made for Leora's birthday.

A week before her big day, Jordana and I had a rapid-fire e-mail planning session.

"Should I do something at the apartment? My parents will be home but I guess I could kick them out." (She was living at her parents' place again, temporarily.)

"Pull a Phoebe?" I replied. "Well, what's your dream birthday celebration? Let's start there."

Jordana kept going back and forth between small dinner parties and big cocktail parties, meals at the apartment and meals out. The guest list shrunk to thirteen, then bounced up to thirty-five.

"You're heading into the-more-the-merrier territory," I wrote, thrilled at the prospect of cooking for so many people. "But that's finger food—the best kind of party to throw."

With all the confidence in the world, I volunteered Phoebe to help cook, apparently not giving a thought as to whether she'd actually be willing and free. The two of us were always talking about food anyway, constantly chattering at potlucks and in text messages about menus, kitchen tools, and dinner party guest lists even though we weren't roommates or dining together all the time. We each seemed to have expertise the other sought. In college, while I'd been spending someone else's money on prosciutto and winter strawberries to make my gourmet open-house concoctions, Phoebe was becoming a pro at crowd-pleasing cooking that was a little more down-to-earth. She'd call me up to gush about how she managed to feed a group of twenty for under $50, and I'd ask her to hold on for a second while I scanned the grocery shelves, trying to choose between Callebaut and Valrhona chocolate for the cookies I was baking.

The week before Jordana's, we combed through our wish list for her birthday, toning down some of the high-concept finger food I thought I wanted to make. In the end, we created a quarter-life-friendly vegetarian menu of crostini and quesadillas, dips and skewers, making two variations of some dishes to streamline the prepping. We did keep on a few involved items: the infamous Manchurian Cauliflower, which had to be fried on the spot, and Jordana's beloved peanut noodles, whose ingredients I tracked down in Chinatown. For dessert, we served cupcakes piled with icing and decorated with candles, and bowls of cold

Pretzel-Toffee Chocolate Bark (page 45). I felt like I was back in the saddle, planning menus again.

When our friends began arriving, Phoebe and I were still in cooking garb (Jordana's old T-shirts) and we were in the midst of grabbing hot trays out of the oven and julienning basil to garnish large platters of crostini. By the time we emerged from Jordana's room in our party clothes, every last cauliflower floret had been inhaled, and people were drinking and getting into the party. We gathered for a photo with a bunch of our Mag Club friends by the beautiful windows that overlook the Hudson. In it, we've got our arms around each other and we're caught mid-laughter, making us look more sixteen than twenty-four.

We watched Jordana—wearing lace and chiffon and basking in her birthday glory—bend over the tray of cupcakes to blow out her candles with a giant *whoosh.*

After most friends had left to head back downtown, Phoebe and I stood alone in the medium-size kitchen. Though I was exhausted, I was as satisfied as I'd been in a while. I thought about standing in my own kitchen after 11 p.m. the night before, getting covered in peanut sauce as I scraped out my blender, and being completely content with the fact that I was spending the better half of a long day of work in my kitchen. I was certain Phoebe and I could and should keep cooking and feeding others—and keep on talking about it.

Two weeks later, Phoebe bought the domain name for *Big Girls, Small Kitchen,* and we started the blog.

noodles with bgsk peanut sauce

Makes 4 servings

This is among our most-requested dishes, especially when Jordana is doing the requesting. We wouldn't recommend eating this with your fingers, but you can make it part of a cocktail spread by serving the noodles in individual bowls or Chinese take-out containers with chopsticks in them.

1 tablespoon diced peeled fresh ginger

1 clove garlic, coarsely chopped

¼ cup sugar

1 teaspoon chili paste, Sriracha sauce, or ½ teaspoon crushed red pepper flakes

½ cup smooth peanut butter, preferably natural

¼ cup soy sauce

2 tablespoons Worcestershire sauce

1 tablespoon rice vinegar

2 tablespoons toasted sesame oil

¼ teaspoon salt (optional)

¾ pound fresh udon noodles, spaghetti, or linguine

1 tablespoon vegetable oil

1 bunch scallions (green parts only), chopped

1 cucumber, peeled, seeded, and julienned

1 tablespoon sesame seeds, toasted (see page 305)

1. Pulse the ginger, garlic, and sugar in a food processor or blender until the mixture resembles a paste. Add the chili paste, peanut butter, soy sauce, Worcestershire sauce, rice vinegar, and sesame oil. Process until smooth. Add ⅓ cup water, and pulse to combine. Taste, and add the salt if needed. Set the sauce aside for at least 1 hour to let the flavors meld, or refrigerate it overnight. (If the sauce thickens when you refrigerate it, just add a few tablespoons of boiling water to thin it.)

2. When you're ready to make the dish, bring a large pot of salted water to a boil. Cook the noodles, following the package directions. Then drain, rinse with cold water until chilled, and toss with the vegetable oil.

3. In a large mixing bowl, toss the noodles with the peanut sauce. Serve in individual portions, topped with the scallions, cucumber, and toasted sesame seeds.

the crostini consultant

Phoebe, Fall 2008

The practice of loading crusty bread with savory toppings entered my repertoire back in 2005, when I was living in Rome. Our student apartment, where my first experimentations with fancy Pesto Panino (page 39) took place, was one of the most claustrophobic spaces I have inhabited in my short span of urban rentals. Six of us—my guy friends from college, Al and Wish, and three girls from our program—lived right off Campo dei Fiori, the site of an exquisite outdoor market and the city's best source of inexpensive produce. There was no dishwasher, a bona fide mini-fridge, and barely enough utensils and plates for all the roommates to enjoy a meal at the same time.

Regardless, Al and Wish would constantly invite over large groups of our classmates for Italian family-style dinners. These affairs were BYOP (bring your own plate) in addition to BYOB, though this was not as bad as it sounds since most of our fellow students lived in the very same three-story walk-up.

About thirty minutes before people were supposed to arrive at any given party, I would inevitably notice the boys floundering about in the kitchen. They'd be prodding two wimpy chicken breasts and staring blankly at various cheeses and meats, wondering how to arrange them in a presentable manner and, more importantly, how to make the rather meager quantities stretch to feed twelve mouths.

At this point, I would usually be pulled in as a consultant, and since the kitchen really fit only one person at a time, the boys would scatter. I'd put the undercooked chicken back in the skillet and put Al and Wish to work at the dining room table. Exiled, they would sit there slicing loaves of *pane rustico* into thin, bite-size pieces until I'd join them to top each one with a slice of gorgeously ripe tomato, some buffalo mozzarella or fontina, and a piece of prosciutto—whatever ingredients hadn't made it into my sandwich that afternoon. Then I'd carry the assembled crostini back to the tiny kitchen and toast them in the oven until crusty, melty, and ready for the masses who'd arrived and were hanging out on our living room floor drinking jug wine out of water glasses. Their appetites appeased by the numerous courses of crostini, our dinner guests always left full enough not to notice that they hadn't really been served a meal at all.

Back at Jordana's twenty-fourth, I noticed how fast the platters of eggplant crostini were emptying. I looked across the room and saw someone loading up a large paper plate. It was none other than my old roommate Al, who, thanks to my matchmaking prowess, was dating Jordana at the time. I walked over to join them, and to steal some of the dwindling supply of crostini from Al's plate. He was smiling, eating, and telling Jordana about the Roman family-style dinner parties we used to throw, with friends on the floor and crostini lining every other available surface.

sweet pea crostini

Makes 30 to 40 bites

It's funny how recipes trickle down to us. This topping was inspired by a dish made by Jenny, a friend of Cara's sister Jill, which we heard about but didn't taste—but credit where credit is due. Don't over-cook the frozen peas. You want them green and vibrant, not olive-colored and limp.

2 tablespoons unsalted butter or olive oil

1 small yellow onion, diced

½ teaspoon crushed red pepper flakes

Two 20-ounce bags frozen peas

¼ cup white wine

1½ teaspoons salt, or more if needed

1 baguette, cut into ½-inch-thick rounds

½ cup fresh basil or mint leaves

¼ cup grated Parmesan cheese

1. In a large nonstick skillet, melt the butter or heat the oil over medium-low heat. Add the onion and red pepper flakes, and sauté until the onions are translucent but not yet brown, 5 to 10 minutes.
2. Preheat the broiler.
3. Arrange the baguette rounds on cookie sheets and toast under the broiler until they are lightly toasted on top, but not hard.
4. Add the peas and white wine, and raise the heat to medium-high. Bring the liquid to a boil, stirring the peas around so all of them defrost, 5 to 7 minutes.
5. When the mixture is heated through, transfer it all to a blender or food processor and add the salt. Blend until the peas are about the consistency of hummus, adding water if the puree is too thick to process. Taste for salt and correct to your preference.
6. Scoop 1 tablespoon of the pea mixture onto each toasted baguette round, and garnish with the chopped basil and grated Parmesan.

eggplant caponata crostini

Makes 30 to 40 bites

2 tablespoons olive oil, plus extra if needed

2 pounds eggplant (2 medium), cut into ½-inch cubes

1 large sweet or yellow onion, finely diced

3 cloves garlic, minced

1½ teaspoons salt

½ teaspoon crushed red pepper flakes

One 15-ounce can diced fire-roasted tomatoes

½ cup golden raisins, soaked in hot water for 10 minutes and drained

2 tablespoons balsamic vinegar, plus extra for drizzling

¼ cup coarsely chopped fresh basil

1 baguette, sliced into ½-inch-thick rounds

1. Coat a large cast-iron skillet or Dutch oven with the olive oil. Add the eggplant and onion, and sauté over medium heat for 15 minutes, until the eggplant is soft but not falling apart, adding more olive oil as needed. Add the garlic, salt, and red pepper flakes and cook for another 2 minutes. Add the tomatoes and their juices, raise the heat to medium-high, and cook for 10 more minutes, until the acidity of the tomatoes has cooked off and the eggplant is beginning to fall apart. Off the heat, add the golden raisins, balsamic vinegar, and half of the basil. Stir to combine. (The eggplant mixture can be made 2 days in advance and kept in the fridge. Bring to room temperature before using.)

2. Preheat the broiler.

3. Arrange the baguette rounds on cookie sheets and toast under the broiler until they are lightly toasted on top, but not hard.

4. Scoop the eggplant mixture onto individual baguette slices, arrange the crostini on a large platter, and scatter with the remaining basil. Drizzle a little balsamic vinegar and olive oil over the crostini, and serve.

how to plate crostini

Crostini defines the art of finger food and can be served at classy and casual affairs alike. We have a few basic guidelines for serving these bites at any party.

get the bread toasty

Cut slices of baguette on a slight diagonal with a serrated knife. Each slice should be about ½-inch thick. You want the bread to support your toppings even if it gets a little soggy, but you also want your guests to be able to bite into it easily. Toast the bread slices under the broiler for a few minutes.

the more surfaces, the better

At large parties, these little bites will be inhaled faster than you can replenish them. It's best to cover all your plates, platters, and cutting boards so that once the party starts, you can stay out of the kitchen. Since the bread soaks up most of the moisture from the topping, there is rarely much more than a smudge or two on the serving plates, making cleaning all those surfaces no big deal.

plate sparingly

Crostini aren't the easiest bites to cram onto one plate, which makes tip #2 that much more important. When you plate your crostini, make sure you use only the flat interior of the platter or plate, and follow its shape when you line up your pieces. If the platter is round, arrange the crostini in concentric circles starting at the edge. Square platters are easier: just line the crostini in rows, as many as will fit without seeming cramped.

alternate flavors

If you are using two or three different toppings, alternate the pieces on one platter so that guests can try both. If the platter is round, alternate every other piece. If square, do one row of each.

garnish

If you are not alternating types of toppings, the repetition of one singular color (green pea) or non-color (eggplant) can be a little drab. It's best to brighten up the plate by adding a handful of coarsely chopped fresh herbs or some other crumble, sauce, or flourish. This can be a drizzle of olive oil or vinegar on the plate, or a scattering of bacon, a small dollop of crème fraîche, or spoonfuls of pesto on the crostini themselves.

four hands, two fillings

Phoebe, Spring 2008

When I was still living at home, my parents were somehow cool enough to let me have friends over to their apartment, and cool enough that for anticipated special occasions like my twenty-second birthday, they volunteered to leave. The party I threw featured a few types of crostini to wash down my vile cocktail offerings ($9.99 Karkov vodka), and as the night got going, the food seemed to do its part to minimize the rowdiness, at least to the extent that there was no wine spilled on the Turkish rug in the living room (there may have been people smoking cigarettes in my childhood bathroom, like teenagers). Still, by the end of the night, I was exhausted. It was too much work for one person, especially the birthday girl, to cut up all those baguettes, spoon out all those fillings, and replenish all the platters when people had plowed through the first round.

While I was attempting to cohabit with my parents, Caitlyn, my roommate-to-be, was working at an orphanage in Tanzania. She was teaching English, tending to kids starved for attention in the classroom. The long e-mails she wrote about her adventures indicated nothing but happiness, but as I learned later, she was grappling with her own hunger, too. The orphanage's meals were mainly made up of *ugali*, a bland, unappetizing dough that was used, like my baguettes, to supplement other meager offerings by filling the children up with carbs. When Caitlyn returned, she told me the things she missed most were running water and bread.

Our apartment was a happy medium between my parents' place uptown and an African hut. After we moved in, I struggled to stock my own pantry and cope with not having a dining room table, and Caitlyn adjusted to having friends her own age in our living room, and furniture (albeit floor pillows) for them to sit on. The faucets, though, took far less time for her to re-embrace.

That first week, I made dinner for the two of us. As I slowly caramelized onions over a low flame, I told Caitlyn about North, my then boyfriend, and how the relationship had unfolded that fall—visiting his family over Labor Day, our recent trip to Argentina, and all the fights in between. She sat at the kitchen counter pulling apart pieces of a dinner roll and listened patiently. I realized how much I had missed having a friend around to talk to.

When it came time for our first party, our housewarming, I knew there would be plenty of friends coming through our front door. But thankfully, now that Caitlyn was in the picture, there was someone else there to man the room, and also another set of hands with which to tackle making hors d'oeuvres.

At 8 p.m. the night of the party, I was still running around in a towel, straightening framed pictures of Kilimanjaro in our living room. The kitchen counters were covered with flour and scraps of puff pastry, and the bowl of roasted butternut squash had yet to be touched. Caitlyn, seeing that I had abandoned my post and that I still lacked both eye makeup and presentable clothing, got to work filling rounds of puff pastry with the two types of fillings. As I raced upstairs to grab my iPod speakers, Caitlyn methodically brushed all the rounds with egg wash and folded them into far neater half-moons than I ever could have made.

At around 9 p.m., our first guests arrived just as a tray of empanadas was coming out of the oven. My friend Mark's eyes lit up when he saw the food. He handed me a bottle of Bitch—his new favorite wine—and proceeded to fill up a napkin with the two types of bites.

A few hours into the party, I was replenishing the last platters of butternut squash and chicken empanadas when there was a crash. Some unidentified friend who had had too much to drink had knocked over our Ikea bookshelf. Caitlyn leapt to attention, herding people out of the way with a calm authority she had honed during crises in her last home.

Later, in our new living room, I cleaned up the worst of the mess—the coffee table was littered with cups, there were two new red wine stains on the carpet, and one of Caitlin's picture frames was cracked. But I left the dishes in the sink, happy to know that there was another set of hands willing to help me wash them, with the help of running water, when we got up in the morning.

three fillings, three ways

As I've learned from cocktail parties past, it's best to offer your guests some variety. For this reason, it's great to have a few go-to fillings in your repertoire, and a few ways to assemble them so you don't become known as the eggplant crostini girl (though I've come dangerously close to earning that title). Here are three of my favorites—spiced corn, roasted butternut squash, and leek confit—followed by directions for using them in quesadillas, crostini, and empanadas. You can mix and match, but I'd recommend choosing one dish (such as empanadas) and two fillings (such as butternut squash and spiced corn). All three fillings can be made days in advance, leaving plenty of time for assembly the night of. Just try to make sure there is an extra set of hands to help you.

{spiced corn}

Makes about 2 cups

2 tablespoons unsalted butter

2 cloves garlic, minced

1 shallot, minced

One 15-ounce can corn kernels, rinsed and drained (or, if in season, the kernels from 5 ears of fresh corn, or use defrosted frozen corn)

1 teaspoon ground cumin

1 teaspoon salt

Dash of cayenne pepper

1. In a medium saucepan or skillet, melt the butter over medium-low heat. Add the garlic and the shallot and cook until fragrant, being careful not to burn the garlic, 1 to 2 minutes.
2. Add the corn, cumin, and salt. Sauté gently until the corn is hot and the flavors are melded, 3 to 5 minutes.

{roasted butternut squash}

Makes about 1 cup

One 1½-pound butternut squash, peeled, seeded, and cut into ½-inch cubes (see page 304)

1 tablespoon olive oil

1 teaspoon sugar

½ teaspoon salt

1. Preheat the oven to 400°F.
2. Combine the squash, olive oil, sugar, and salt in a medium mixing bowl and toss to combine. Arrange the squash cubes in an even layer on a baking sheet lined with parchment paper.
3. Roast in the oven until caramelized, 20 to 30 minutes, redistributing the squash once during the cooking process to make sure the pieces brown evenly.

{leek confit}

Makes about 1 cup

2 tablespoons unsalted butter

2 large leeks (white and light green parts), cut in half lengthwise, thinly sliced, and cleaned (see page 298)

½ teaspoon salt

> *Note: The leek confit also works really well when mixed with either the roasted butternut squash or the spiced corn filling. If you don't mind the extra work, try a hybrid version.*

1. In a small lidded saucepan or Dutch oven, melt the butter over medium-low heat. Add the cleaned leeks and sauté for 3 to 5 minutes, until translucent.
2. Add ¼ cup water and the salt, reduce the heat to low, cover, and cook for 20 to 25 minutes, stirring occasionally, until the leeks are completely soft and taking on an almost jamlike texture.
3. Take the lid off and cook, uncovered, until most of the liquid has evaporated, about 5 more minutes.

quesadillas

Makes 6 appetizer servings

{ 6 medium flour tortillas
1 cup shredded white cheddar or Monterey Jack cheese

{ 1 cup Spiced Corn, Butternut Squash, or Leek Confit filling (or a combination) }

1. Preheat the oven to 425°F.
2. Place 1 tortilla on a cutting board, and sprinkle it with 1 to 2 tablespoons of the cheese and 1 to 2 tablespoons of the filling. Fold the tortilla in half and push down on it so the quesadilla is properly sealed and the filling is evenly distributed. Repeat with the remaining tortillas.
3. Arrange the quesadillas on a cookie sheet and bake until they are browned on top, 10 to 15 minutes. Cut each quesadilla in thirds, and serve immediately.

crostini

Makes 30 to 40 bites

{ 1 baguette, sliced into ½-inch-thick rounds

{ 2 cups Spiced Corn, Roasted Butternut Squash, or Leek Confit filling (or a combination) }

1. Preheat the broiler
2. Arrange the baguette rounds on cookie sheets and toast under the broiler until they are lightly toasted on top, but not hard.
3. Spoon the filling on top of the crusty slices, arrange the crostini on a large platter, and serve.

empanadas

Makes 18 empanadas

If you don't want the hassle of making empanada dough from scratch, you can easily substitute 2 sheets of puff pastry.

{
2¼ cups all-purpose flour

1½ teaspoons salt

8 tablespoons (1 stick) very cold unsalted butter, cut into ½-inch cubes

1 egg

⅓ cup very cold water

1 tablespoon white wine vinegar

1 cup Spiced Corn, Roasted Butternut Squash, or Leek Confit filling (or a combination)

1 egg, beaten
}

1. Make the dough: In a large bowl, stir the flour and salt together with a fork. Add the butter cubes, and with your fingers, rub the butter into the dry ingredients. The mixture will start to look like crumbs. (Try to touch the dough as little as possible.)

2. In a small bowl, beat together the egg, cold water, and vinegar with a fork. Add this to the flour mixture, stirring until just incorporated.

3. Lightly flour your cutting board or countertop, and transfer the dough to the work surface. Knead the dough with heel of your hand until it comes together. Form it into a flat disk and cover with plastic wrap. Chill in the fridge for at least 2 hours.

4. When you are ready to use the dough, roll it out on a floured surface until it is about ½-inch thick, and cut it into 6 sections. Roll each section until it is very thin (about ⅛-inch thick), and using a 3-inch round cutter, cut the dough into rounds.

5. Preheat the oven to 400°F.

6. Place a little less than 1 tablespoon of the filling in the middle of each pastry round, and fold the round in half. Seal with a fork, then crimp the edges with your fingers. Arrange the empanadas on a cookie sheet. Combine the egg and 2 tablespoons water in a small bowl, and brush the empanadas with this egg wash. Cut a few slits on top of each. Bake for 20 to 25 minutes, until browned on top.

the dip party

When we started *Big Girls, Small Kitchen*, it was all in good fun. We figured we naturally cooked enough to keep up with the writing, and we were already one step ahead because there were two of us. After founding the blog in November, we trekked through December, lazily posting when we remembered to take and upload photographs from weekday packed lunches, cocktail parties, and dinners for one, and to jot down the recipes we invented.

In January, we buckled down. We brainstormed the kind of cooking information our demographic would find useful; we polled our friends to find out who they were when faced with a frying pan. We met for sleepy but enthusiastic planning sessions after long days at work. And we cooked and entertained and then cooked some more.

By March we noticed we had whipped each other into shape. Our friends had started to turn to us as experts. "What should I cook for a date?" "Do you have a good brownie recipe?" "Will you make me some cookies?" The questions poured in.

We were as grateful to our friends and parents for their excitement about the blog as we were to our kitchens, our friendship, and our boredom with our jobs for getting the ball rolling. A launch party to celebrate our new project seemed judicious if not downright obligatory.

We planned for cheap wine and snacks at Phoebe's apartment. As parties past revealed, her centrally located duplex allows for a decent number of friends to show. But when we thought about what we'd serve, we ran into a dilemma. Even reducing the guest list from all our friends to only friends who'd expressed a vested interest in the blog, there were more people than we could economically wine and dine. We had to figure how to translate the kind of reasonable, limited-resources meal we were used to blogging about into a spread that would be satisfying to a roomful of twenty-somethings but also a worthy output for the launch party of a cooking website. At a food blogger's apartment, guests were bound to expect a lot of very good food. As for the wine, we bought a few big bottles but counted on our friends to bring more.

A creative arrangement of dips was our saving idea. Phoebe deconstructed classics and reconstructed them into interesting, conversation-worthy dishes like Chipotle Hummus and Panko-Crusted Spinach Dip. We put massive bowls on every available surface and paired each with its own dipping morsel, knowing full well how carbs can extend a meal. Cara baked two kinds of oatmeal chocolate chip cookies—the competing recipes that we were baking back in high school—and packed them into ribbon-tied baggies, blue for Cara, green for Phoebe. Only a few partygoers, arriving on very empty stomachs because of the food-blogger expectation, got a little more drunk than anticipated with nothing more than pita to absorb their intake of booze. But most guests persisted in eating, scraping the last bits of dip from the bottom of each bowl in order to get their fill.

From then on we were never intimidated by a party, whatever its size, budget, or other limitations. We realized that the chef's toques (literally, gifts our friend Mike presented to us at the party) we'd be donning from now into eternity meant we'd always have to feed people. But we didn't mind. We'd always have dips. We'd always have cookies. We'd always be able to pull together crostini, quesadillas, peanut noodles, and chocolate bark. And our friends would always bring us wine.

panko-crusted spinach dip

Makes 10 to 15 servings

Serve this while it is still hot, with tortilla chips for dipping.

FOR THE DIP
Three 16-ounce bags frozen spinach, defrosted and drained (see page 299)

8 ounces (1 cup) sour cream

½ cup mayonnaise

⅔ cup grated Parmesan cheese

½ teaspoon crushed red pepper flakes

2 cloves garlic, minced

1 teaspoon salt

Two 8-ounce packages cream cheese, at room temperature

FOR THE TOPPING
¼ cup panko

¼ teaspoon salt

¼ cup grated Parmesan cheese

Note: The dip can be made up to step 2, then kept covered in the refrigerator for 1 to 2 days prior to finishing and serving.

1. Preheat the oven to 350°F.
2. In a medium mixing bowl, combine the spinach, sour cream, mayonnaise, Parmesan, red pepper flakes, garlic cloves, and salt. Add the cream cheese to the bowl and stir until all the ingredients are fully incorporated. Pour the mixture into a cast-iron skillet or ovenproof baking dish.
3. Combine the topping ingredients in a small bowl. Sprinkle the topping over the dip mixture in an even layer.
4. Bake for 20 minutes, until bubbling. Raise the heat to 450°F and bake for another 5 to 10 minutes, until the top is golden brown. Serve immediately. Though this is best hot, it turns out to be delicious at room temperature, too.

chipotle hummus

Makes 4 servings

You can make this hummus several days in advance and store it in the refrigerator. Triple this recipe for a big party. Serve it with toasted pita triangles, torn baguettes, or mini carrots.

One 15-ounce can chickpeas, rinsed and drained

2 cloves garlic

2 tablespoons tahini

Juice of ½ lemon

¼ teaspoon ground cumin

¼ teaspoon paprika

1 teaspoon salt

1 teaspoon chopped canned chipotle chiles in adobo (about 1 chile)

1 tablespoon adobo sauce from the can, or more if needed

Paprika or chili powder, for garnish

Olive oil, for garnish

1. In a food processor, a mini food prep, or a blender, combine the chickpeas, garlic, tahini, lemon juice, cumin, paprika, salt, chipotle peppers, and adobo sauce. Puree the mixture, adding water as needed (up to about ¼ cup and 2 tablespoons) to thin it. Taste for seasoning, and add additional adobo sauce if you want the hummus to be spicier. When the hummus has a smooth consistency, spoon it into a serving bowl.
2. Garnish the hummus with a couple dashes of paprika or chili powder and a drizzle or two of olive oil.

Classic Hummus: Simply omit the chipotle peppers and adobo sauce and increase the tahini to 3 tablespoons. Optional: Add 2 tablespoons olive oil with the tahini.

white bean and rosemary dip

Makes 4 to 6 appetizer servings

{ One 15-ounce can cannellini or
white beans, rinsed and drained

Juice of ½ lemon

2 teaspoons fresh rosemary leaves

1 clove garlic

1 tablespoon olive oil, or more if
needed

½ teaspoon salt. }

In a small food processor or blender, combine the beans, lemon juice, rosemary, garlic, olive oil, and salt. Puree, adding another tablespoon of olive oil if the mixture is still coarse, until smooth. (The dip can be stored in the refrigerator for up to 1 week.)

black bean dip

Makes 6 appetizer servings

{ 1 clove garlic

½ small shallot

One 15-ounce can black beans,
rinsed and drained

1 canned chipotle chile in adobo
sauce

1 tablespoon adobo sauce from
the can

¼ teaspoon ground cumin

¼ teaspoon chili powder

Juice of ½ lemon

1 teaspoon salt

Chopped fresh cilantro, for garnish

Sour cream, for garnish }

1. Combine the garlic, shallot, beans, chile, adobo sauce, cumin, chili powder, lemon juice, and salt in a small food processor. Add ¼ cup warm water, and puree until smooth and creamy.
2. Spoon the dip into a bowl, garnish it with cilantro and sour cream, and serve.

party punch and other ways to wet the whistle

Though the food tends to take center stage at our cocktail parties, we can't ignore the real reason for having them. Quarter-lifers tend to want to kick back after a long week of work, loosen their proverbial ties, and drink. Most of the time, you can rely on the tenets of BYOB (see page 83) to make sure your coffee table winds up littered with bottles. But for special occasions, it's fun to offer one specialty cocktail. Mix a large quantity and make sure your guests drink their full. Alcohol isn't called a social lubricant for nothing. (Note from our editor: Drink responsibly!)

boozy cider

Makes about 50 drinks

At Kate's holiday party, our group of friends couldn't get enough of this wintry cider, and Phoebe was incredibly grateful when Kate's mom, Barb, offered her a paper to-go cup of it as she left to head to another event.

{ 3 gallons apple cider
10 cinnamon sticks

3½ cups Jack Daniel's (one 750-milliliter bottle) }

Slowly warm the apple cider and cinnamon sticks in a large pot set over medium-low heat. Add the Jack Daniel's and remove from the heat. Serve in heatproof cups, with or without the cinnamon sticks.

adam's big kid hot chocolate

Makes about 25 drinks

Phoebe's friend Adam began a movement with this playful twist on a childhood classic. It requires only three ingredients, and if paired with breakfast burritos (page 167), it is sure to get you on your feet for a long day of cold-weather drinking.

{ 2 cups hot chocolate mix (Adam buys a 22-ounce container of Nesquik and uses about three-quarters of the container)

One 750-milliliter bottle of Bailey's Irish Cream

One 60-ounce handle of vodka (you're not going to use the whole thing, but you can probably figure out something to do with what's left over) }

1. Fill a large pot with 4 quarts water and set it over high heat.
2. Dump in the hot chocolate mix and stir to incorporate. Bring to a simmer, then reduce the heat to very low. When the hot chocolate is cool enough to drink—not before, or you'll burn off the alcohol—pour in the full bottle of Bailey's and a little less than half of the vodka. Give it a taste. If it's a bit watery/vodka-y, pour in more hot chocolate mix. Stir, and add more vodka if you see fit. Then let the good times roll.

Hot Chocolate from Scratch: Mix 1 cup unsweetened cocoa powder with 1½ cups sugar in a large saucepan. Pour 2 cups boiling water over this mixture, then whisk to create a smooth paste. Add 4 quarts milk and heat slowly over low heat. Add vodka and Bailey's to taste as per the directions above. For *Mexican Hot Chocolate*, simply add 1 tablespoon ground cinnamon to the from-scratch hot chocolate or Nesquik mix.

spiked lemonade

Makes 6 drinks

You have to squeeze a lot of lemons for this, so it's better for small afternoon parties than crazy shin-digs. If you want to make something similar for a crowd, see the recipe below for Spiked Arnold Palmers.

{
¾ cup sugar

4 large strips lemon zest (from about ½ lemon)

1 cup freshly squeezed lemon juice (from 8 or 9 lemons)

6 ounces (¾ cup) vodka

½ cup fresh mint leaves

Lemon slices, for garnish
}

1. Make a simple syrup by combining the sugar, lemon zest, and ¾ cup water in a small saucepan. Cook over medium-high heat until the sugar dissolves. When the mixture bubbles, reduce the heat and simmer for 2 to 3 minutes, just until it becomes slightly more syrupy. Remove from the heat and let the syrup steep for 15 more minutes; then remove the lemon zest.
2. Combine the lemon juice and the sugar syrup in a large bowl or pitcher. Add 3½ cups water and the vodka. Taste, adding more water or vodka as needed.
3. Serve over plenty of ice, garnished with the mint leaves and lemon slices.

Spiked Arnold Palmer: Combine 1 part Firefly Sweet Tea Vodka with 1 part lemonade (store-bought for a group, homemade for a smaller number). Serve over ice.

DATING & FOOD

The old adage about hearts and stomachs being connected may or may not be true, but when you date someone, you end up eating with that person at least on occasion. This chapter is about our past experiences with men and food, from breakfast to dinner. We also wanted to find out what happened in other people's relationships behind closed kitchen doors, so we asked our friends for their opinions on the subject and uncovered a few rules of thumb to keep in mind when feeding the opposite sex.

date night

Spring 2009

In the spring of 2009, when the birds were chirping and all the in-love couples were walking around in the sunshine kissing and holding hands, we got to thinking about date food. Cara had just had her first date with Alex (they sat at a restaurant bar 'til 10 p.m., but she was too shy to order dinner) but had yet to invite him into her home for a meal. Phoebe was lost in the chaos that is the New York singles scene, finding herself across the table from a series of suitors at a series of Italian restaurants. Up until then we hadn't thought that much about cooking for men, and we had little experience with the question of what we'd like to have men cook for us.

Then Phoebe's friend Dave asked her to recommend an easy menu to wine, dine, and impress his date, recession-style, in the comfort of his apartment. Phoebe, thrilled to know that men like Dave exist, even if she has yet to date one, went into quarter-life coaching overdrive.

Dave's date was hot. But with her long skinny legs came an equally long list of dietary obstacles. She did not eat steak. She did eat bacon. She did not eat lamb or pork besides bacon. She did not eat pasta. But she did eat seafood. Phoebe recommended what she herself would like to eat on a date if she ate fish but no meat or wheat-based carbs: shrimp risotto with spring veggies. She sent Dave extremely detailed instructions filled with minutia about prepping, timing, and serving. She waited anxiously for the verdict.

Dave called the next day to report that the dinner had been canceled. The potential love interest had complained that she'd eaten a big lunch, and therefore she was no longer per-mitting herself to have dinner. As it turned out, Dave's date not only didn't eat red meat or chicken, she really didn't eat much of anything at all. Since Dave comes from a large Jewish family where people get sick only from overeating, their compatibility seemed unlikely and the date was not rescheduled. But the scenario made us realize a few things about cooking for men, cooking for women, and how much we would never want to cook for men or women who don't eat.

For more insight on the subject, we surveyed our friends. We asked them slightly inap-propriate questions about how they saw the relationship between food and the hearts of the opposite gender. Our friend Keith was particularly enthusiastic, and helped us discover what men want out of their at-home dates with women. Phoebe's boss, Stephanie, also relayed a particularly adorable example of an enviably thought-out first date, one that proves that making something meaningful is always better than making something impressive. (See page 124 for these insights.)

In the end, the idea that women want to eat salads and health foods on a date is silly. What we do want is to be fed something that is easy to eat and will not leave us worrying that we have basil in our teeth or reek of spice rather than perfume. But we also don't want something that is expected. Many of our guy friends, including Phoebe's boyfriend-to-be, Will, told us that they'd made seared tuna on first food dates. Yes, tuna steaks are delicious and expensive, and seemingly impressive for those reasons. But something about seared tuna just screams trying too hard.

We prefer it when a guy whips up something that is casual yet romantic—something that he likes to eat too. But the best is when you can tell that the meal was the result of an extra effort, an effort he would put in only for a date he cared to impress, a dish he would make only for you.

shrimp risotto with sweet peas and leeks

Makes 2 servings

Risotto has a bad reputation for being hard to make, but it is actually fairly straightforward. This combination of fancy and homey is a great note to strike when cooking for a woman. You can give yourself a head start with the risotto and cook it until the rice is almost done (through step 7) and it is time to add the shrimp and other ingredients. Turn the heat off and wait for your date to arrive. After you have given her a glass of wine to drink while you finish making dinner, continue with the recipe. She will be all the more impressed, watching you cook. End the meal with a chocolaty dessert (like Brownies on page 174 or the Chocolate-Flecked Clafoutis on page 242).

We've overcompensated in this recipe, addressing the cooking level of a fledgling male cook, and included instructions for all the prep work. If you are more experienced, you can skim the in-depth prep explanations and proceed with the main part of the instructions.

{
½ pound peeled and deveined shrimp, fresh or frozen (thawed if frozen; see Note)

1 large shallot

1 leek

2 cloves garlic

2 tablespoons chives

½ cup dry white wine

2½ cups chicken or vegetable stock, warmed

1 tablespoon olive oil

¾ cup Arborio rice

Salt

½ cup peas, fresh or frozen

Juice of ½ lemon
}

Note: It can be much cheaper to buy shrimp in their shells. For instructions on peeling and deveining shrimp yourself, see page 300. If the shrimp are frozen, allow them to thaw in the fridge for 1 hour first.

to prep

1. Rinse the shrimp, and pat them dry with a paper towel.
2. On a large cutting board, peel the shallot and thinly slice it. Trim, slice, and clean the

leeks according to the instructions on page 298, about ¼-inch thick. Set the leeks and shallots aside.

3. On another section of the cutting board, finely chop the peeled garlic and the chives. Reserve for later.

4. Open your wine.

5. Pour the stock into a large glass measuring cup or a saucepan. Heat the stock in the microwave for 3 to 4 minutes, until it is very warm, or heat it in a saucepan over low heat.

to cook

6. In a large skillet or a medium Dutch oven, sauté the shallot and leek in the olive oil over medium heat until translucent, 3 to 5 minutes. Add the chopped garlic and sauté for an additional minute. Add the rice and stir so it becomes coated in the oil. Cook for 2 to 3 minutes to lightly toast the rice. Add ½ teaspoon salt and the wine and cook, stirring, until the wine has nearly evaporated, about 2 minutes. Turn the heat to low. Add ½ cup of the warm stock and cook, stirring occasionally, until the rice has absorbed the liquid.

7. This portion of the cooking process will take some attention and instinct. You don't need to be constantly stirring, but you also want to make sure that the rice does not stick to the bottom of the pan: Continue adding the stock, ½ cup at a time, cooking until each addition has been absorbed before adding the next, until the risotto has only a slight bite to it. This is not a precise science; the risotto may require 2½ cups, or more or less. The total cooking time will be 25 to 35 minutes.

8. Add the peas, shrimp, and lemon juice along with any extra stock as necessary. Cook until the shrimp have taken on a pinkish tint and the peas are cooked through, about 3 minutes. Add the chives, taste for salt, and serve immediately.

hearts and stomachs

Though we don't fancy ourselves anthropologists, when it came to the subject of dating and food, we wanted some concrete answers and evidence. The following lessons, advice, and stories are the product of a questionnaire we sent to some of our friends. We liked many of the anecdotes so much, we decided to leave them in our friends' own words.

inside jokes are great flirtation devices

My boyfriend, Cooper, actually cooked for me first. He made guacamole (and strawberry daiquiris), but it wasn't just ordinary guacamole, it was awesome. . . . The idea for this date actually started a long time before he made the guacamole. Cooper and I met in a bar. I was with some friends when a drunk weirdo sidled up next to me and was falling off his stool. Cooper, my knight in shining armor, pushed him out of the way with a "Watch it, man." Ah, love. Many drinks later, Cooper kissed me outside of the bar. But I told him that I had never kissed a boy who hadn't taken me out to dinner. So we went in search of food. Pizza was closed so we stumbled into a Mexican restaurant, ordered guacamole, and told them we were having our wedding reception in the back room. In Spanish. While we danced. (Cooper now rarely speaks Spanish, wears suits, or impromptu dances). At the bar, I asked for his card and he told me he would make me guacamole (clearly, I now know, because his was way better).

—Stephanie, Phoebe's boss

gender stereotypes can be misleading

I think one of the first meals I ever cooked for a girl was a pasta dish. . . . I wasn't a very skilled chef at this point (not that I've gotten all that much better), and I had heard the old adage that girls don't really eat on first dates. So pasta made sense: something quick, easy, and tasty. A lot of guys might say if you're going to cook for a lady, cook girl food: fish, salads, etc. I agree in general, but would also contend that making something that fills her up pleasingly and quickly leaves more time to devote to conversation and boozing. I started with some gnocchi, grilled a couple of chicken breasts, chopped some garlic, onions, and veggies, and mixed the components together with copious quantities of cream and freshly grated Parmesan cheese. The concoction, while unquestionably heavy, is also too simple to mess up and quite pleasing to the taste buds. As expected, the lady in question ate daintily, drank copiously, and we had a great time.

—Keith, future founder of the Chili Cook-Off (see page 196)

be adventurous and take charge

My husband does most of the cooking, to the great chagrin of our assorted male friends whose wives and girlfriends wonder why they can't "be more like Tony." He taught me how to make red sauce when I was in college and we were still just dating, once telling me that to marry into his family of Italians, I had to learn how to do it, and well. . . . He's pretty adventurous in the kitchen and tends to stray from recipes, which can often be delicious but disastrous on my waistline.

—Christina, Cara's coworker

clean your plate when on a date

I'm a pretty big eater so I need a guy to out-eat me, lest I feel like a total pig.

—Caitlyn, Phoebe's roommate

tailor to the taste of your mate
(otherwise known as being thoughtful)

My boyfriend is a great cook. There are nights when I don't necessarily feel like cooking or would be satisfied with simple veggies, but on those nights Evan typically insists on cooking for me and it's really nice. I once begged him to re-create a salmon dish I had at an Italian restaurant. Evan was never really that into salmon, so for a while it was off the table. Then all of a sudden (the millionth time I asked) I convinced him to try it. The fish was just as good as I had remembered it. But the dish was the key to my heart because I knew he had made it just for me.

—Sarah, Mag Club member

the frenchman

Phoebe, Summer 2009

In mid-July, after seven months of blogging, I was in the midst of emotional turmoil about whether food was going to be my next chapter in life and how much guilt I should feel about leaving my current job. After a week on vacation, I handed Stephanie my resignation letter. In the end the decision was an easy one, but the letter was the most difficult message I've ever had to deliver. Between the two of us, many tears were shed in her office. When I left, I expected to breathe a sigh of relief. Instead, I walked down 5th Avenue feeling utterly shaken.

I am not usually someone who reaches out to people during times of vulnerability, but that evening, I really didn't feel like being alone. I called Adam, and upon hearing the quiver in my voice—evidence of crying most males can recognize—he met me at Rockefeller Center for a drink. He ordered himself a Diet Coke and forced a shot of tequila into my hand. I drank it. And then began to cry again, so he gave me another.

Adam returned to his office building to finish up work, and I called my next victim: Cara. I pulled up to 17th Street, and she was perched in the window of the bar we'd picked out, smiling. Cara's excitement made me remember my own. We toasted to our future together, to *Big Girls, Small Kitchen*, and to her imminent departure from her office job. We clinked our glasses of whiskey on the rocks, and I finally exhaled.

It was in this extreme state of emotional unbalance, under the influence of numerous varieties of hard liquor five hours later that evening, that I met the Frenchman. I had ended up at my old college housemates Nathalie and Lydia's apartment. They were throwing another college friend a going-away party, and as was usually the case at these occasions, I knew fewer than half of the people in the room. Luckily, aside from the group of boarding school girls wearing pearls, most of them were cute, vaguely European men.

The next thing I remember is making out with the Frenchman in Nathalie and Lydia's stairwell. I think he smelled like Acqua di Gio.

"Can I have your mobile?" he asked, as we walked out onto the street. I blink-blinked, before realizing it was my number he wanted. He had trouble pronouncing my name as he entered it into his phone, and I had trouble understanding anything he said afterwards.

The next morning I went into my soon-to-be-former office at a French cosmetics company, hungover and reeking of cologne. I was fairly pleased, though, that my general outlook on French culture had been rectified, even if I had no plans for a future with the Frenchman. In college, I had plenty of male European acquaintances, but I never took the leap to actually dating one due to the language barrier, which usually meant—even if they could craft flawless sentences—the inability to understand sarcasm. Since I could barely understand anything the Frenchman said, I thought our time together would begin and end in the stairwell.

In the days following, the Frenchman was quite persistent. His calls led to coffee, then to brunch, and then eventually to an offer to cook me the cuisine of his land in the comfort of my own apartment. The offer had a catch: I had to do the shopping, and he'd cook from my ingredients.

Aside from a burger or steak on the grill, I'd never had a man cook for me, nor had I gone on any dates outside the traditional restaurant venue during my year of singledom. I labored over the surprise ingredients in my shopping cart, carefully choosing eggplant and zucchini, which, in his hands, just might become ratatouille. As I asked the butcher to wrap up a pound of expensive lamb, I thought that I might have misjudged the Frenchman's intentions. A man who was willing to cook for me? Maybe this could go somewhere.

He arrived on my doorstep an hour late, bearing a bottle of red wine. It was not French, but a Malbec I had urged him to try on our previous date. As he surveyed the kitchen, I asked him questions about the restaurant he had owned in Paris and the girl he had left behind there when he decided to take a job in New York. He took a look at the ingredients I had purchased—vegetables, potatoes, and the lamb—and furrowed his brow. He peeled away the butcher paper and smelled the meat. His nose stayed wrinkled. My face burned hot and pink.

"Is there something wrong with the meat I bought?" I said in my best over-simplified English.

"I don't know if I should use this," he replied. "All the lamb in your country is no good. The best lamb comes from my village in Auvergne."

I asked him what he cooked for himself in New York, if he didn't like the meat and vegetables in our supermarkets. "Pasta," he said. "And I make a nice ratatouille sometime."

He left the zucchini and eggplant in the fridge, and instead got to work chopping and sautéing potatoes in my skillet. He was distressed that I did not have twine for him to tie together the asparagus. And when I showed him my vinegar options, he smiled. "This is what we use to clean the silverware in France," he said, holding up the bottle of clear white liquid.

I smiled too, and thought how the evening was slowly becoming the worst date of all time. As his cooking progressed, he told me that my olive oil, cast-iron skillet, Sancerre, and stove were not up to his standards. Eventually we sat down to a meal of braised not-French lamb, sautéed *pommes de terre*, and steamed asparagus with vinaigrette. In my opinion, the food was sub-par for a man who had graduated from French culinary school. I spent the following week cooking my way through the ingredients he had rejected (I made quite a nice ratatouille myself) and replaying the meal misfires in my head.

It turned out that the Frenchman had had a great time and thought not only that the date went well, but that we were in love. This led to an invitation to join him on a wine tour of the French countryside, where I would get to meet his grandparents. I had no desire to meet his grandparents. Instead, I wished him well on his trip and promised to watch *Ratatouille* with him upon his return. The Frenchman loved this idea. A part of me wished I loved the Frenchman too.

By the time he returned, I had packed up my cube and started that next chapter, with less emotional turmoil than expected. I had also just met Will.

ratatouille for two

Makes 2 generous servings

Most classic ratatouille recipes, Julia Child's particularly, require you to cook each of the vegetables separately. And because of the many different types of vegetables involved, most recipes are designed to feed more than six mouths. I've pared down the ingredient list and simplified the technique so that the entire dish can be cooked stovetop and doesn't require hours of simmering. This version serves two, but I wouldn't necessarily recommend making it for your Frenchman.

To round out the meal, top the ratatouille with a few slices of grilled chicken or lamb.

{
2 tablespoons extra virgin olive oil

1 small yellow onion, diced

1 small orange or yellow bell pepper, diced

1 small (1 pound) Italian eggplant, cut into 1-inch cubes

1 small zucchini, quartered and cut into thin slices

1 small yellow squash, quartered and cut into thin slices

2 cloves garlic, minced

2 plum tomatoes (½ pound), cored, seeded, and coarsely chopped

1 bay leaf

1 teaspoon salt

¼ teaspoon crushed red pepper flakes

¼ cup finely chopped fresh basil leaves
}

1. Coat a large lidded pot or a Dutch oven with the olive oil, and sauté the onion and bell pepper over medium heat until soft and beginning to brown, about 8 minutes.
2. Add the eggplant and sauté for 5 minutes, until it is beginning to soften.
3. Stir in the zucchini, yellow squash, and garlic, and sauté for 5 minutes more.
4. Mix in the tomatoes, bay leaf, salt, and red pepper flakes. Reduce the heat to medium-low, cover, and cook, stirring occasionally, until the vegetables are tender and the tomato juices have concentrated, about 30 minutes.
5. Discard the bay leaf and stir in the basil. Taste for seasoning, and serve hot, at room temperature, or cold.

the invention of "hangry"

Cara, Summer 2009

I met Alex on a subway platform. We saw each other a few times, waiting for the number 2/3 train, emerging from morning-commute hazes for a moment of eye contact and a smile. The first day we actually talked, I was completely panicked that he would notice I smelled like a bakery. I'd been making a cake for Jessy's birthday, which we were celebrating at a high school potluck that night. Only an hour before the train ride, I had prepped the icing so it would be ready to assemble when I got home from work. I was convinced, therefore, that I reeked of chocolate—my hands, my hair, my clothes. When Alex grabbed the pole next to me, pointed at the gadget I was holding, and asked, "What's that?" (it was a Sony e-reader, a perk of working in publishing), I was sure he'd be able to smell the icing on my breath. What kind of girl smells like chocolate at eight in the morning? We talked for the whole forty-five-minute commute.

In the weeks that followed, I saw Alex two more mornings on the train. The first time, we boarded at opposite ends of the car and didn't see each other until the train emptied at Fulton Street. During the three seconds before the next horde of commuters got on, he sprinted across the entire car to grab the pole next to where I was standing. We talked for the rest of the ride. The next time, as we walked up the stairs in Grand Central, he asked for my number.

By the end of June, we'd been seeing each other for a couple of weeks, and I'd learned a lot about him. I was intrigued by the fact that he could program computers, that he was an aspiring photographer who scoured the city for photogenic scenes, and that he'd left behind his post-college life in Maryland to move to New York and start over.

Apparently, I was also already comfortable enough with him to reveal my ultimate flaw: indecision.

Figuring out plans on the phone one Saturday, I simply could not decide what on earth we should spend the afternoon doing. It was cold and rainy, even though it was supposed to be summer, and eventually we settled on a movie. Of course there was no way I could pick which one to see. I think we finally decided based on the time of the showing.

I put on a skirt, since I find overdressing to be a tried-and-true way of dispelling the effects of a gloomy afternoon, and headed out to meet Alex. It was then that the indecision got worse. We'd said we'd meet at Grand Army Plaza, but suddenly I couldn't decide whether meeting at Grand Army Plaza meant finding each other at the subway stop, the platform, or the plaza itself.

I waited for a few minutes across from the arch aboveground, where we had convened when we went for a walk in Prospect Park on our fourth date. Then I waited for a few more minutes at the entrance of the subway stop. Eventually I went downstairs, swiped through, and found Alex impatient on the stairs, just a few yards from where we first met. A train was pulling away from the station.

One indie-movie happy ending later, I forgave him for his part in my bad mood (in my grumpy mind, he had had one). When we left the theater, it had stopped raining, and I suggested that we walk home through the charming streets of Fort Greene and down Prospect Heights' bar-lined boulevard, Vanderbilt Avenue. It was pleasant and smelled like rain, and I was content just to be where I was, walking down the street holding hands with Alex.

That's when Alex got hungry. When he gets hungry, he gets really, really hungry, the kind of stupor where blood sugar drops and the world suddenly spins, and you can't even remember why you feel so bad, or what eating means. Alex was *hangry*. He offered to make dinner; he had kidney beans in the pantry, he said, and a green pepper in his fridge. I would later learn how delicious Alex can make a can of beans taste, but you can imagine how I felt about this offer. Kidney beans happen to be my least favorite legume.

"We could go out and grab something," I said, looking around at all the bars and restaurants.

"You said you bought stuff at the market this morning? If you have all those vegetables, I don't want them to go to waste."

"I'd love to make something," I said, meaning, "Please let's just make a decision!"

"Do you mind cooking?"

"Not at all. So you want to come over?"

We walked toward my place, and immediately I was jolted out of our analysis of the movie and into the many possible permutations of carbs and veggies that I wanted very much to turn into an early dinner. I had never cooked for Alex before.

I fed him raw sugar snap peas while I chopped and sautéed. With no room for him in the tiny kitchen, Alex used the food-found energy to zap around the rest of my studio, coming back only when in need of another dose of raw vegetable. I passed him yellow peppers, string beans, and carrots, all before I put them into the pan. He told me he has no self-control when it comes to baby carrots.

Eventually, the warming scents of golden onions, heated olive oil, and a big mess of vegetables filled the apartment. The pasta was almost done, and the sauce too. I drained the pasta into the colander, siphoning off about a cup of it into a tumbler ready on my counter.

He returned to the doorway of the kitchen.

"What are you doing with that?" he asked about the extra water, curious like a kid.

"Saving the pasta water," I explained. "It helps the vegetables become a sauce for the pasta."

"Wow," he said, and he was genuinely, adorably impressed. "You really do know what you're doing."

We sat down to eat at the table, and he took a big helping of linguine. Fifteen minutes later, as he scraped his fork tines around the perimeter of my cast-iron skillet (producing the kind of sound that would have made a lesser woman cringe), picking up the last shards of melty veggies, he complimented me again. "It's just so much better than anything I make."

Even the beans? I wondered but didn't say.

He was no longer hungry and I was no longer indecisive. We sat at my little table and talked for hours. Eventually, we got up. Alex offered to do the dishes, but I refused to let him. "Some other time," I said, making sure he'd want to come back.

pasta primavera

Makes 2 servings

- 1 bunch asparagus, trimmed and sliced into 1-inch pieces, or ½ head broccoli, cut into florets
- Olive oil
- Salt
- 1 small onion, chopped
- 1 clove garlic, minced
- 2 cups mixed vegetables, cut into bite-size pieces (I like to use carrots, sugar snap peas, zucchini, and yellow bell peppers)
- Freshly ground black pepper
- Pinch of crushed red pepper flakes
- ¾ pound linguine (regular or whole wheat)
- 1 large bunch leafy greens (spinach or arugula; if you use dandelion greens, kale, or chard, parboil them first), trimmed and torn into bite-size pieces
- ¼ cup freshly grated Parmesan cheese (optional)

1. Preheat the oven to 350°F.
2. On a baking sheet, toss the asparagus or broccoli with 2 teaspoons olive oil. Roast for 30 minutes, until cooked through and browned. Sprinkle with ½ teaspoon salt, and set aside.
3. Bring a large pot of heavily salted water to a boil.
4. Meanwhile, in a large skillet, heat 2 tablespoons olive oil over low heat. Add the onion and garlic, and sauté until soft, about 5 minutes. Add the mixed vegetables, starting with the longest-cooking (carrots) and ending with the shortest (snap peas). As each vegetable softens, add the next. Season with salt, the black pepper, and the red pepper flakes.
5. Cook the pasta until al dente. Drain, reserving 1 cup of the pasta water.
6. Add ½ cup of the pasta water to the sautéed veggies. Stir in the asparagus or broccoli and the leafy greens.
7. Add the pasta to the skillet. Add more pasta water if it seems dry. Then add half the Parmesan, if using. Taste for salt, and serve with a sprinkling of good olive oil, and the rest of the cheese on the side.

meat and potatoes

Phoebe, Fall 2009

My mom and I were sitting on stools at the island in my parents' kitchen, eating an array of vegetables—broccoli with lemon, peas in olive oil, and roasted beets—with our fingers.

"What was the first meal you made for Dad?" I asked casually. I had been dating Will for a few months at this point, but had yet to cook for him. I had, however, been doing a lot of recon on the subject, and my parents' narrative was not exempt from my investigation into the stomach of the opposite sex.

"A frittata," my mother replied. "Haven't I told you that story?" I remembered but asked her to tell it again anyway.

When my parents met, my father was a longtime bachelor. They were thirty-five or thirty-six at the time—a bit beyond quarter-life, enjoying the comfort of established careers and the houses afforded by them. A few months into their relationship, they took a trip up to my father's cottage in Hudson, New York. There was traffic, and by the time they arrived around dinnertime, my dad was cranky and starving (otherwise known as hangry). The only option was to cook, and the only ingredients to work with from the bachelor's fridge and pantry were eggs, onions, and an old chunk of Parmesan. So my mother grabbed one of her future mother-in-law's frying pans hanging on the wall and got to work on a frittata.

I won't say that those few eggs changed everything, but somehow, I know they mattered. I don't think my father has cooked for himself since.

My mother had never entered her previous boyfriend's kitchen. "I never wanted him to date me just because I cooked," she said, pausing for a moment to lick olive oil from her index finger. "But I regretted it for a while after it ended."

The man in question was kind of a homebody, and my mom's domestic prowess might actually have kept the relationship alive. But instead they dined out night after night for years, and eventually, lucky for my father and lucky for me, they fizzled.

My hesitation with Will was fairly typical. I always obsess over determining the right point in a relationship to cook for a boy for the first time. I overanalyze the timing, putting much more pressure on the impression, the meaning, and the menu than I ever do on all the dates at restaurants combined. I delay the process, naturally, until a moment when I really feel it is *right*. These instincts never really lead me astray: every man I've ever cooked for, I've ended up dating. Some, I wish I had never let in the front door, but I don't think that can be blamed on the food.

Even with all the advance planning, the first cooking experiment didn't always result in perfection. In fact, quite the opposite. I've made every possible mistake. I've overcooked meat, undercooked rice, and made so much food I could have fed five boyfriends. But even if the food was perfect, nothing my date could do would satisfy my too-high expectations— shy of licking the serving platter clean.

This was a particular problem when it came time to feed North, my previous boyfriend. If we had eaten together more often in college, perhaps I would have predicted that he'd leave three whole homemade meatballs sitting on his plate from the spaghetti dinner I slaved over. His eyes were far bigger than his stomach when faced with anything but penne with vodka sauce, and his appetite shrank even more when he drank. I have never encountered anyone who claims fullness from red wine. But that was North, neurotic and easily satiated, usually leaving half the food on his plate at restaurants (which I would then happily consume).

Still, I obsessed over the uneaten meatballs for months. I had given him the leftovers to take home, and I was haunted by the image of that Tupperware container sitting in his fridge, untouched, a week later. It took the better part of the year before I attempted to cook for him again, this time in my new apartment kitchen with Caitlyn by my side for moral support.

As I pounded chicken thin and peeled potatoes for a gallette, Caitlyn told me about the first time she cooked for her boyfriend Matt. We were all in college at the time, and the special dinner she had planned went horribly awry. By the time the meal was done, it was about ten (she was aiming for eight), the chicken was rubbery, the asparagus was soggy, and Caitlyn was in tears. "I was not even speaking to Matt by the time we sat down to eat because I was so embarrassed and frustrated," she told me. "Which, of course, made for a lovely dinner."

Caitlin and I were obviously trying to play our cards right, to make our guys realize how lucky they were to have tough, independent girlfriends who could also wield a frying pan. We both proved not so tough. But failed meatballs, chicken, and asparagus aside, our relationships lasted long enough for us to get a second chance in the kitchen. Even if my second chance involved burnt chicken.

Will and I met for the first time at a bar, where we were celebrating Date Night Dave's birthday. I had just finished my last day of work, and when he asked me what I did for a living, I thought for a moment and then replied "I'm a writer, I guess."

For the first few months of dating, I gathered all the evidence I could as to Will's tastes and eating habits. More important than his relationship with his mother was the fact that she made incredible flank steak (note to self: do not attempt flank steak). By the time I finally asked Will to dinner, the safe options were numerous—pretty much anything that didn't involve mayonnaise. I decided to make one of my mom's dishes, one of her few that didn't involve a cup of the stuff.

I was nervous the day before the meal, even though I had made my Beer Beef Stew in advance and knew it was perfect. Unlike with prior relationships, my cards were already on the table when it came to cooking. Will had been reading the blog since that first night at the bar—over a month before we even went on our first date. This time, I wasn't cooking to impress him with my food, but to express to him how much I wanted him to be there to enjoy it with me.

An obstacle arose the night before our date. Caitlyn had swine flu, and our apartment suddenly became plagued by disease. I swabbed the kitchen counters, plates, and utensils with hand sanitizer. Then I broke the news to Will and offered to bring the stew over to his closet-size apartment for us to eat on his couch. Too embarrassed to say that I had already made the whole meal, I tried my best to dodge his suggestion to reschedule.

He ended up coming over anyway, bringing two packets of Emergen-C for dessert. As he helped himself to a second portion of Semi-Sweet Potato Mash, I told him about the origins of the dish at my family's Thanksgiving, which was less than a month away. I went to grab another bottle of wine, and Will, already sick of the evening's soundtrack (my one playlist, on repeat), went onto my iTunes to download an indie band that would "change my life."

We finished the pot of stew and our second bottle of red with the Dirty Projectors playing in the background. The evening was some sort of perfect. But then, as I've come to realize, cooking for men is not about perfection.

The next morning, Will woke up without swine flu. Unafraid of sickness and failure, I offered to make him breakfast.

semi-sweet potato mash with spiced caramelized onions

Makes 2 to 4 servings

If you have leftovers, try appropriating the excess into Mashed Potato Croquettes (page 268).

Olive oil

2 large Vidalia onions, halved and thinly sliced

1/4 teaspoon ground cumin

1/4 teaspoon hot smoked paprika

1/4 teaspoon chili powder

Dash of cayenne pepper, or to taste

Salt

1 pound russet potatoes, peeled and cut into 2-inch chunks

1 pound sweet potatoes, peeled and cut into 2-inch chunks

2 tablespoons unsalted butter

2 to 4 tablespoons stock (chicken or vegetable)

1. Coat a large cast-iron skillet with olive oil, and sauté the onions over medium heat, stirring very infrequently. Once they soften and begin to brown, reduce the heat to low and allow the onions to slowly caramelize, about 40 minutes (see page 297). When the onions are dark brown but not burnt, add the cumin, paprika, chili powder, cayenne, and salt to taste. Set aside. (These can be made a few days in advance.)

2. In the meantime, place the russet and sweet potatoes in a large pot of salted water and bring to a boil over high heat. Cook the potatoes until tender, 15 to 20 minutes. Drain the potatoes in a colander, return them to the pot, and mash them (see page 303). Add the butter, and season with 1/2 to 1 tablespoon salt, adding a dash of cayenne, if desired, to give them some heat.

3. Add the stock, a tablespoon at a time, until the potatoes reach the desired consistency.

4. Spoon the potatoes into a large baking or casserole dish and spread the onions evenly over the top. Serve piping hot.

beer beef stew

Makes 2 to 3 servings

This is one of my mother's best stews. What really makes the whole thing come together in comforting perfection is the beer. Just saying the words *beer* and *beef* in one sentence is enough to get most men to pay attention. I once made this stew for a larger group, and Date Night Dave asked me to marry him. Serve egg noodles or a simple potato mash (see page 137) alongside.

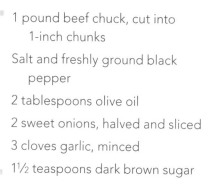

1 pound beef chuck, cut into
    1-inch chunks
Salt and freshly ground black
    pepper
2 tablespoons olive oil
2 sweet onions, halved and sliced
3 cloves garlic, minced
1½ teaspoons dark brown sugar

3 sprigs fresh thyme, tied together
    with kitchen string, or
    ½ teaspoon dried thyme
1 bay leaf
1 cup beef broth
1 cup beer (preferably Belgian ale)
1 tablespoon whole-grain mustard

1. Preheat the oven to 325°F.
2. Pat the beef dry. Season with salt and pepper.
3. Coat a large Dutch oven with the olive oil, and brown the beef, in batches, over high heat (see page 297). Set the beef aside.
4. Reduce the heat to medium, add the onions to the pot, and sauté for about 10 minutes, making sure to scrape up any browned bits left over from the beef.
5. Add the garlic and the brown sugar, season with 2 teaspoons salt and ¼ teaspoon pepper, and sauté for an additional 2 minutes, or until fragrant.
6. Raise the heat to high, return the beef and any juices to the pot, and add the thyme and bay leaf. Pour the broth and the beer over the top and bring to a simmer. Stir in the mustard.
7. Cover, transfer to the oven, and cook for 2½ hours, or until the meat is fully tender. Remove the thyme sprigs and bay leaf, taste for seasoning, and serve.

men and pancakes

Cara, Fall 2009

To me, seduction is awkward. I have an innate desire to be delivered an engraved invitation to parties, friendships, and conversations, so if you haven't formally asked me to seduce you, I probably won't. In other words, I don't enjoy the chase.

Yet, the one dating book I ever read seemed to imply that, unbeknownst to me, I actually do know something about seduction.

The book was on the "take shelf" at the publishing house where I worked, and I smuggled it under my sweater to the locked drawer at my desk and, eventually, home. I hadn't read dating books before, so I was genuinely curious to see what wisdom I'd come across. I skimmed most of the two hundred pages, but I took only one thing away from that book: it said that if you like a man enough to let him spend the night, you'd better like him enough to cook him breakfast. Now this may sound less like seduction and more like manners, or even like a good barometer of your feelings about someone, but there's more to breakfast than that. It has the power to win people over, and it just might be the one form of seduction I am comfortable with.

In high school, I had a boyfriend named Aaron. We flirted in math class, at parties, and during the free periods when he hadn't run off to IHOP with his friends. Once we started "officially" dating, Aaron would come over to my house after school, ostensibly to do home-work. Aaron loved pancakes more than anyone I'd ever known. We'd get home from classes hungry, and I would make batches of pancakes as our after-school snack. My mom couldn't believe how fast we started to go through maple syrup. When Aaron and I broke up, amica-bly, after sophomore year in college, I sent him away to his summer job in Boston with bag-gies of homemade pancake mix and instructions for adding milk, eggs, and butter. The following semester, I coincidentally met the girl who'd been one of his summer roommates. We talked for about thirty seconds before she recognized me as the pancake ex-girlfriend.

The guy I dated on and off in college and beyond, for far longer than I should have, was a slippery one. One minute I could have sworn we had a future together, the next I was certain I never wanted to see him again. I think in the end I didn't understand Jack because he was far less complicated than I was able to imagine a person could be. That, and he didn't like sweets (except my brownies). As might be expected, for breakfast Jack ate fried eggs and toast. I have the clearest memory of sitting in his off-campus house the summer before my senior year, diligently buttering the toast all the way to the edges while he fried eggs, two for me and three for him. It got to the point where I couldn't imagine Jack ordering a pancake to save his life.

After college, Jack moved abroad and our relationship dwindled down to the occasional e-mail. I figured that was it, but he reappeared in New York ten days after I moved to Brooklyn, and he came over for drinks. We talked into the night, sitting on my brand-new couch, a series of The Shins albums playing on my laptop. In the morning, I made him fried eggs and toast. Bread, butter, eggs, and coffee were all I had in my new kitchen, but they were enough to satisfy Jack.

Alex, a man who would be after my own heart if he hadn't already won it, has the most wonderful taste in breakfast. Most days, he eats cereal (two bowls), and he has introduced me to some of the best out there: oat and honey granola, and Peanut Butter Panda Puffs, an organic cereal marketed to kids but clearly appealing to us pseudo-adults. During the summer that we started seeing each other, Alex would always offer me cereal when I slept at his place, as if he too had read my dating book.

It took me a while to reciprocate, but one morning breakfast inspiration finally struck. Alex likes pancakes even more than he likes cereal, but since he can't eat dairy, I wasn't sure I could pull them off. I wound up using a browning banana, a can of coconut milk, and a bunch of standard baking ingredients to make a batch of heart-winning banana coconut pancakes. He gobbled them down. Since then, I've gone on to make oatmeal pancakes with apple compote, and I've branched out from pancakes into quick breads, muffins, and yeast breads (especially Jim Lahey's no-knead bread, which rises while you, um, sleep).

The moment I knew that my homemade breakfasts had become about more than mere hunger fulfillment was on a Sunday morning in November or so. I was awake, drinking coffee and going about the business of blogging, writing, and reading the real estate section. I whipped up a loaf of banana chocolate chip bread with yet another bunch of browning bananas. I was just pulling it out of the oven when I heard Alex stir. I set it down on my makeshift cooling rack (a pan propped on top of a pot) and went over to say good morning.

"This is the first time I've ever woken up because of a smell," he said drowsily as he disentangled himself from the sheets, tying to get up to find out what the smell was. He reached out and hugged me. It was so cute and loving, I vowed to myself that I'd keep on making breakfast if he'd keep on waking up with that smile on his face, directed not just at the meal but at me.

plain jane pancakes

I like crepe-like pancakes, but I know some people prefer them fluffy. Use the larger amount of milk if you're like me, and the smaller amount if fluffy's your bag.

The first pancake is often a throwaway—don't despair if it comes out under- or overcooked. It's really a gauge of the temperature of the pan and the consistency of the batter, so adjust the heat and the thickness of the batter to your liking before you make pancake #2 and so on.

{
1 cup all-purpose flour
2 teaspoons baking powder
1 tablespoon sugar
¼ teaspoon salt
1 large egg, beaten
¾ to 1 cup whole milk

1 tablespoon unsalted butter, melted, plus more for the pan (optional)
Canola or other neutral oil, for the pan (optional)
Butter, for serving
Maple syrup, for serving
}

1. Combine the flour, baking powder, sugar, and salt in a small bowl or on a piece of wax paper.
2. In a medium mixing bowl, whisk together the egg, milk, and melted butter.
3. Pour the dry ingredients into the bowl and fold until just incorporated. Don't worry if there are a few bubbles of flour—better to undermix than overmix.
4. Heat a cast-iron skillet over medium heat. Brush it lightly with oil or butter. Make one pancake to test the heat of the skillet by spooning out ¼ cup of the batter. Let it cook until bubbles appear on the surface, about 3 minutes. Then flip it over and cook for 2 to 3 minutes on the second side, until lightly browned. If the pancake doesn't flip easily, that means the pan wasn't hot enough.
5. Repeat with the remaining pancake batter. Serve hot, with slices of butter and a pitcher of maple syrup.

coconut banana pancakes

Makes 6 to 8 pancakes

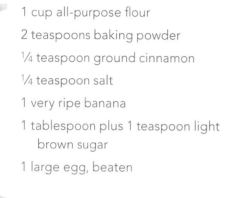

1 cup all-purpose flour

2 teaspoons baking powder

¼ teaspoon ground cinnamon

¼ teaspoon salt

1 very ripe banana

1 tablespoon plus 1 teaspoon light brown sugar

1 large egg, beaten

¾ cup coconut milk, preferably light

1 tablespoon canola or other neutral oil, plus a drizzle for the pan (optional)

Butter, for the pan (optional) and for serving

Maple syrup, for serving

1 ripe banana, sliced, for garnish (optional)

1. Combine the flour, baking powder, cinnamon, and salt in a small bowl or on a piece of wax paper.
2. In another small bowl, combine the banana with the brown sugar. Mash slightly—you don't want to turn the banana into a gluey mess, though. Add the egg to the banana mixture, along with the coconut milk and the oil. Stir to combine. Sprinkle the flour mixture over the banana mixture, and then fold together gently. Don't worry if there are still some pockets of flour. It's better to undermix than to overmix.
3. Heat a heavy-bottomed skillet over medium heat. Brush it lightly with oil or butter.
4. Make one pancake to test the heat of the skillet by spooning out ¼ cup of the batter. Let it cook until bubbles appear on the surface, about 3 minutes. Then flip it over and cook for 2 to 3 minutes on the second side. If the pancake doesn't flip easily, that means the pan wasn't hot enough. If the pancake begins to brown too quickly, adjust the heat to medium-low.
5. Make the rest of the pancakes this way. Serve hot, with slices of butter and a pitcher of maple syrup. Garnish with banana slices if you happen to have an extra banana lying around.

eating together

My former boss's wife used to call every day around 4 p.m. Though he let most other calls go through to voice mail or to me, when Amy's cell showed up on the caller ID, he always picked it up by the second ring. I couldn't hear through the wall of his office, but I imagined the conversation went something like this: Amy: "Hi, I'm home . . ." (She was a teacher and arrived home before him).

Boss: "Not such a busy day. I'll be home at six."

Amy: "What would you like to have for dinner?"

Of course, this was very '60s sitcom-esque of my imagination, and I found it hard to picture this ever happening to me—this repetitive, ordinary conversation. And then it did, only on Gchat, not on the phone. If it's a Tuesday night dinner at stake, this conversation is quite simple. I think about what's in my fridge and suggest a dinner based on that and on my day's reading in the food blogosphere. When Alex has something approaching its expiration date in his fridge, we'll be sure that's an ingredient too. Then he stops for cilantro and fruit for dessert or I run out for lemons and ginger, and a meal makes its way to the table.

Before the era of the 3:30 p.m. Gchat, I had two modes of cooking: I cooked for myself or I cooked for others, emphasis on the plural. That contrast was the genesis of our blog categories "Cooking for One" and "Cooking for Others." It was rare that I cooked for only one other person, and if I did, my co-diner was someone like Jordana or Lisa, my roommates, or Phoebe. The meals I made them were definitely closer to what I'd make for company than to what I'd eat alone.

Since meeting Alex and beginning to eat with him on a regular basis, I've added a third mode. While the temptation is always there to make something involved, I do try to tone things down when it's just us needing to be fed. I don't want to overspend on groceries or exhaust myself in front of the stove. But deep down I do still want to impress. I don't feed Alex cereal for dinner or crackers and cheese, and I add little extras here and there—a garnish, some spice, a sprinkle of the truffle salt he gave me as a gift. Occasionally we will make a special meal, and occasionally we'll cook it together. Once in a while, Alex cooks for me.

When you eat, or cook, with a boyfriend (or anyone) often, you have to take into account not only the contents of his fridge, but also his preferences, habits, and dietary restrictions. I find the added parameters of someone else's appetite to be enjoyable, like extra pieces in the "what should I make for dinner?" puzzle. When it's just me, I'm stuck listening to my cravings, which tend to be unreliable. In college, I used to leave my dorm room hungry, walk halfway to the Thai place, decide I wanted pizza, walk toward the pizza place, realize I was craving a burrito, and stand on line to order before doing a 180 and buying a sandwich (have I mentioned I'm indecisive?). I've done similar bouncing around in my kitchen, opening cabinets and pulling out cartons only to put the cartons back and slam the cabinets shut. The extra constraints actually help me to make up my mind. Without delving further into the overthinking I'm prone to doing, I'll go on to say that our resulting repertoire is a mix of pastas and rice, beans, soups, focaccia, the occasional bit of meat, and stews.

The very first meal I cooked for Alex, pasta primavera, was impromptu, but this meal of barbecued lentils was very much planned. I'd gone through so many variations in my head, most of the riffing done off of our individual dietary restrictions—I was still a pescatarian, and Alex ate dairy-free. I had already learned that Alex likes beans, so the lentils weren't a gamble (if you aren't sure if someone is a bean eater, lentils are probably the road to conversion). The meal I decided on was vegetarian but also hearty enough for a male appetite, easy to make from the pantry, and an excellent answer to the "what's for dinner?" question, which I think I like answering more than the average person when Alex is the one who's asking.

barbecue lentils

Makes 2 generous servings

I like to serve these lentils piled on top of a slice of cornbread (see page 191), accompanied by a garlicky chard (see page 149). You can make Lentil Sloppy Joes by using split dinner rolls or hamburger buns.

½ cup (4 ounces) black (French) lentils

2 cloves garlic; 1 whole, 1 minced

2 teaspoons salt

1 tablespoon olive oil

½ small onion, diced

1 small sweet potato, peeled and diced (about ¾ cup)

⅛ teaspoon cayenne pepper

⅛ teaspoon ground ginger

¼ cup ketchup

1 teaspoon Dijon mustard

2 teaspoons dark brown sugar, or more if needed

⅓ cup balsamic vinegar, or more if needed

Dash of Worcestershire sauce (optional)

1. Combine the lentils, 4 cups of water, and the whole (peeled) clove of garlic in a saucepan or Dutch oven, and bring to a boil. Reduce the heat and simmer, uncovered, for 30 to 35 minutes, until the lentils are soft but still hold their shape. Toward the end of cooking, add ½ teaspoon of the salt.

2. Drain the lentils, reserving ½ cup of the cooking water, and discard the garlic clove.

3. Wash and dry the pot you used to simmer the lentils. Heat the olive oil in the pot over medium heat. Add the onion and minced garlic, and sauté until soft and lightly browned, about 5 minutes. Add the sweet potato and cook until softened, 7 to 10 minutes.

4. Stir in the cayenne and ginger. Then add the ketchup, mustard, brown sugar, vinegar, Worcestershire sauce, if using, and the remaining 1½ teaspoons salt. Bring to a simmer.

5. Add the lentils and the reserved cooking water to the pot. Simmer until the sauce coats the lentils and the mixture is no longer soupy. Taste for balance of flavors, adding more brown sugar or vinegar if necessary.

garlicky swiss chard

Makes 2 servings

{ 1 bunch (about ¾ pound) Swiss chard

1 tablespoon olive oil

3 cloves garlic, thinly sliced

½ teaspoon salt, or more if needed }

1. Wash the Swiss chard well. Trim off the lower stems and discard. Cut the leaves into ribbons and the stems into bite-size pieces and set aside.

2. In a Dutch oven, warm the oil over low heat. Add the garlic and allow it to become golden, 3 to 4 minutes. Add the chard leaves and stems, tossing them as you go—the pan will be quite crowded at first. The chard will turn a brighter green as it hits the heat.

3. After a minute or two, add ½ cup water and the salt, and raise the heat to medium. Once the water boils, lower the heat to a simmer and cook, covered, for 10 minutes, until the Swiss chard is tender.

4. Remove the cover and boil off any extra water. Then taste for salt, and serve.

BRUNCH

Brunch is a New York institution. People love to sit for hours over coffee and mimosas, at outside tables if the weather is nice. We think brunch is a meal that's best extracted from the restaurant and reinvented at home—and not just because we like wearing our pajamas all day long.

sunday breakfast in bed

Phoebe, Spring 2008

Without dining halls at our disposal, meals with my former college roommates have become fewer and further between. However, one thing I can rely on to bring the six of us around a table is brunch. Regardless of the intensity of our day jobs, and our weekend rituals to forget about them, I can rest assured that at noon on a Sunday all of my girlfriends will be in the same place: bed. And though it's an enticing place to stay, the promise of an indulgent French toast will lure even my laziest of girlfriends (Salima) across and/or downtown for a 1 p.m. rendezvous, complete with bloody Marys and plenty of coffee.

Back in college, we got together for brunch a bit earlier, mainly because our meeting place was slightly more convenient. Salima's room was on the first floor of our house senior year and was around the size of my current apartment. The layout included a king-size bed she inherited from Jamie, the 6'7" frat boy who had lived in the room the year before. Though she managed to find the girliest king-size comforter ever, she also managed to keep the rest of the room, bed included, in a state of squalor not unlike the one that had become customary during the reign of the house's former tenants. The seven of us were of course partially responsible for this, and our weekend morning routine was to blame.

Every Saturday and Sunday morning, the first one awake would make a run to Bagel Gourmet down the block and come back with a large brown bag filled with all of our individual favorites. I think I could walk in there tomorrow and still accurately order each item: for Salima, a whole wheat bagel with low-fat scallion cream cheese and sliced tomato; scrambled eggs with extra butter and one slice of Muenster on an everything bagel for Lydia; a small breakfast burrito with extra cheese for Caitlyn; a plain bagel with sausage, egg whites, and provolone for Ali; and so on.

Creatures of habit we were, and as unchanging as our bagel choices was where we chose to eat them. After brushing our teeth and removing the mascara from under our eyes, we would trickle downstairs and sandwich ourselves around Salima while she stayed nestled under her covers. By one in the afternoon, the seven of us would have finished recapping our antics from the night before, the bagel wrappers crushed and lying in a pile in the middle of the bed, underneath a thick layer of Nathalie's poppy seeds, Jillian's dried onion bits, and my crumbs.

After a year in the real world, I sometimes think I would happily give up my own perfectly white sheets to have my friends, sesame seeds and all, greet me in bed every Sunday.

One day in the fall, an e-mail from Nathalie arrived in our in-boxes. "You guuuuuys, can we please go eat bagels in Salima's bed this weekend?" Fearing that in her adult life Salima might be a little less willing to sully her comforter (even though it's the same one she had in college), I decided to open my kitchen to the girls.

Knowing I would be reluctant to get out of bed in the morning, I prepared the bulk of the meal the night before, leaving only the scrambling of eggs and toasting of bread for the morning of. As it turned out, the work over the skillet required less effort than the old bagel run, especially with a mimosa in hand. I might have been the only one in pajamas, looking as disheveled and happy as I did in Salima's bed, but our civilized living-room brunch had all the comfort of the old days because, well, we were together. By four we were done catching up, full of eggs and mimosas, with all the crumbs caught on the plates below.

creamy mushroom tartines with chive scrambled eggs

Makes 10 servings

A tartine is an open-faced sandwich that should be eaten with a knife and fork, so if you're serving this to a large group, be sure to pick up plastic utensils when you do your grocery shopping. You can also serve this buffet-style. Just instruct your guests how best to plate the meal.

{
1 to 2 loaves rustic country white bread, sliced ½-inch thick (10 slices)

2 tablespoons unsalted butter, melted

Salt

2 tablespoons olive oil
}

{
2 dozen large eggs, beaten

1 cup grated white cheddar cheese

⅔ cup chopped fresh chives, plus extra for garnish

Freshly ground black pepper

Creamy Mushrooms (recipe follows)
}

1. About 45 minutes before your guests are due to arrive, preheat the oven to 350°F.
2. Arrange the bread slices on a cookie sheet. Brush the top of each slice with the melted butter, and sprinkle with a little bit of salt. Toast in the oven until golden brown but not hard, 5 to 8 minutes.
3. In the meantime, coat a large nonstick skillet with the olive oil and heat it over medium heat. Add the eggs and slowly scramble, scraping the bottom of the pan as the eggs begin to cook. If the bottom is quickly forming chunks, turn the heat down. For best results, this should be a fairly slow, tedious process (see Joanne's Soft Scrambled Eggs, page 37).
4. When the eggs are nearly cooked, add the cheese and the chives, and season generously with salt and pepper. Cook for another minute or two, until the cheese melts and the eggs are no longer runny.
5. To serve, spoon a helping of the Creamy Mushrooms over each piece of toast, followed by a scoop of scrambled eggs. Garnish with chopped chives.

{creamy mushrooms}

Makes 2 to 3 cups

2 tablespoons unsalted butter

1 large sweet onion, finely chopped

4 cloves garlic, minced

1 pound cremini mushrooms (if cremini are criminally expensive, use half cremini and half regular white mushrooms), stems discarded, caps cleaned (see page 298) and finely chopped

1 cup white wine

¼ teaspoon dried thyme

¼ teaspoon crushed red pepper flakes

1 teaspoon salt

¼ cup heavy cream

> *Note: The mushrooms can be made 2 days in advance and stored in the fridge. Reheat before serving.*

1. In a large skillet or Dutch oven, melt the butter over medium-low heat. Add the onion and garlic, and sauté until soft, about 4 minutes.
2. Add the mushrooms and cook for 5 to 10 minutes, until they begin to soften.
3. Add the white wine and cook until the alcohol has evaporated and the liquid has reduced by half, about 5 minutes. Add the thyme, red pepper flakes, and salt. Simmer the mushroom mixture, uncovered, stirring occasionally, until the liquid is nearly all gone, about 5 minutes.
4. Add the cream and cook for another 3 minutes, until slightly reduced.

baked french toast with berry compote

Makes 10 servings

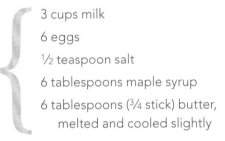

3 cups milk

6 eggs

½ teaspoon salt

6 tablespoons maple syrup

6 tablespoons (¾ stick) butter, melted and cooled slightly

2 teaspoons butter, at room temperature, for the pan

1 loaf challah or brioche, cut into 10 to 12 slices (about 1½ inches thick)

1. In a large bowl, whisk together the milk, eggs, salt, maple syrup, and melted butter.
2. Butter a baking pan that is large enough to fit all the bread slices. (You'll probably need a 9 × 13-inch pan plus possibly a smaller square or round pan. Improvise!) Arrange the bread in it.
3. Pour the egg mixture over the bread, flipping each piece to make sure it's submerged. Let rest for 1 hour at room temperature, or longer (even overnight) in the fridge.
4. About 20 minutes before you are ready to bake, preheat the oven to 400°F.
5. Bake the French toast for 25 minutes, or until the bread is golden and crusty and the slices are cooked through (cut open and peek if you're not sure).
6. Serve with maple syrup and confectioners' sugar, and pass a bowl of Berry Compote (page 158).

Cinnamon French Toast with Apple Compote: Add 1 teaspoon ground cinnamon to the egg mixture before soaking the bread. Top the French toast with Apple Compote (page 159) before serving.

berry compote

Makes 1½ cups

{
1½ cups frozen blueberries or raspberries, or a mix

3 tablespoons sugar, or slightly more, depending on how sweet the berries are

2 teaspoons cornstarch

Pinch of salt
}

1. Combine 1 cup of the berries and the sugar in a small saucepan. Bring to a boil over medium heat, and then reduce the heat and simmer for about 5 minutes, until the blueberries have released quite a lot of juice.
2. Meanwhile, in a small bowl, make a cornstarch slurry: mix the cornstarch with 2 tablespoons water until dissolved.
3. Add the cornstarch slurry to the berries and stir to combine. Cook for another 2 minutes, until the compote has thickened.
4. Add the remaining ½ cup berries, cook for 1 minute, and then set aside. If necessary, rewarm before serving.

apple compote

Makes 2 to 3 cups

Granny Smith apples work well here, but you can use any apple that's available.

{ 6 apples, peeled, cored, and cut into eighths

1 cup sugar
Grated zest of 1 lemon }

1. In a medium pot or saucepan, combine the apples, sugar, zest, and 1 cup of water. Bring to a boil. Then reduce the heat and simmer, stirring occasionally, until the apples are just tender, 10 to 15 minutes.
2. With a slotted spoon, transfer the apples to a bowl. Continue to cook the liquid until it has reduced and is quite syrupy, about 15 minutes.
3. Pour the syrup over the apples. Serve warm, or store in an airtight container in the fridge.

how to host brunch (and still sleep 'til noon)

If you take some rules into account, you can turn out a great brunch and still get the weekend beauty rest you deserve. Here are a few good calls and bad calls with regard to popular brunch choices, and our best calls for keeping weekend mornings friend-filled, delicious, and stress-free.

First:

- Don't give yourself more than an hour of prep work the morning of.
- Only attempt to cook one item on the stove. That's it. Dealing with sautéing hash browns and scrambling eggs, all the while entertaining the first few arrivals, is just a disaster waiting to happen.
- Choose one item that requires attention the day of (scrambled eggs or hash browns), one that requires assembly (salad or sandwiches), and another that can be made start to finish the night before (quick breads or coffee cake), and brunch will be a breeze.

eggs

good call: Eggs are cheap, traditional, and tasty, and they are easy to double and triple according to your party size. If you are scrambling a large pan of eggs, you can do all the cracking and beating the night before, and then slowly scramble them just before your guests arrive. This isn't stressful like frying, and can be done painlessly right before the meal.

bad call: They are also perhaps the trickiest and most time-sensitive thing to cook. This means lots of stress if the right menu choice isn't made. Don't attempt omelets for ten people. That's just crazy talk.

the best call: If you don't go for a simple scramble, choose an egg dish that only requires baking in the oven. Frittatas (like the Swiss chard version on page 32), savory puddings, and stratas are great choices. In the case of the last two, they can be completely assembled the night before and baked the morning of.

hash browns

good call: Potatoes are probably more comforting for a hangover than either Advil or hair of the dog (booze). If you can whip up a decent batch of hash browns in large quantities, you might become the most popular person ever.

bad call: Hash browns take a long time to cook and are traditionally done in a large skillet on the stove, meaning they require attention and have the potential to become a huge pain.

the best call: Parboil your potatoes the night before and they will take no time at all the day of. They don't need to be straight out of the skillet like eggs, so feel free to keep them warm in the oven while waiting for your guests to arrive. Also, roasted potatoes, instead of hash browns, are easy and equally delicious. Simply halve baby Yukon Gold or red potatoes, toss with salt and olive oil, and roast at 425°F for 50 minutes.

breakfast meats

good call: A little sausage and bacon never disappoints.

bad call: Again, the skillet issue.

the best call: Bake your bacon and sausage in the oven. Most recipes will advise using a draining rack, but who actually owns one of those? You'll be fine using a regular rimmed baking sheet lined with foil. Make sure to drain the bacon afterwards on paper towels, as you would if you fried it in a pan.

bread

good call: A loaf of crusty artisan bread is a great cheap way to bulk up a meal and to keep people occupied, restaurant-style, while you finish cooking. Understandably, at 1 p.m. your guests may be a little hungover and ornery, so this gives them something to nosh on right when they walk in the door.

bad call: If you buy your bread the day before, with the rest of the ingredients, it could be a little stale by brunch time—especially if you buy a baguette, which always tastes best freshly baked.

the best call: Buy bread in advance, then toast the whole loaf in a preheated 350°F oven for 10 or 15 minutes before slicing and serving it. Rubbing a little water on the crust with your hands will help crisp it up if it has gotten rubbery and soft.

sandwiches

good call: Any type of sandwich that doesn't require too many made-to-order hot ingredients is a good option. They can be assembled in advance, and it doesn't take much more effort to make fourteen than four. Try making the Pesto Panino on page 39 and keeping it warm in the oven, or the Pesto Chicken Salad Sandwiches (page 64), which can be easily assembled the morning of.

bad call: Some people may feel cheated out of standard breakfast fare if you just serve sandwiches.

the best call: Pair sandwiches with something that is more traditional, like an eggy savory bread pudding or muffins, or choose a more breakfast-oriented sandwich (see below for eggy ideas).

egg sandwiches

good call: There's a good reason every corner deli in the world sells some variation of an egg sandwich. They taste good if you use humble ingredients, but they can also be gussied up with a few simple embellishments.

bad call: You don't want to have to fry a billion individual eggs.

the best call: Allow people to make their own egg sandwiches buffet-style, as we do with the Breakfast Burritos on page 167. Other easier egg preparations are frittata sandwiches, egg salad sandwiches, and egg pizzas, which are cooked directly in the oven and then cut into slices.

french toast

good call: French toast can be an incredibly easy, cheap brunch option.

bad call: Frying up individual slices of French toast is a huge pain.

the best call: Try the Baked French Toast on page 157. It can soak as long as it needs to, so you can make it the night before if your schedule allows. Tweak it with cinnamon, nuts, and berry compotes to make it special.

pancakes

good call: Take your friends back to childhood with every bite. It's easy to create variety with these—just add some chocolate chips or fresh fruit and you can have pancakes two ways. For recipes, see pages 143 and 144.

bad call: Messy messy messy, and a pain.

the best call: Make pancakes only if you have four or fewer guests. If serving a crowd, go with baked French toast instead.

fruit

good call: Fruit satisfies light eaters, and it can brighten up an otherwise monochromatic brunch plate. Fruit salads are easy and can be made in advance.

bad call: Be careful, as these can get pricy if you are serving a lot of people.

the best call: If you want to offer fresh fruit, cut up one large melon or pineapple and serve it on a big platter in the middle of the table. Compotes for pancakes and baked French toast are a great way to make your dish more elegant and special without spending too much. They can be made the night before and reheated the morning of. Better yet, you can use frozen berries if the fruit is not in season, or just as an inexpensive alternative. Because the flavor is concentrated, a little compote goes a long way. See pages 158 and 159 for fruit topping ideas.

baked goods

good call: Quick breads, coffee cake, and muffins are a great addition to any brunch, and can be made in advance. They are also fairly inexpensive, as long as they don't involve too many nuts.

bad call: Crumbs! Make sure to provide proper napkins. Also, if the treat must be baked the morning of (scones taste best this way), make sure to plan the rest of your meal accordingly. If your bread needs to be toasted and your frittata cooked, there may not be room for a muffin pan in the oven.

the best call: Try our Apple Bread recipe (page 187) baked as muffins, or a loaf of Zucchini Bread (page 186), both made the night before. See pages 186 and 187 for even more options.

caffeine

good call: If you own a coffee maker, great. Buy an inexpensive roast and whip up a pot. Have milk and sugar readily available.

bad call: How many of your friends actually do own a coffee maker?

the best call: If you're short a coffee pot, don't bother with the powdered stuff—it's nasty. Some people will grab a coffee on their way over. For those really in need of caffeine, make sure you have some tea on hand and offer them that instead. You will be surprised at how many closeted tea drinkers there are.

booze

good call: Mimosas, Bloody Marys, and Bellinis are what make brunch worth believing in. Especially when you're at someone's home and they don't cost $10 a glass.

bad call: Champagne is the most popular breakfast alcohol, and that can get expensive.

the best call: Try to get your friends to chip in by bringing a bottle (see page 83 for BYOB tips); you can supply orange juice or other mixers, or ask someone to get that too. Otherwise, there are some other fun brunch-friendly cocktails that are cheaper for large parties; see page 113 for Big Kid Hot Chocolate and other ideas.

feeding the masses

Phoebe, Summer 2008

My mother has always been incredibly skilled at cooking for unexpected crowds. She practiced this while I was growing up, during summers spent at my grandparents' house on Martha's Vineyard with our whole extended family. My dad would grow sick of making small talk with my mom's relatives and on a whim invite ten people over for dinner, notifying my mother about half an hour before their arrival. Disgruntled but willing, she'd run to the seafood store and manage to turn out a huge, beautiful baked fillet of salmon just in time. She would often ask me to lend a hand, but I was usually relegated to tiny tasks like washing and chopping herbs for the tarragon-butter sauce.

In rebellion against her total kitchen control during those summer vacations, I opened Phoebe's Restaurant—a one-day-only affair where I exhibited shameless only-child, attention-seeking behavior and indulged in a burgeoning multiple-personality disorder, playing both the surly waitress, Shirley, and a greasy-spoon short-order cook, Bob, and

Phoebe, 1990

dishing out breakfast to my parents, aunts, uncles, and cousins. The placemats were finely crafted from the most refined fax-machine paper, the menus written in bold crayon, and the food (evidence that line cooks on egg duty have the most difficult job in the kitchen) was always a disaster.

It took a few years, and some very patient family members, but eventually I learned from my mistakes and began taking a more totalitarian approach by offering only one item on the menu. There was nothing particularly remarkable about Phoebe's Famous Breakfast Burritos, nor anything particularly burrito-like, come to think of it—just scrambled eggs in a warm flour tortilla. But they were easy, and when you are functioning as both surly waitress and greasy short-order cook, you learn to simplify.

I'm not sure when it happened, exactly, but at some point between college and when we started the blog—years after I discovered the peas in my mother's freezer and began feeding large groups of people with bowls of chili and many pieces of crusty crostini—I became known amongst my friends as the official Hostess of the Masses. As I've had time to reflect on the pounds upon pounds of avocados I've mashed for guacamole and the dozens upon dozens of eggs I've scrambled in dangerously full skillets, I realize where my love of mass production began. It was at age seven, with the breakfast burrito.

Last summer, I returned to my grandparents' house for Labor Day weekend. This time, instead of relatives, the rooms were filled with my friends, who were more than happy to wait while I made them the grown-up incarnation of my childhood signature dish: the hangover burrito buffet. Caitlyn was the first one up. She came downstairs and began mixing mimosas. As I got the eggs going in a large skillet, she handed me a glass of champagne with a splash of orange juice—a signature ratio she likes to call "the Papa John," after her father. By this point, Adam (brewer of Big Kid Hot Chocolate) and Jamie (frat boy whose bed Salima inherited) were standing eagerly at my side, waiting for their mimosas to kick in, peering over my shoulder as I continued to scrape the egg from the bottom of the pan. I decided to retire the Shirley act, and my guests served themselves straight from the pan, plopping down on the lawn outside to devour their burritos.

Adam and Jamie were far more enthusiastic about my egg-scrambling abilities than any family member had ever been, and as soon as we returned to the city, I found myself reopening Phoebe's Restaurant in the comfort of their apartment (which they share with a third roommate, Date Night Dave). The boys recruited me for all manner of "special" occasions—a warm Saturday in October, St. Patty's Day one week early in Hoboken, or just because the promise of my famous breakfast burritos gets our friends out of bed like nothing else I know. Best of all, now that I've worked my way up the restaurant food chain, I can simply sip Big Kid Hot Chocolate (page 113) while I scramble, and order Dave to slice tomatoes and Adam to chop the herbs.

breakfast burrito buffet with all the fixings

Makes 20 to 25 servings

These breakfast burritos are enlivened by homemade guacamole and pico de gallo. Because each burrito uses a small amount, you don't need to make huge batches of these condiments. The amounts specified in the recipes that follow are right for this size buffet.

Three 15-ounce cans black beans, rinsed and drained

1 teaspoon chili powder

½ teaspoon ground cumin

4 dozen eggs, beaten (see Note)

1 cup caramelized onions (see page 297; optional)

1 pound Monterey Jack cheese, grated

Salt and freshly ground black pepper

25 medium (8-inch) flour tortillas

Guacamole (recipe follows)

Pico de Gallo (recipe follows)

Note: It's best to crack all the eggs the night before and store them in a large airtight container, or in a bowl covered tightly with plastic wrap, in the fridge. Then, the day of, beat them.

1. Preheat the oven to 325°F.
2. Combine the beans, chili powder, and cumin in a small saucepan or Dutch oven. Keep the mixture warm over low heat while you cook the eggs.
3. Wrap the tortillas in aluminum foil and let them warm in the oven until you are ready to serve.
4. Pour the beaten eggs into a large nonstick skillet, making sure it is not so full that eggs will overflow as you scramble. If necessary, use two skillets. Set the pan(s) over high heat. There are a lot of eggs, so it will take some time before the mixture as a whole is warm enough to start forming solid clumps. When curds begin forming at

the bottom, turn the heat down to medium-low and cook, regularly scraping them up from the bottom, until the eggs are still runny but nearly cooked through, 20 to 30 minutes.

5. Add the onions (if using) and 1 cup of the grated cheese, stirring to combine. Season with salt and pepper. Cook for a few minutes to let the cheese melt and the whole mixture firm up slightly.

6. Serve immediately from the pan, alongside the warmed tortillas, beans, remaining cheese, guacamole, and pico de gallo.

{guacamole}

Makes 8 to 10 servings as an appetizer, 20 to 25 as part of a buffet

2 cloves garlic, pushed through a press or finely minced

Juice of 3 limes

½ cup finely diced red onion

3 medium plum tomatoes, cored, seeded, and finely chopped

1 tablespoon minced pickled jalapeños (about 8 slices)

8 ripe avocados

1½ teaspoons salt

¼ teaspoon cayenne pepper

1 cup chopped fresh cilantro leaves

1. In a medium mixing bowl, combine the garlic, two-thirds of the lime juice, and the red onion, tomatoes, and jalapeños. Stir to combine. This mixture will keep up to a day.

2. No more than 2 hours before serving, halve the avocados and, with a large kitchen knife, remove the pits by wedging your knife into them and twisting. Reserve 4 pits. Use a large spoon to scoop the avocado flesh out of its skin. If you have a masher, add the avocados to the bowl and mash them together with the other ingredients. If not, roughly chop the avocados and add half to the bowl. With the flat side of your knife, smash the remaining avocados against the cutting board until they become a

coarse mush. This will be a little messy, but the result will be a great texture, smooth but not overly pureed. Using your knife, scrape all the avocado mush from the cutting board and add it to the bowl. Mix together with a fork, mashing the large chunks of avocados until the guacamole reaches the desired consistency. Mix in the cilantro.

3.   Squeeze the remaining lime juice over the top of the mixture and submerge the 4 pits just below the surface of the guacamole. Cover tightly with plastic wrap. This should prevent the guacamole from browning for at least an hour or two.

4.   To serve, remove the pits, stir, and taste for seasoning.

{cherry tomato pico de gallo}

Makes 2 cups

2 pints cherry or grape tomatoes, quartered

¼ cup finely chopped red onion

2 cloves garlic, minced

2 fresh jalapeños, minced (see page 300)

Juice of 2 limes

1 tablespoon olive oil

1½ teaspoons salt

¼ teaspoon cayenne pepper

¼ cup chopped fresh cilantro leaves

1.   Combine the tomatoes, onion, garlic, jalapeños, lime juice, olive oil, and cayenne in a small bowl. (This can be done up to a day in advance.)

2.   Just before serving, mix in the cilantro and taste for seasoning.

GIVING

Food can bring such pleasure, and sweets may be the easiest treat to share. We make cookies and cakes and give them away as gifts for all kinds of reasons. Knowing how to cook is a gift in itself, one for which we're grateful to our parents and friends, who have provided key tips and kitchen lessons along the way.

tins of treats

We send off treats when we want to express an emotion or make a gesture that we're not eloquent enough to put into words. We bake, box, and deliver, and poof—we've conveyed how we feel.

Nearly any box can become a vessel for delivering treats. Shoeboxes lined with foil or parchment can be charming. Oatmeal and coffee canisters work. Save boxes that gadgets come in—Cara once sent off birthday brownies in her Flip camera's old home. Then there are real tins, the most proper for gift giving when the recipient is your boyfriend's mom, though unnecessary when you're sending treats off to your sister. If you find tins for cheap, stock up. They will come in handy.

If possible, mail sweets early in the week by two-day mail. It usually costs more to pay for one-day shipping or guaranteed delivery, but if you send on a Monday and the cookies are one day late, they'll still be fine. If you send on Thursday and the cookies sit in delivery purgatory for the weekend, it may be too late.

lotus blondies

Makes 24 blondies

atonement

recipient: Kate, Cara's sister

occasion: Holding on to jewelry your sister lent you for much longer than she intended—so long, in fact, that she accuses you of stealing. When you finally take off the necklace, embarrassment hits: "How could I have been such a jerk?" you ask yourself.

treat: Lotus Blondies. The necklace has little gold lotus leaves hanging from a chain. Cara put white chocolate and roasted cashews in her classic blondie recipe and named the bars appropriately.

{

2½ cups packed light brown sugar

8 tablespoons (1 stick) unsalted butter

2 large eggs

1 teaspoon vanilla extract

1 cup all-purpose flour

½ teaspoon salt

1 cup roasted, unsalted cashews, chopped

1 cup white chocolate chips

¼ cup semisweet chocolate chips

}

1. Preheat the oven to 325°F. Grease a 9 × 13-inch baking pan with butter and line it with parchment paper.
2. Combine the brown sugar and the butter in a small saucepan, and heat over medium heat until the butter is melted and the whole mixture is just beginning to bubble. Transfer it to a medium mixing bowl and let cool to room temperature. This will take about 20 minutes; speed it up in the fridge if need be.
3. When the butter mixture has cooled, beat in the eggs and vanilla.
4. Add the flour, salt, nuts, and chips, and fold together.
5. Pour the batter into the prepared baking pan and bake for 25 to 30 minutes, until the top has gotten slightly puffed and crusty. Let cool in the pan, and then cut into 24 bars.

resignation brownies

Makes sixteen 2-inch brownies

guilt

recipient: Stephanie, Phoebe's boss, who miraculously became one of the most important people in her life. In a good way.

occasion: Quitting. Bosses are the best scapegoats around, so most people don't feel guilty when leaving a job. But Phoebe did.

treat: The first Monday Phoebe was gone, Stephanie got a batch of Cara's fudge brownies instead of her right-hand woman.

8 tablespoons (1 stick) unsalted butter, plus extra for the pan

2 ounces unsweetened chocolate

½ cup granulated sugar

½ cup packed light brown sugar

2 large eggs, lightly beaten

½ teaspoon vanilla extract

1 teaspoon instant espresso powder (optional)

¼ cup all-purpose flour

¼ teaspoon salt

1 cup add-ins: chocolate chips, white chocolate chips, Heath brand toffee bits, or chopped toasted nuts

Note: If you only have a 9 × 13-inch baking dish, double this recipe. It just means lots more brownies!

1. Preheat the oven to 325°F.
2. Butter an 8-inch square baking pan. Clear a space in the freezer for the pan, and line the space with a dish towel.
3. Melt the chocolate and butter together in a saucepan over low heat (this can also be done in the microwave) just until both are melted. Remove from the heat. Stir in both sugars.
4. Add the eggs, vanilla, and espresso powder (if using), and mix until smooth.

5. Stir in the flour, salt, and nuts/chips/candy, and mix until smooth. Pour into the prepared baking pan.
6. Bake for 25 to 30 minutes, until the top is crackly but the brownies are still quite moist.
7. Place the whole pan in the freezer and leave it until thoroughly cool, 1 to 2 hours, or leave it overnight. Cut the brownies into 16 squares and let come to room temperature. Eat, serve, or send.

thin and snappy ginger cookies

Makes 36 cookies

love

recipients: Alex and Will

occasion: Whenever. If Phoebe makes a batch of treats for another reason, she saves a cookie or two for Will. Her most flagrant withholding was of the two best Christmas cookies at Kate's holiday party, which she smuggled away in a napkin. Cara's boyfriend, Alex, can't eat dairy, and it is truly an act of love that she makes him cookies, brownies, and cakes with oil and almond milk.

treats: Gingersnaps

⅔ cup canola oil

1 cup packed light brown sugar

½ cup molasses

1 egg

2½ cups all-purpose flour

1 teaspoon baking soda

1½ teaspoons ground ginger

¾ teaspoon ground cinnamon

¼ teaspoon ground cloves

¼ teaspoon ground nutmeg

¼ teaspoon salt

1. Preheat the oven to 325°F. Cover three baking sheets with parchment paper.
2. Mix together the oil, brown sugar, and molasses in a large bowl. Add the egg and beat to combine.
3. In a separate bowl, whisk together the flour, baking soda, spices, and salt until combined. Sprinkle the dry ingredients over the wet, then fold in until just absorbed.
4. With slightly wet hands, roll tablespoon-size balls of the dough—the dough will be a bit gooey. Drop them on the prepared baking sheets, spacing them 3 inches apart. Each baking sheet should hold 12 cookies.
5. Bake, rotating the sheets 180 degrees halfway through the baking time, for 15 minutes or until the snaps are flat and round. Cool on the sheets for 5 minutes, then transfer to plates and let cool completely.

butterscotch pecan cookies

Makes 24 to 30 cookies

gratitude

recipient: Pancake-loving Aaron, our blog's temporary tech consultant

occasion: Website tutorial. When we set up *Big Girls, Small Kitchen*, we didn't know how to abbreviate our past posts so they didn't fill up the whole page. Aaron hacked Blogger to set up the "read more" feature.

treat: Butterscotch Pecan Cookies

2 cups (8 ounces) pecan halves

2 cups plus 2 tablespoons all-purpose flour

1 teaspoon baking soda

½ teaspoon salt

1 cup (2 sticks) unsalted butter, at room temperature

⅔ cup granulated sugar

⅔ cup packed light brown sugar

1 egg

¾ teaspoon butterscotch extract (see Note)

2 teaspoons vanilla extract

⅛ teaspoon instant espresso powder

FOR COATING THE COOKIES

⅓ cup granulated sugar

1¼ teaspoons salt

Note: If you can't find butterscotch extract, use ¾ cup butterscotch chips and decrease the pecans to 1¼ cups.

1. Preheat the oven to 375°F. Line 2 to 3 baking sheets with parchment.
2. Spread the pecan halves on a baking sheet and toast them in the oven for about 10 minutes, checking every minute or so after 5 minutes have passed. You want the nuts to be fragrant and sweet but not burnt. Set aside to cool. (You can do this step up to a week in advance.)
3. Put ¾ cup of the cooled pecans in a food processor. Pulse on and off until the pecans are just ground—you don't want to turn them into a paste.

4. On a cutting board, chop the remaining 1¼ cups pecans into small pieces. Put the ground and chopped nuts in a small bowl and add the flour, baking soda, and salt. Stir to combine, and set aside.
5. In a large mixing bowl with a handheld mixer, cream the butter with the sugars until light and fluffy.
6. Add the egg and beat until combined. Then mix in the extracts and espresso powder.
7. Pour the dry ingredients into the butter mixture and mix just until the flour is incorporated.
8. Prepare the coating: mix together the sugar and salt on a shallow plate. Form the dough into 2-inch balls, and roll the balls in the sugar-salt mixture until coated. Place the balls on the baking sheet, spacing them 3 inches apart.
9. Bake the cookies for 8 to 10 minutes, until the bottoms are golden and the tops are just barely firm. Let cool on the baking sheet for 10 minutes; then gently transfer them to plates to cool completely.

classic chocolate chip cookies

Makes 24 to 30 cookies

pity

recipients: Anonymous. But how much more humane is it to say "Here, have a cookie" than "Man, your life blows"?

occasion: A friend got dumped, lost employment, had a fight with a roommate.

treat: Classic Chocolate Chip Cookies

{
⅔ cup granulated sugar

⅔ cup packed light brown sugar
(you can substitute dark)

1 cup (2 sticks) unsalted butter, at
room temperature

1 large egg

2 ¼ cups all-purpose flour

1 teaspoon baking soda

½ teaspoon salt

1 cup semisweet chocolate chips

1 cup milk chocolate chips
}

Note: You can use just one kind of chocolate chips, but the cookies are best this way, with half semisweet and half milk chocolate chips, a trick Cara owes to her friend JoJo.

1. Preheat the oven to 375°F. Line 2 or 3 baking sheets with parchment.
2. Combine both sugars and the butter in a large mixing bowl. With a mixer, a handheld beater, or a very strong arm, beat until creamy.
3. Add the egg and beat until the batter is fluffy and light.
4. Stir in the flour, baking soda, and salt until just combined.
5. Mix in the chocolate chips.
6. Drop rounded tablespoonfuls of the dough onto cookie sheets, spacing them about 2 inches apart.
7. Bake for 6 to 8 minutes, until just barely set. Let cool on the cookie sheets for 5 to 10 minutes. Then transfer the cookies to plates to finish cooling.

baking by heart

Cara, Spring 2009

For Jessy's twenty-fourth birthday, I baked my mother's best chocolate cake (see page 184) and brought it to a high school potluck. A few days later, we gathered again for a low-key cocktail hour at our friend Sami's apartment to celebrate.

A bunch of girls were sitting around, and I had started telling them about the guy I had just met on the subway (Alex), when I took a bite of the banana chocolate chip bread sitting on the coffee table. I stopped talking. The banana bread was amazing. It was a world away from the loaf I had always made. It was gooey, not just with an excess of chocolate chips, but with a dense, buttery, banana-y crumb. It reminded me of the best banana bread I'd ever had before this night—the one made by Phoebe's mom.

"Who made this?" I asked accusingly.

Sami pointed at Ali, Jessy's roommate.

"This is the best banana bread I've ever had," I told her. "Can I have the recipe?"

Ali looked happy for the compliment, but also not entirely surprised. Somehow I could tell that it wasn't the first time she'd heard it.

"Well, not really," Ali said.

I have to admit that seemed a little weird. I've never been one for secret recipes—I tend to believe that good food, and the way to create it, should be shared.

"I don't use a recipe," she went on. "Just proportions."

Oh, I sighed to myself. That made a lot more sense.

Thankfully, Ali shared her rule of 1-2-3: One part fat. Two parts sugar. Three parts flour. Then, a couple of bananas, a couple of eggs, a pinch of salt, chocolate chips, and "something to make it rise," she explained. It didn't matter exactly what the fat was, if the sugar was white or brown, or if the leavening was powder or soda. The bread came out fabulously every time.

The potential of this knowledge was so enormous, it felt like a gift. There were so many goodies at my fingertips, now that I knew one simple formula. I baked a lot that spring, loaf after loaf, experimenting. Knowing a recipe by heart is a wonderful way to cook. It may often come with age and wisdom, but I was glad to be learning early.

That's how my mom cooked for us while we were growing up: from memory. Sure, she would open a cookbook and try something new, but she had memorized the recipes for our tried-and-true favorites: chicken cacciatore, corn muffins, pancakes, and most important, chocolate cake. These were more complicated than 1-2-3, but my mom has a gift for keeping track of numbers and directions, albeit sometimes to irrelevant ends. (She is known for memorizing license plates.)

Early on, Mom taught my sisters and me some dishes we could make without recipes, like scrambled eggs and macaroni and cheese. For the more complicated dishes, though, there were times when even my mom could have used a refresher. For example, she always made a perfect chocolate cake, the cake I'd made for Jessy a few days before the banana bread feast. It is a delicious three-layer confection, flavored with a bit of coffee, and, back in the day, sometimes fully covered with M&Ms. It originally came from a recipe published in *Bon Appétit* in the late '70s or early '80s, and my mom served it three or four times a year, at birthdays and holidays. As far as I can gather, by the time I was eating the chocolate cake, the recipe was already lost. But true to form, my mom re-created it from memory year after year, to the point where waking up to the smell of chocolate cake may be my most vivid childhood memory. Eventually, though, my mom started to lose track of the exact proportions of the cake. She'd swap the icing's two eggs for the cake's three, and dessert wouldn't be as perfect as any of us had remembered.

One day in 2008, I got an e-mail from my mom, with a file attached. Google had recovered the recipe! Mom baked the cake for Christmas that year, and I was in heaven. It tasted just the way it always had, but better. After I'd eaten two slices at the table, my cousin Jessie and I stood at the kitchen counter directing forkfuls of the remaining cake into our mouths.

While I will always love Mom's chocolate cake, I will probably never know how to make it by heart. Knowing a simpler formula—Ali's 1-2-3 miracle—lets me bake up a storm even when I have no recipe. It has come in handy when I'm away for the weekend with friends, or when I have few ingredients in the apartment and need to improvise. And though I am giving a recipe for Banana Chocolate Chip Bread here, the point of including this recipe at all is to encourage invention and playing around. Because, of course, it's the playing around that keeps me in the spirit of baking long after I'm tired of washing dishes and tired (temporarily) of eating.

banana chocolate chip bread

Makes 1 loaf

Ali uses melted butter in her loaf, but I usually opt for oil. See pages 186 and 187 for quick bread variations.

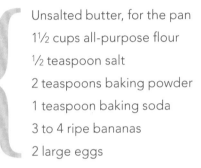

- Unsalted butter, for the pan
- 1½ cups all-purpose flour
- ½ teaspoon salt
- 2 teaspoons baking powder
- 1 teaspoon baking soda
- 3 to 4 ripe bananas
- 2 large eggs
- ½ cup granulated sugar
- ½ cup packed light brown sugar
- 1 teaspoon vanilla extract
- ½ cup safflower oil or other neutral oil, or melted butter
- 1 to 1½ cups semisweet chocolate chips

1. Preheat the oven to 350°F. Butter a loaf pan and line the bottom with parchment paper.
2. In a medium mixing bowl, stir together the flour, salt, baking powder, and baking soda.
3. In a large mixing bowl, mash the bananas with a fork or masher into large chunks (you don't want it to be totally smooth—the banana should still have texture). You should have 2 cups.
4. Add the eggs, both sugars, the vanilla, and oil, and beat until thick.
5. Fold in the dry ingredients and stir until just blended—don't overbeat! Stir in the chocolate chips.
6. Pour the batter into the prepared pan. Bake for 1 hour, or until the loaf has risen and a knife or skewer inserted in the middle comes out clean. Cool in the pan for 15 minutes. Run a knife or offset spatula along the edges and invert onto a rack or a plate. Peel off the parchment paper and invert again. Eat warm or at room temperature.

Carrot Cake: Substitute 3 cups grated carrots for the banana, and 1 cup chopped walnuts plus ½ cup raisins for the chocolate chips. Add 1½ teaspoons ground cinnamon and ¼ teaspoon ground ginger to the dry ingredients.

Pumpkin Bread: Substitute 1 can (15 ounces) unsweetened pumpkin puree for the banana, and reduce the eggs to just 1. Add 1 teaspoon ground cinnamon and ½ teaspoon each of ground nutmeg, cloves, and ginger to the dry ingredients. You can either omit the chocolate chips or use them to make **Pumpkin Chocolate Chip Bread.**

Zucchini Bread: Substitute 1½ cups shredded zucchini for the banana, and add 2 teaspoons ground cinnamon to the dry ingredients. Use 1½ cups chopped walnuts instead of the chocolate chips.

Orange Loaf: Cream ½ cup (1 stick) room-temperature butter with 1 cup granulated sugar (omit the brown sugar) and the grated zest of 1 orange; then beat in the eggs. Leave out the banana and the chocolate chips. In thirds, alternate adding the dry ingredients with ½ cup whole milk. Optional: Fold in ¾ cup dried cherries.

Apple Bread: Substitute 1 cup applesauce for the mashed banana. Use 1 cup whole wheat pastry flour and ½ cup all-purpose flour. Add 2 teaspoons ground cinnamon to the dry ingredients. Instead of chocolate chips, use 1 cup chopped pecans and 2 Granny Smith apples, peeled, cored, and diced. Sprinkle the top with sugar or cinnamon-sugar before baking.

Yogurt Cake: Reduce the oil to ⅓ cup, and substitute ¾ cup plain yogurt (not low-fat) for the banana. Use all granulated sugar, and add 1 tablespoon rum in addition to the vanilla extract. Optional: Fold in 1 cup fresh raspberries or blueberries.

baking variations

To turn any 1-2-3 cake into **muffins or cupcakes**, fill the muffin tins three-fourths full with batter and bake for 20 to 25 minutes (for **mini muffins**, bake for 12 to 15 minutes). To make a **sheet cake**, bake in a 9×13-inch baking pan for 25 to 30 minutes.

cream cheese frosting

To frost your muffins/cupcakes or sheet cake, beat together 12 ounces room-temperature cream cheese, 12 tablespoons (1½ sticks) room-temperature unsalted butter, 1½ cups confectioners' sugar, and 1 teaspoon vanilla extract. Add 1 to 2 tablespoons maple syrup—enough to reach a fluffy, spreadable consistency. Wait until the cake/cupcakes have cooled completely before frosting.

THE DINNER PARTY

We're convinced that entertaining doesn't have to be about twenty-five-year-olds morphing into practiced, competent hosts. It can be about twenty-five-year-olds relying on the resources we do have, like the energy to forge ahead even when we get stuck at work and have only twenty minutes to prepare before friends arrive. In hosting dinner parties that shake off tradition, we're concocting our own low-key methods for having people over, for concentrating on one another and on the food, on leaning back and digging in. This is the most food-centric section of this book, a resource for entertaining with recipes to mix, match, and make again and again.

sitting on the floor

I moved to Brooklyn sort of for the hell of it, winding up in a neighborhood—Park Slope—that was everything the East Village wasn't: quiet, clean, beautiful. I left to the East Village the memory of my first year in the real world and to my East Village neighbors my nearly destroyed first-year furniture. By the second week in October, my new studio had little in it besides a just-purchased multicolored striped rug. It had no official dining area, but apparently this didn't bother me—I'd already invited someone to dinner.

I had gone to my mom's house to salvage a dresser and night table, and on my way back I confirmed plans with Kirk, a college friend who lived in my new neighborhood. I planned a simple dinner around my farm-stand purchases—the season's final yield of corn, tomatoes, zucchini—and I had cornbread in the oven to pair with some sliced mozzarella when Kirk rang the buzzer. I let him in. He said something like "What a great . . . space." I accepted the compliment because there wasn't all that much else to say. I had a rug, a bed on a cotlike frame, and a white all-purpose wood bench with steel legs, the one piece of furniture that had made it out of my last apartment and into my new one. I also had two desk chairs that my landlords had left when they sublet their place to me, but no table of appropriate height at which to set them.

When I took the cornbread out of the oven (the vegetables had to be roasted first, and this was my first clue to how interesting it would be to time a meal when your oven contains only one rack), I looked around for a place to set it. With a minuscule counter and no table, the surface options were limited, and I ended up filling our plates in the kitchen. We ate on the striped rug and set our plates on the white all-purpose bench, which we had dragged to the middle of the room.

Kirk didn't protest being fed at a bench, just as he'd never have commented that my simple vegetarian meal was a bit strangely conceived (cornbread and mozzarella?). He was a twenty-something whose friend had invited him over and then fed him, and I don't think he cared where or what he ate (what he cooks for himself is a dish he calls "slop"). As hosts with limited resources, we all have our hang-ups, but in these tiny apartments and at our age, inviting friends to dine on the floor shouldn't be one of them.

cornbread

I like my cornbread the way I like my dessert: sweet. So if you're looking for southern-style cornbread, this might not be the recipe for you. If you don't have a large cast-iron skillet, you can substitute a 9-inch cake pan.

{
- 2 teaspoons canola oil
- ½ cup all-purpose flour
- 1½ teaspoons baking powder
- ¾ cup yellow cornmeal
- ¼ cup sugar
- ¼ teaspoon salt
- 4 tablespoons (½ stick) unsalted butter, melted and cooled
- ½ cup whole milk
- 1 large egg
- ½ cup corn kernels, fresh, canned and drained, or defrosted frozen (optional)
- Butter and honey, for serving (optional)
}

1. Preheat the oven to 375°F. Pour the oil into a large cast-iron skillet and place it in the oven.
2. Into a large bowl, sift together the flour, baking powder, cornmeal, sugar, and salt.
3. In a smaller bowl, whisk together the cooled melted butter, the milk, and egg.
4. Pour the wet ingredients over the flour mixture and fold to combine. Don't worry if there's some flour still showing. Stir in the corn kernels, if using.
5. Remove the hot skillet from the oven. Carefully use a brush to distribute the oil all around and up the sides of the skillet. Pour the batter in, and use a spatula to smooth the top.
6. Bake for 10 to 12 minutes, until the edges are crisped and a toothpick inserted into the center of the cornbread comes out clean. (If you use a 9-inch cake pan, the cornbread will take 15 to 20 minutes to bake.)
7. Slice the cornbread in the skillet and serve it warm, with butter and honey if you desire. To reheat it, place the skillet in a preheated 350°F oven and bake for 8 to 10 minutes.

how to set the coffee table

There is nothing formal about eating with a plate on your lap. But when you own mismatched dinner plates, use soupspoons to serve salad, and have your dining room practically in your bedroom, formal is already out the window. Still, there are simple ways to make the environment around a coffee table not uncivilized. Even if it's a place you usually reserve for single slices of pizza and reruns of *Sex and the City*, any flat surface can make the transition to dinner table with just a few small adjustments.

We've geared the tips below to the dining-room-less city dweller, but they are just as good for setting a real table, too.

rainbow napkins

Whatever your coffee table's surface, a bunch of bright napkins can make it look festive. We tend to use three of one kind of napkin and three of another (some of which may actually be dish towels). We've inherited many of these elements from parents and former roommates who, no doubt, had no use for them anymore. But you know what? We've come to appreciate the hodgepodge look of a table set with multicolored napkins, as long as there is some color or tone that's consistent among them. At $2.50 a pop, buying an extra napkin or two is also pretty feasible, since embracing multicoloredness means we don't feel compelled to buy a set.

candles

You'd be surprised how much mood lighting can impact an at-home dinner, whether or not romance is at stake. We like to put out a few lit pillar candles (unscented), especially when we're hosting at the coffee table and want a touch of elegance. Scented candles are great to dispense of any unwanted smells after the meal is finished, but wait until after dessert. No one wants to be inhaling lavender while taking a bite of steak.

flowers

Like candles, a simple bouquet can completely change the tone of an otherwise makeshift table setting. For a vase, use an empty jar, drinking glass, milk jug, beer, wine, or whiskey bottle—or, of course, a vase. We like to buy a mixed bouquet or something unusual at the farmers' market when we can get there, but a $6.99 bunch from the corner deli works well, too. Sunflowers, in particular, can brighten a dinner party even on the dreariest day of the year.

serve family-style

Serving the main course on a large platter set in the middle of the table is compatible with our entertaining ways. Trying to plate restaurant-style can be overwhelming and takes you out of the swing of things, relegating you to the kitchen for a while. Make abundant platters and garnish them with green herbs. Then, as long as the group can fit around the table comfortably without squeezing, set the platter down in the center.

or set up a buffet

If space at the coffee table is limited, keep the big serving dishes off of it. Use another surface—a regular table if you have one, or a cleared-off desk or counter if you don't—for the pots of food. Let people serve themselves before taking a seat on the floor. For more on buffet dining, see page 194.

buy a tablecloth

Phoebe bought a tablecloth. It was a strange moment because it felt like an avoidable expense—much, in our opinion, like a ladle. But she finds it's worth having one simple, cheap tablecloth because it immediately translates to a more refined vibe, covering the table surface altogether. You can spend less than $20 on the whole cloth, and you only have to launder it if it gets especially dirty at dinner. If it's just slightly soiled, shake it out in the hallway or stairwell (as long as your neighbors aren't looking).

the buffet

Phoebe

When I got back from studying in Rome and moved into my first off-campus house, I started hosting themed dinner parties. I judged an evening's success by how thoroughly the platters were licked clean and how many Solo cups needed to be picked up the next day. Eventually I stopped trying to fit mismatched chairs around the dining room table and realized that these dinner parties were meant to be casual, with the emphasis on the "party." My college friends are peculiarly motivated people, and they tend to show up in unexpected numbers whatever the occasion. Keep in mind the following rules of thumb when hosting a crowd of your own, and the dinner portion of your party will be a success.

Choose one involved dish—broiled fish, chili—that can stand as the centerpiece, and fill out the meal with smaller preprepped items. **Cut corners:** buy preshredded cheese for your burritos, deveined shrimp for your tacos, and precooked rotisserie chicken for your enchiladas. When serving more than ten people, **switch to disposable** cups, plates, and utensils. (Plan on three cups and two plates per person. Once people start drinking and eating, they put down their original cup, lose it among the sea of empty red cups, then get a new one five minutes later.) Be sure to **recruit helpers;** in favoring quantity over quality, your guacamole will not suffer in the hands of a less seasoned cook. Last but not least, **have fun**. Don't forget that it's *your* party. And if the dip runs out, it's not that big a deal.

the fish taco buffet

Cara and I and a big group of college friends went to Costa Rica for spring break our senior year. We shared an apartment there with four others, and the two of us would start the morning off right for our roomies with a Costa Rican incarnation of the Breakfast Burrito Buffet (see page 167 for more on this). Soon enough, as these things tend to happen, we would have residents of another apartment showing up at our door at 9 a.m., wondering what we were up to. We were eating, of course, and naturally they joined us.

The last night of the trip, for my friend Ben's birthday, Cara and I decided to have the whole forty-person group over for dinner. We went down to the seaside fishmonger and bought ten pounds of nameless fluffy white fish. Cara fit it into rusted baking pans and then inside the small oven we had at our disposal, while I doctored cans of beans with cumin and Costa Rican hot sauce and chopped fresh mango for the salsa. The apartment was soon packed with people eating, drinking, and celebrating the trip. The platters were not completely licked clean, but the next morning at 7 a.m., as we scrambled to get our luggage together, the last stragglers showed up at our door to pack the remaining fish tacos to eat in line at customs.

the chili cook-off buffet

One December night, I had my friend Keith and a few others over to my apartment for a bowl of chili. It was a quiet evening, quieter than most of the nights or mornings when Keith had experienced my cooking in college, and the chili really hit the spot.

As we were sinking into our food comas, the idea of leaving the apartment for a Saturday out on the town seeming more and more unlikely, Keith looked over at me and said: "Hey, your chili is pretty good. But the question is . . . is it better than my chili?"

I laughed. "Is that a challenge?"

"Maybe so."

A few weeks later, we e-mailed a crowd of friends to come judge a cook-off. I hurried home from work to reheat the veggie chili I had made the night before. Keith showed up at my doorstep with two versions of his Spiked Meat Chili—one lethal, one milder—and set them up on the remaining burners. I made the mistake of trying the lethal version first, and I asked if his intention was to do away with his competition by way of heart attack. Keith smiled, taking my reaction as a sign that Claire, his girlfriend, who touted her tolerance for spice, would buckle under the heat.

I set up the spread around the stove and told the guests to grab a bowl or two, serve themselves, and load up on condiments. I also mentioned that one pot of Keith's chili should probably be treated as a hot sauce, rather than a dish. When I mentioned that my version was vegetarian, most of the guys in attendance turned up their noses. "Humph. Veggie? Can that even be considered chili?" I had apparently forgotten that vegetables are for sissies.

Fifty beer cans, dozens of Solo cups, and many glasses of water later (for those cocky few who mixed too much of Keith's lethal batch into their portion of the mild), the Chili Cook-Off proved a rather successful weeknight party.

As people got their coats to leave and my disgruntled downstairs neighbor looked on disapprovingly, several guys whispered in my ear, "I know it wasn't really a competition, but just for the record, your veggie chili was my favorite."

Keith gave me a hug on the way out, his arms full of empty pots and a shit-eating grin on his face for having made his girlfriend cry spicy chili tears. "Can we do this again some-time?" he said.

Two weeks later, we met for round two: stew. (See the chicken tagine on page 210 for my competing pot, which is also great in a buffet lineup.)

lime-marinated fish tacos with mango salsa and all the fixings

Makes 10 servings

To make this dinner party a seamless one, make the mango salsa and the crema a day in advance. Bake the fish just before your guests arrive, and lay out all the elements on a table (the fish, tortillas, cabbage, and condiments) so people can assemble their own tacos. See page 168 for our guacamole recipe if you want an extra condiment for the buffet, or an appetizer to nosh on beforehand.

FOR THE FISH

2 cloves garlic, minced

Juice of 6 limes

2 teaspoons hot sauce (Sriracha works well)

2 tablespoons olive oil

1 tablespoon sugar

2 teaspoons salt

3 pounds white fish fillets (mahi mahi, snapper, striped bass, catfish, or tilapia), skin removed

FOR THE TACOS AND FIXINGS

Ten 8-inch flour tortillas

½ head purple cabbage, shredded (about 4 cups)

2 limes, sliced into wedges

2 avocados, pitted, peeled, and sliced (optional)

Mango Salsa (recipe follows)

Cilantro-Lime Crema (recipe follows)

1. Preheat the oven to 400°F.
2. Prepare the fish: In a small bowl, combine the garlic, lime juice, hot sauce, oil, sugar, and salt.
3. Place the fish in a 9 × 13-inch baking dish and pour the lime mixture over it, flipping the fish once to make sure it is coated with the marinade. Marinate for 15 to 30 minutes (any longer and the fish will begin to cook in the lime juice and become a ceviche).
4. Bake the fish in the oven for 5 to 10 minutes, until cooked through. Serve directly from the pan, or transfer to a platter and pour the marinade over the fish to keep it moist.
5. Arrange the fish and all the taco fixings on a table.

{mango salsa}

Makes 2 cups

2 cups diced mango (1 to 2 medium mangos)

1 clove garlic, minced or pushed through a press

¼ cup finely diced red onion

Juice of 1 lime

½ teaspoon hot sauce (preferably Sriracha)

½ teaspoon salt

½ cup fresh cilantro leaves, roughly chopped (optional)

Combine the mango, garlic, onion, lime juice, hot sauce, and salt in a medium mixing bowl and toss. When you are ready to serve, stir in the cilantro, if using. This can be made the day before.

{cilantro-lime crema}

Makes 1 cup

Juice of 1 lime

8 ounces (1 cup) sour cream

1 clove garlic, minced or pushed through a press

¼ cup chopped fresh cilantro leaves, plus extra for garnish

¼ teaspoon salt

¼ teaspoon ground cumin

Pinch of cayenne pepper

Combine all the ingredients in a small bowl and stir to combine. Garnish with some cilantro leaves. The crema can be stored, covered, in the refrigerator for up to 2 days.

smoky chipotle vegetarian chili

Makes 10 servings

To turn this chili into a full buffet party, bake a pan or two of Cornbread (page 191). Set up bowls of the garnishes (avocado, cheese, sour cream, cilantro, and lime wedges) on a countertop or table, preferably near the stove. Set bowls, spoons, and napkins next to the pot of chili, and have people load up.

CHILI

1 tablespoon olive oil

2 large sweet onions, chopped

1 red bell pepper, chopped

1 yellow bell pepper, chopped

1 orange bell pepper (if unavailable, double up on red), chopped

2 medium zucchini, diced

1 yellow summer squash, diced

3 cloves garlic

Stems from 1 bunch cilantro (reserve the leaves for the garnish)

One 7-ounce can mild green chiles

2 or 3 canned chipotle chiles in adobo sauce

2 cups vegetable stock

Three 15-ounce cans diced fire-roasted tomatoes (we prefer Muir Glen)

Two 15-ounce cans kidney beans, rinsed and drained

One 15-ounce can black beans, rinsed and drained

One 15-ounce can pinto beans, rinsed and drained

2 teaspoons salt

2 tablespoons chili powder

2 tablespoons ground cumin

1 tablespoon dried oregano

1 bottle dark Mexican beer (Negra Modelo if you can find it)

GARNISHES

Leaves from 1 bunch fresh cilantro

8 ounces (1 cup) sour cream

1 cup shredded Monterey Jack cheese

2 limes, cut into thin wedges

2 avocados, seeded, peeled, diced, and tossed with lime juice to prevent browning

Note: The chili is best if made the night before and can keep in the refrigerator for up to a week.

1. Heat the olive oil in a large pot over medium heat. Add the onions and peppers, and sauté until they are beginning to caramelize, about 8 minutes.
2. Add the zucchini and yellow squash, and sauté until tender, about 5 minutes.
3. In the meantime, combine the garlic cloves, cilantro stems, green chiles, and chipotle chiles in a small food processor, and process until minced (or mince by hand). Add ½ cup of the stock, and pulse to combine.
4. Add the tomatoes and the chile mixture to the pot, and bring to a simmer.
5. Add all the beans and the salt, chili powder, cumin, oregano, beer, and the remaining 1½ cups stock. Simmer, uncovered, stirring frequently, until the liquids thicken and the vegetables have begun to break down, about 30 minutes.
6. Place the garnishes in bowls, set them near the pot of chili, and call your guests.

dirt-cheap dinners

As hosts, we want to impress. Our guests, as New Yorkers, are not so easy to impress. If we succumbed to their every desire, we'd be spending far beyond our means. Courageously, we ignore fancy ingredients at the store and aim to feed, and please, in more creative ways than with simply the best cut of meat.

It's not just about steering clear of expensive price tags. We've been to the store and spent $100, all on things that individually were cheap. Cara has even thrown simple burrito buffet parties that cost more than going to Mexico, because (this was when she first started entertaining) she couldn't resist the little accoutrements—the smidgeon of sour cream, the bag of gourmet tortilla chips, the three extra avocados. This was silly, and she has since learned to be better. In fact, she now polices other friends when they attempt to overbuy on grocery trips.

When you host a dirt-cheap dinner, you don't have to tell anyone how little you spent—at least until afterwards. If you served oatmeal for dinner, everyone would know you were cutting corners. But Polenta Steaks with Asparagus Pesto? Provençal Baked Chicken? Those don't sound cheap, and that's our point.

Be wary of what side dishes you choose. If you decide to serve your polenta with a salad made up of endive, pine nuts, and shiitakes instead of freshly tossed greens, you'll still be spending too much. On the other hand, you can use our dirt-cheap staples to pick up the slack if you've overspent elsewhere—on wine and dessert, for example.

The most important thing is to forge ahead, even if your wallet is thin. Don't be fearful of cheap cuts of meat, small portions of protein (and big portions of carbs), and vegetarian dishes (all of ours in this book are dirt cheap). Don't forget to stock your pantry when favorite items are on sale, since it'll save you money in the long run. When we spend less, we entertain more.

polenta steaks with asparagus pesto, cherry tomatoes, and burrata

Makes 8 to 10 servings

Budget under: $30

Using such a tiny amount of cheese per serving is the easiest way to lower the cost. Feel free to substitute fresh mozzarella for the burrata if you can't find any.

FOR THE POLENTA

2 tablespoons unsalted butter, plus extra for the baking dish

2 cups polenta or coarsely ground yellow cornmeal

1 quart water or chicken stock

1 quart milk

1 tablespoon salt

Olive oil

FOR THE PESTO

1½ pounds fresh asparagus, trimmed

1 cup fresh mint leaves

2 cloves garlic

Juice of 1 lemon

⅓ cup pine nuts, toasted (see page 305)

¼ cup olive oil

½ teaspoon salt

½ cup grated Parmesan cheese

FOR THE TOPPING

1 pint cherry or grape tomatoes, halved

½ pound burrata or mozzarella cheese, coarsely torn

1 tablespoon olive oil

1 teaspoon salt

1. Butter a 9 × 13-inch baking dish, and set it aside.
2. In a large Dutch oven or stockpot, bring the water and milk to a boil. Add the polenta in a gentle stream, whisking as you pour. Reduce the heat to medium-low and continue to whisk the polenta until it has thickened, about 10 minutes. Add the butter and salt, and continue to whisk until most of the liquid has evaporated, about

3 minutes. Pour the polenta into the prepared baking dish, and smooth it with a spatula to make an even layer. Cover with plastic wrap and chill in the refrigerator for 2 hours or up to 2 days.

3. Preheat the oven to 450°F.

4. Cut the polenta into 12 "steaks," and pat each one dry with a paper towel (there may be some condensation from the fridge).

5. Brush both sides of each polenta steak with olive oil. Place the steaks on a baking sheet and bake in the oven for 30 to 40 minutes, until the tops have browned.

6. Meanwhile, prepare the pesto: Bring a pot of heavily salted water to a boil. Blanch the asparagus in two batches until bright green and just tender, 1 to 2 minutes. Use tongs to transfer the asparagus to an ice bath, or put them in a colander and rinse under cold water. Drain.

7. Cut the asparagus into 1-inch pieces. Put 2 cups of the stalk pieces in a small food processor, reserving the tips. Add the mint, garlic, lemon juice, pine nuts, olive oil, and salt, and pulse. Add 1/3 cup water, and pulse until the mixture has the consistency of pesto. Mix in the Parmesan, and taste for seasoning.

8. Place the reserved asparagus tips in a mixing bowl, and toss with the tomatoes, burrata, olive oil, and salt.

9. To serve, place a warm polenta steak in the center of each plate, and top it with a generous dollop of pesto and a spoonful of the cherry tomato topping.

vietnamese fisherman's stew

Makes 4 servings
Budget under: $20

To keep this cheap, we reduced the amount of fish and bulked up the stew with potatoes. You can stretch this even further by serving it with white rice (see page 298).

2 tablespoons vegetable oil

2 small onions, thinly sliced

5 cloves garlic, thinly sliced

2 tablespoons minced peeled fresh ginger (from a 2-inch knob)

2 carrots, peeled and cut into thin slices on the diagonal

2 tablespoons curry powder

1/2 teaspoon cayenne pepper

2 teaspoons salt

2/3 cup mirin or white wine

One 14-ounce can coconut milk

1 1/2 pounds waxy potatoes (red or Yukon Gold), peeled and cut into 1 1/2-inch pieces

6 bunches baby bok choy, washed and trimmed

1 1/2 pounds hake, catfish, cod, or tilapia or other mild white fish, cut into 8 pieces

2 limes: 1 juiced, 1 quartered

1. Heat the oil in a lidded pot over medium-low heat. Add the onions, garlic, and ginger; cook until soft but not browned, 8 minutes. Add the carrots and cook for another minute.

2. Sprinkle in the curry powder and cayenne, and cook for 1 minute, or until fragrant. Add the salt and mirin, and bring to a boil. Let it simmer for 3 minutes, until slightly reduced. Pour in the coconut milk and 2 cups water, and bring to a boil.

3. Add the potatoes, return the liquid to a boil, and then turn the heat to low and cover the pot. Simmer for 10 to 12 minutes, until the potatoes are easily pierced with a fork. (You can make the stew ahead to this point.)

4. Add the bok choy and toss to distribute. Then add the fish pieces and arrange them so they are fully covered by the liquid. Cover the pot and simmer for 4 minutes, until the fish is cooked through but not falling apart. Add the lime juice to the stew.

5. Ladle the fish, vegetables, and broth into bowls, and garnish with the lime quarters.

provençal baked chicken

Makes 6 servings
Budget under: $15

These ingredients may seem to represent what your Mediterranean great-aunt would find if she cleaned out her fridge and pantry, but in fact the combination is more deliberate than that. The brine of the olives, the pungency of the vinegar, the sweetness of the dates, and the richness of the olive oil come together to make a fantastic, impressive chicken dish. This produces a lot of sauce, too, so find a makeshift gravy boat (a bowl or glass) and be sure everyone gets to try some.

Great accompaniments include orzo tossed with butter and minced parsley, plain rice, or good crusty bread.

¼ cup red wine vinegar

3 tablespoons olive oil

5 dried dates, pitted and chopped (about ¼ cup)

3 tablespoons chopped pitted Kalamata olives

2 bay leaves

3 tablespoons garlic, crushed, minced with 1 teaspoon salt (see page 302)

1½ teaspoons dried oregano, or 2 tablespoons fresh oregano

Freshly ground black pepper

3 pounds bone-in, skin-on chicken thighs, preferably organic

1 small onion, thinly sliced

4 plum tomatoes, each cut into 6 wedges

3 tablespoons packed light brown sugar

¼ cup dry white wine

2 tablespoons minced fresh parsley (optional)

Note: You can bake the chicken ahead of time and reheat it. After baking, refrigerate the chicken in the pan. Reheat it together with its sauce in a 350°F oven or in a pot over a low flame. (If you do this, you'll also get a chance to skim a bit of the fat off the sauce while it's cool.)

1. Combine the vinegar, olive oil, dates, olives, bay leaves, garlic, oregano, and black pepper to taste in a large container with a lid. Add the chicken and toss well to coat. Let this sit overnight in the fridge (or at least 6 hours).
2. Preheat the oven to 350°F.
3. Arrange the chicken in one layer in a casserole dish or baking pan. Pour all the marinade from the container over the chicken. Scatter the onion slices between the chicken pieces, and wedge the tomatoes into crevices around the pan. Sprinkle each piece of chicken with some of the brown sugar; then evenly pour the wine around the dish and over the chicken. Bake for 1 hour, or until the chicken's juices run clear, the tomatoes are browned, and the onions are soft.
4. Sprinkle the fresh parsley over the chicken, and transfer into a platter if you're not serving it in the baking dish.
5. Pour the juices from the pan into a small serving bowl and pass this sauce with the chicken.

saving on space: one-pot meals

Small kitchen disasters are directly proportional to the number of dishes it takes to cook a meal. Fewer pots equals fewer disasters.

Our one-pot meals are meant to maximize small kitchen space without giving up flavor or complexity. When we say one pot, we mean one pot: all these meals can be served simply as they are, without any side dish whatsoever. Plant your Dutch oven on the table, and let everyone dig in.

chicken tagine with sweet potatoes and golden raisins

Makes 10 servings

The summer after she graduated, Phoebe and her mother traveled around Morocco together. She invented this sweet and savory chicken stew shortly after she got back, and it was her contribution to the second cook-off with Keith, captured on the blog in January 2009. Since then, she has revised this tagine to include sweet potatoes, which means you don't need another carb to make it a complete meal. Still, couscous and quinoa are great (if you don't mind another pot), but a loaf of crusty bread to soak up the juices works even better.

3 pounds boneless, skinless chicken thighs, each halved

Salt and freshly ground black pepper

Olive oil

3 medium yellow onions, diced

4 cloves garlic, finely chopped

1 tablespoon ground cumin

2 teaspoons ground turmeric

1 tablespoon ground ginger

½ teaspoon ground nutmeg

½ teaspoon ground cinnamon

¼ teaspoon cayenne pepper

1 ½ tablespoons salt

One 28-ounce can diced tomatoes, with their juices

One 15-ounce can chickpeas, rinsed and drained

About 1 quart chicken stock

2 pounds sweet potatoes, peeled and cut into 1-inch chunks

½ cup golden raisins

¼ cup fresh cilantro leaves, roughly chopped

Juice of ½ lemon

¼ cup slivered almonds, toasted (see page 305; optional)

Note: You can make the stew through step 5 and then refrigerate it overnight. Just reheat it for 30 minutes over medium-low heat before your guests are due to arrive, and continue with the remaining ingredients.

1. Season the chicken thighs with salt and pepper. Coat a large pot or Dutch oven with a thin layer of olive oil. Heat it over high heat and brown the chicken, in batches, making sure not to crowd the pot. If the chicken sticks to the bottom, don't worry—this will help develop the flavor of the sauce. Remove the browned chicken from the pot and set it aside in a mixing bowl. (See page 297 for tips on browning.)

2. Add the onions to the same pot, reduce the heat to medium-low, and sauté until translucent, making sure to scrape up any remaining drippings from the chicken, about 7 minutes.

3. Stir in the garlic, cumin, turmeric, ginger, nutmeg, cinnamon, cayenne, and salt. Cook until the spices are fully incorporated and aromatic, about 2 minutes. Return the chicken to the pot, and add the tomatoes and chickpeas. Toss to combine.

4. Pour in enough stock to submerge all the contents (this may be less than 1 quart, depending on the size of your pot) and bring to a simmer. Turn the heat back down to low and cook, uncovered, for at least 2 hours, the longer the better.

5. During the last 30 minutes or so of cooking, add the sweet potatoes, submerge them in the liquid, and cook until tender.

6. Add the raisins, half the cilantro, and the lemon juice. Simmer for 10 minutes.

7. Spoon the tagine into individual bowls. Garnish each bowl with some of the remaining cilantro, sprinkle with the almonds (if using), and serve.

Vegetarian Squash Tagine: Omit the chicken, and substitute 3 to 4 diced zucchini or yellow squash. Double the chickpeas, and use vegetable stock instead of chicken.

green lasagna

Makes 8 servings

Using no-boil lasagna noodles empowers you to make this multistep dish without taking out all your pots and pans.

{
3 cloves garlic

1 teaspoon salt

One 16-ounce container whole-milk ricotta

1 egg, beaten

¼ teaspoon ground nutmeg

¼ teaspoon crushed red pepper flakes

1 tablespoon olive oil, in a small bowl

5 ounces baby spinach

One 16-ounce package no-boil lasagna noodles

1 pound fresh mozzarella, grated

½ cup freshly grated Parmesan cheese
}

1. Preheat the oven to 350°F.
2. Mince the garlic with the salt to create a paste (see page 302).
3. In a small bowl, mix the ricotta with the garlic paste, egg, nutmeg, and red pepper flakes until well combined. Set aside.
4. Brush the bottom of a 9 × 13-inch baking dish with some of the olive oil. Sprinkle a handful of spinach across the bottom. Fit a layer of lasagna noodles on top of the spinach. Drop ¾ cup of the ricotta mixture, in spoonfuls, across the noodles, and spread it with a spatula or a knife to cover the surface of the noodles. Top with a large handful of spinach and ¾ cup of the grated mozzarella. Repeat the layers of noodles-ricotta-spinach-mozzarella twice more, using up all the ricotta and spinach but reserving some mozzarella. Arrange a final layer of noodles, and top with the remaining mozzarella. Brush a piece of aluminum foil with some of the olive oil, and drizzle the remaining oil on top of the lasagna.

5. Sprinkle ¾ cup water evenly over the pan, cover it tightly with the foil, oiled side down, and bake for 45 minutes.

6. Remove the baking dish from the oven and take off the foil. Sprinkle the Parmesan over the lasagna and return it to the oven. Bake for 10 to 15 minutes, until the cheese is bubbly and melted. Let the lasagna rest for 10 minutes, and then cut it into 12 squares and serve.

scallop, chorizo, and artichoke paella

Makes 8 servings

Classic paella usually contains multiple varieties of seafood and meat. To pare down the shopping list, we went with Spanish chorizo from the land and scallops from the sea. From the garden (with a little detour in between) are frozen artichoke hearts. (You can always use canned; just make sure to drain and rinse them well.)

{
- 2 to 3 tablespoons olive oil
- 1 pound sea scallops
- 1 pound chorizo in its casing, cut diagonally into 1½-inch pieces
- 1 large sweet onion, diced
- 4 cloves garlic, minced
- 8 to 10 scallions, white and green parts chopped separately
- 2 cups Arborio rice
- ½ cup dry white wine

- One 15-ounce can crushed tomatoes
- One 9-ounce package frozen artichoke hearts, or jarred or canned unseasoned artichoke hearts packed in water
- 2 teaspoons smoked Spanish paprika (pimentón)
- 1 teaspoon salt
- 3 to 4 cups chicken stock
- Lemon wedges, for garnish
}

Note: To reheat leftovers, add ½ cup chicken stock and warm over medium heat. The rice will soak up the stock (and not burn onto the bottom of the pan) and gently reheat.

1. In a large cast-iron skillet or a Dutch oven, heat 2 tablespoons of the olive oil over medium-high heat until the oil is shiny and just about to smoke. While the oil is heating, quickly pat the scallops dry and remove and discard the tough side muscles. Sear the scallops, in batches, in the hot oil until browned and crusty on both sides, about 2 minutes per side.

2. Transfer the scallops to a plate. Add the chorizo to the skillet and brown it, turning it on all sides, 2 to 5 minutes. Set the chorizo aside.

3. Reduce the heat to medium and sauté the onion in the remaining fat until translucent, scraping up any drippings in the skillet. Add the garlic and the white part of the chopped scallions, and cook for another 2 minutes. Add the rice and stir to coat it in the onion mixture, allowing it to get covered in the oil and begin to toast, 3 minutes. Add the wine, and cook until the liquid has reduced by nearly half, 2 to 3 minutes. Use your spatula to help deglaze the pan and lift up any caramelized bits.

4. Stir in the tomatoes (and their juices), artichokes (rinsed and drained if jarred or canned), paprika, and salt.

5. Return the chorizo to the skillet, and add enough stock to submerge the rice mixture. Bring the liquid to a boil. Then reduce the heat to medium-low and simmer until the rice is cooked through, all the liquid has been absorbed, and the rice is beginning to become crusty around the edges, 25 to 30 minutes.

6. Using the back of your spoon, make indents in the top of the rice and arrange the scallops in them. Pour the scallop juices over the skillet, and cook until all the liquid has been absorbed.

7. Garnish with the chopped scallion greens and lemon wedges. Serve warm, straight from the skillet.

cooking for veggie-carnivore crowds

When Cara became a vegetarian after college, she got the inside scoop on what it was like to be labeled the picky eater. Everywhere she went, it was as if there was a warning label: DO NOT FEED MEAT TO THIS HUMAN. Phoebe was an especially friendly host, and she went out of her way to feed Cara mushroom Bolognese instead of beef, or black bean chili instead of turkey.

Our patience with the dietary restrictions of our guests began in high school, when we had as many vegetarian friends as carnivores. For potlucks, it was easy enough to end up with a spread that catered to both groups. But after college, with Cara joining the vegetarian ranks along with Jordana, Leora, and Carolyn, we had to learn to throw dinner parties that had two main-course options, lest we resort to that veggie staple that chefs seem to assume carnivores would, if pressed, consume: Eggplant Parmesan.

We're devoted to the side-by-side approach. We make two dishes that use the same prepped ingredients, require the same spices and herbs, and are topped with the same sauces and garnishes. The only difference? The main ingredient. While Jordana (veg) and Al (carnivore) were dating, this was a particularly handy tactic. For Al's birthday, Phoebe put together a Mediterranean-themed lamb burger for the guest of honor and, using the same base flavor additions and ingredients, created a chickpea burger for Jordana.

In theory, picky eaters are a host's worst nightmare. But with veggie-carnivore duos like the ones here, feeding and pleasing both crowds isn't a big deal. And since, in the end, we don't really care why our guests eat what they eat, we feel it pays off in friendship points to be tolerant and accommodating.

chickpea and walnut burgers

Makes 4 servings

If you are planning on making both the chickpea and the Mediterranean Lamb Burgers (page 220) for one meal, prep all of the ingredients at the same time—you'll notice that they call for many of the same components.

½ cup walnut halves

2 cloves garlic, roughly chopped

1 shallot, roughly chopped

⅓ cup fresh mint leaves

One 15-ounce can chickpeas, rinsed and drained

1 tablespoon extra-virgin olive oil

1 large egg

Juice of ½ lemon

½ teaspoon salt

½ teaspoon ground cumin

¼ teaspoon paprika

Dash of cayenne pepper

½ cup fresh breadcrumbs (see Note)

2 to 3 tablespoons vegetable oil

4 burger buns

Mint Raita (page 221), for serving

Fresh parsley or mint leaves, for garnish

Note: Pulse half a burger bun in a food processor to generate fresh crumbs.

1. Preheat the oven to 350°F.
2. In a small, dry sauté pan over low heat, toast the walnuts in a single layer until they are browned and fragrant, about 5 minutes. Keep an eye on these. Nuts are the easiest things to burn. Set aside.
3. Combine the garlic, shallot, and mint in a food processor and pulse until finely chopped. Add the toasted walnuts, chickpeas, and olive oil, and pulse until coarsely chopped.
4. In a medium mixing bowl, beat the egg with the lemon juice, salt, cumin, paprika, and cayenne. Add the chickpea mixture and the breadcrumbs. Fold everything together until well blended.

5. Form the mixture into 3 or 4 patties, depending on how large you like them. Chill, covered, in the refrigerator for 1 hour. (The patties can be prepared the night before, then covered and chilled overnight.)

6. In a large skillet, heat the vegetable oil (enough to coat the bottom of the pan) over medium heat. Cook the patties on both sides until nicely browned, 3 to 5 minutes per side. Transfer them to a baking sheet.

7. Arrange the buns, cut sides up, around the burgers on the baking sheet, and toast in the oven at 350°F for 3 to 5 minutes, until lightly browned.

8. To serve, place each chickpea patty on a toasted bun and top with a spoonful of Mint Raita and a few leaves of parsley or mint.

mediterranean lamb burgers

Makes 4 servings

Ground lamb is pretty affordable, but it sounds more special than beef or chicken.

1 tablespoon olive oil

1 large shallot, minced

3 cloves garlic, minced

1 tablespoon minced peeled fresh ginger

1½ pounds ground lamb

⅓ cup finely chopped fresh mint

Juice of ½ lemon

1 teaspoon salt

½ teaspoon ground cumin

¼ teaspoon paprika

Dash of cayenne pepper

1 tablespoon vegetable oil

4 burger buns, toasted

Mint Raita (recipe follows), for serving

Fresh parsley or mint sprigs, for garnish

1. Heat the olive oil in a small saucepan over low to medium heat. Add the shallot, garlic, and ginger, and sauté until soft and fragrant, about 3 minutes. Remove and let cool in a medium mixing bowl.
2. Add the lamb, mint, lemon juice, salt, cumin, paprika, and cayenne to the bowl. With clean hands, fold the ingredients together until well incorporated. Form the mixture into 4 patties.
3. In a large skillet, heat the vegetable oil (enough to line the bottom of the pan) over medium heat. Add the burger patties to the skillet and cook on both sides until beautifully browned and cooked through to medium-rare, about 5 minutes on the first side, 10 minutes on the second, making sure to turn the heat down if either side is burning.
4. To assemble, place each patty on a toasted hamburger bun and top with a dollop of Mint Raita and a couple sprigs of parsley or mint.

{mint raita}

If you are making both burgers at the same time, make sure to double this recipe. Any leftovers can be used as an excellent dipping sauce for crudités. This will keep in a sealed container in the refrigerator for a week.

Makes 1 cup

1 cup plain Greek yogurt

½ cup fresh mint leaves

2 tablespoons lemon juice

½ clove garlic

½ teaspoon salt

Combine the yogurt, mint, lemon juice, garlic, and salt in a small food processor, and puree.

chicken enchiladas and black bean–zucchini enchiladas, with creamy green chile sauce

Makes 10 to 12 servings

If you are feeding just carnivores, you can mix the fillings together in all the enchiladas instead of serving two types; if serving vegans, omit the cheese and the green chile sauce, and top the black bean enchiladas with a good store-bought red enchilada sauce. The fillings and sauce can be made up to two days in advance, and the enchiladas can be assembled the morning of the party.

FOR THE CHICKEN FILLING

2 tablespoons Dijon mustard

1 tablespoon olive oil

1½ teaspoons chili powder

1 teaspoon salt

4 boneless, skinless chicken breasts

FOR THE BLACK BEAN FILLING

Olive oil

1 red onion, chopped

1 pound zucchini (about 2 medium), quartered lengthwise and cut into ¼-inch-thick slices

2 cloves garlic, minced

One 15-ounce can black beans, rinsed and drained

1 teaspoon chili powder

1 teaspoon ground cumin

1 teaspoon salt

FOR THE SAUCE

2 tablespoons butter

2 cloves garlic, minced

2 jalapeños, minced (see page 300)

2 tablespoons all-purpose flour

One 15-ounce can vegetable or chicken stock

16 ounces (2 cups) sour cream

One 8-ounce can fire-roasted mild green chiles

1 teaspoon ground cumin

1 teaspoon chili powder

1 teaspoon salt

Cayenne pepper, to taste

FOR THE ENCHILADAS

Sixteen 8-inch flour tortillas

1½ pounds Monterey Jack cheese, shredded

½ cup fresh cilantro leaves, plus more for garnish

2 limes, cut into 6 wedges each

1. Preheat the oven to 350°F. Line a baking dish with aluminum foil.
2. Make the chicken filling: In a medium mixing bowl, combine the mustard, oil, chili powder, and salt. Add the chicken breasts and toss to coat. Place them in the lined baking dish and bake for 30 minutes, or until cooked through and tender. Allow the chicken to cool slightly, then shred the breasts using two forks. Set the meat aside, along with the juices from the baking dish.
3. Make the black bean filling: Coat a large nonstick skillet with olive oil, place it over medium heat, and sauté the onion until soft, 5 to 8 minutes. Add the zucchini and continue to sauté, stirring occasionally, until the zucchini is tender and browned, another 6 minutes. Add the garlic, beans, chili powder, cumin, and salt, and cook until the beans are tender and the garlic is fragrant, about 5 minutes. Set aside.
4. Make the sauce: Wipe out the skillet with a paper towel. Melt the butter over medium heat, add the garlic and jalapeños, and cook until they are soft but not beginning to brown, about 4 minutes. Add the flour and cook for 1 minute, until incorporated. Add the stock, raise the heat to high, and bring the mixture to a boil. Then reduce the heat and simmer until the liquids have reduced and the sauce has become opaque, about 5 minutes.
5. Transfer the sauce mixture to a blender or food processor, and add the sour cream, chiles, cumin, chili powder, salt, and cayenne. Puree until smooth. (If you don't have a food processor, just mince the chiles by hand and then whisk all the ingredients into the skillet). Coat the bottom of two 9 x 13-inch baking dishes with some of the sauce. Reserve the rest.
6. Assemble the enchiladas: Fill 8 tortillas with the chicken and 8 with the black bean and zucchini mixture. Top the filling with a spoonful of shredded cheese and a sprinkling of cilantro. Roll up the tortillas and place them, seam side down, in the baking dishes.
7. Pour the remaining cream sauce evenly over the enchiladas, and sprinkle with the remaining cheese. Bake in the oven for 30 minutes, or until the sauce is bubbling and the cheese is beginning to brown. Garnish with the extra cilantro leaves and serve with the lime wedges.

the back-pocket "fancy" dinner party

Casual yet refined comfort food goes a long way when entertaining friends, but there may come a time when you want to have, well, a "real" adult at the table. Grown-up meals don't have to be fancy in the traditional sense, but there are certain dishes that look beautiful and incorporate ingredients and flavors that will surely impress your boss, clients, parents, or uber-sophisticated European acquaintances without requiring you to try too hard.

Since the usual restrictions of quarter-life—space, money, time—still apply to even the most special of occasions, we've chosen menus that are accessible. This is the only chapter where we ask you to spend money on one big thing: a pork tenderloin, maybe some seafood. There's a time to splurge, and we'll trust you to know that it's not every day. In addition, some of these dishes have more components than usual, but don't be intimidated—many can be made ahead. Just as there's a time for fancy, there's a mood for complexity, and no one will judge you if on occasion you make pork tenderloin for no reason at all.

cioppino

Makes 4 servings

1 tablespoon olive oil

1 medium onion, diced

1 celery stalk, diced

1 medium carrot, peeled and diced

3 cloves garlic, minced

¼ teaspoon crushed red pepper flakes

1 teaspoon smoked paprika

1 teaspoon salt

¾ cup white wine

One 28-ounce can crushed tomatoes (fire-roasted if available)

One 8-ounce bottle clam juice

8 clams, scrubbed and soaked (see page 298)

2 pounds mussels, debearded, scrubbed, and soaked (see page 298)

1 pound cod, haddock, or other meaty white fish, cut into 2-inch pieces

¼ cup chopped fresh parsley

Crusty bread, for serving

1. In a large pot or Dutch oven, heat the olive oil over medium heat. Add the onion, celery, and carrot, and sauté until they are fragrant, about 5 minutes. Then add the garlic and sauté for an additional minute. Add the red pepper flakes, paprika, and salt, and stir to distribute. Add the wine, tomatoes, and clam juice and bring to a boil. Reduce the heat and simmer for 10 to 15 minutes to allow the flavors to combine.

2. Add the clams, cover the pot, and simmer over medium heat for 10 minutes. Then add the mussels and give them a good toss. Cover the pot and cook for 3 to 4 minutes. A few of the mussels may be open, but most will still be closed.

3. Add the fish and half the parsley, and cover. Cook until all the mussels are open (discard any mussels or clams that fail to open) and the fish is opaque and cooked through but not falling apart, about 5 minutes.

4. Spoon the cioppino into individual bowls, garnish with the remaining parsley, and serve immediately with the bread alongside.

pork tenderloin with roasted fennel and cider jus

Makes 4 servings

This dish exists thanks to Phoebe's former boss Stephanie, who is a big believer in pork tenderloin. If you're looking for a special date-night meal, this one also works well for romance.

FOR THE PORK

2 cloves garlic, minced

1 tablespoon chopped fresh rosemary (1 sprig)

1 tablespoon Dijon mustard

1 tablespoon whole-grain mustard

2 tablespoons lemon juice

2 teaspoons honey

3 tablespoons olive oil

1 teaspoon salt

2 pounds pork tenderloin (2 or 3 loins)

FOR THE FENNEL

2 fennel bulbs, trimmed, outer layer removed

2 tablespoons olive oil

1 teaspoon sugar

1 teaspoon salt

FOR THE SAUCE

1 tablespoon olive oil

2 cloves garlic, minced

2 shallots, minced

1 bay leaf

¼ teaspoon cayenne pepper

2 tablespoons apple cider vinegar

2 cups chicken stock

2 cups apple cider

1 teaspoon salt

2 tablespoons butter

Note: The sauce can be made one day in advance. You can also roast the fennel the day before; just reheat it in the oven before serving (see step 6).

1. The day before your dinner party, marinate the pork: Combine the garlic, rosemary, both mustards, the lemon juice, honey, oil, and salt in a small bowl, and whisk together. Place the pork in a large resealable plastic bag, and pour the marinade over it. Seal the bag, swish the pork around until it is well coated, and marinate in the fridge overnight.

2. An hour before serving time, preheat the oven to 425°F. Line a baking sheet with aluminum foil or parchment paper.

3. Prepare the fennel: Slice each fennel bulb in half and use your knife to cut out the triangular core. Discard the cores. Slice each half into 4 to 6 sections. In a large mixing bowl, combine the fennel, olive oil, sugar, and salt. Spread the fennel on the prepared baking sheet, and roast for 20 to 25 minutes, until browned and tender.

4. Meanwhile, start the sauce: In a saucepan, heat the olive oil over medium heat. Add the garlic, shallots, bay leaf, and cayenne. Sauté for 2 to 3 minutes, until the shallots are tender and beginning to brown. Deglaze the pan with the vinegar and cook for 1 minute. Add the stock and apple cider. Bring the sauce to a boil, then reduce it to a simmer. Add the salt and continue to simmer until the sauce has reduced by half, about 20 to 30 minutes.

5. While the sauce is cooking and after you have removed the fennel from the oven, raise the oven temperature to 500°F. Place the pork tenderloin(s) on an aluminum foil–lined baking sheet and roast in the oven for 20 minutes. The remaining marinade may burn on the foil, but the pork will be tender and nicely browned.

6. Transfer the tenderloin(s) to a cutting board, tent with foil, and allow to rest for 15 minutes. While the pork rests, return the fennel to the oven and heat through.

7. Taste the sauce for seasoning, and right before serving, whisk in the butter.

8. Arrange the caramelized fennel around the edge of a platter. Slice the pork into ½-inch-thick pieces on the diagonal. Transfer the whole sliced pork loin(s) to the center of the platter. Drizzle with some of the sauce, and serve immediately. Serve the remaining sauce separately.

roasted goat cheese and tomato skewers with carrot and white bean puree

Serves 4

The more we thought about what our vegetarian-friendly fancy dinner dish should be, the more we found ourselves stumped. The two biggest challenges with vegetarian food for entertaining are texture and presentation. This dish has a wonderful array of textures, and its presentation—on skewers—is definitely impressive.

1 loaf good country bread

¼ pound goat cheese

2 egg whites

4 tablespoons olive oil, plus more for the cookie sheet

½ teaspoon salt

1 bunch scallions, white and light green parts, trimmed and cut into thirds

2 cups cherry tomatoes

8 sun-dried tomatoes, dry or packed in oil

Eight 8- to 10-inch skewers, soaked in water for 30 minutes

Carrot and White Bean Puree (recipe follows)

Fresh thyme sprigs, for garnish

1. Preheat the oven to 350°F.
2. Remove the crusts of the bread and cut the loaf into 1 ½-inch cubes. You will need 16 cubes for the skewers, and you can make a few more for garnish (or snacking) if you like. Arrange the cubes on a cookie sheet and toast in the oven for about 5 minutes to get them crusty but not brown. Set aside.
3. In a small food processor, combine the goat cheese, egg whites, 3 tablespoons of the olive oil, and ¼ teaspoon of the salt. Process until totally smooth. Pour into a medium bowl and add the toasted bread cubes. Toss to combine, and set aside.

4. In another bowl, combine the scallions, cherry tomatoes, and sun-dried tomatoes (if they weren't packed in oil) with the remaining 1 tablespoon olive oil and ¼ teaspoon salt. Toss to combine.

5. Take one skewer and string the components on it in this order: scallion (perpendicular to the skewer), crouton, cherry tomato, sun-dried tomato. Repeat until the skewer is three-fourths full. Fill the remaining seven skewers in the same way. Line the cookie sheet with parchment paper and brush it with olive oil. Arrange the finished skewers on it.

6. Roast the skewers for 15 to 20 minutes, flipping them once, until the croutons are very golden and the cherry and sun-dried tomatoes are blistery and browned. If they are not browned enough, raise the heat to 400°F and roast for another 5 to 10 minutes.

7. Spoon about a quarter of the white bean puree onto each dinner plate. Arrange two skewers over the puree, garnish with fresh thyme, and serve.

{carrot and white bean puree}

Makes 3 cups

6 cloves garlic, unpeeled

3 medium carrots, peeled and cut into 2-inch pieces

1 tablespoon olive oil

Two 15-ounce cans white beans, such as cannellini

2 teaspoons fresh thyme leaves

6 tablespoons white wine

1 teaspoon salt

2 tablespoons water or vegetable stock, plus more if needed

1. Preheat the oven to 350°F.

2. In a 9 × 13-inch baking dish, toss the garlic and carrots with the olive oil. Roast for 30 minutes, or until the carrots are beginning to brown.

3. Meanwhile, drain the beans in a colander. Pat them as dry as possible with a paper towel.

4. Add the beans, thyme, and wine to the baking dish, toss, and roast for 10 minutes more. Remove the dish from the oven.

5. Place the garlic cloves in a small bowl. When they are cool enough to handle (after 5 minutes or so), pop the roasted garlic cloves from their skins. Transfer the garlic, carrots, and beans to a food processor, and add the salt and the water or stock. Process until smooth, adding more water or stock as necessary. Serve immediately, or reheat in a small pan, adding more water if the puree seems too thick.

side-dish salads

We love salads, and we've been known to get carried away with toppings at midtown lunch spots and in the produce aisle. Lately, however, we've discovered that choosing just a few perfect add-ins makes our side-dish salads better. The key to a cheap, successful salad is really in the dressing, and we've always been big believers in making our own. Here are a few of our favorite vinaigrettes, along with the add-ins and greens they match with best. Choose your own side salad adventure, and mix and match—just don't go crazy. Your wallet, and your guests, will thank you for it.

All of these salads serve four to six people. We haven't included strict preparation instructions, except for the warm vegetable salad, which needs to be tossed together in a pan on the stove. To assemble your side-dish salad, simply combine the ingredients as listed below in a large mixing bowl. To dress, pour 2 to 3 tablespoons of the vinaigrette down the side of the bowl so it falls to the bottom, and then use two large spoons to redistribute the leaves and add-ins. Add more of the dressing to taste. Try to dress your salad less than fifteen minutes before your guests arrive—you don't want the leaves to wilt.

	Baby Spinach with Toasted Pecans, Dried Cranberries, and Balsamic Vinaigrette	Baby Arugula Salad with Radishes, Mango, and Creamy Ginger Vinaigrette	Crispy Romaine with Cherry Tomatoes, Garlic Croutons, and Green Goddess Dressing	Mixed Greens with Avocado, Corn, and Lemon-Herb Vinaigrette
Salad				
Start with	5 ounces baby spinach	5 ounces baby arugula	3 hearts of romaine, chopped (or one 10-ounce package)	5 ounces mixed greens
Add	½ cup coarsely chopped pecans, toasted	1 cup sliced radishes	½ pint cherry tomatoes, halved	1 avocado, pitted, peeled, and diced
Then add	¼ cup dried cranberries	1 small mango, peeled, seeded, and diced	1 cup garlic croutons (see page 301)	1 cup corn kernels (fresh, frozen, or canned)
Dress with	Balsamic Vinaigrette	Creamy Ginger Vinaigrette	Green Goddess Dressing	Lemon-Herb Vinaigrette
For a main-dish salad, top with	4 ounces fresh goat cheese, sliced	Soy-Honey Baked Tofu (page 76)	Roasted chicken (see page 305)	Roasted chicken (see page 305)

balsamic vinaigrette

Makes ½ cup

2 tablespoons balsamic vinegar

1 tablespoon Dijon mustard

½ teaspoon honey

½ teaspoon salt

¼ cup olive oil

creamy ginger vinaigrette

Makes ¼ cup

2 tablespoons mayonnaise

1 tablespoon chopped peeled fresh ginger

2 tablespoons lime juice

½ tablespoon Dijon mustard

1 teaspoon honey

2 tablespoons olive oil

¼ teaspoon Sriracha or other hot sauce

¼ teaspoon salt

green goddess dressing

Makes 1 cup

½ avocado, diced

2 tablespoons white wine vinegar

1 clove garlic, minced

Juice of ½ lemon

1 tablespoon mayonnaise

¼ cup fresh parsley leaves, chopped

2 to 3 scallions (white and light green parts), chopped

½ cup olive oil

½ teaspoon salt

lemon-herb vinaigrette

Makes ⅓ cup

Juice of ½ lemon

½ teaspoon white wine vinegar

½ tablespoon Dijon mustard

½ small shallot, thinly sliced

½ teaspoon salt

½ cup coarsely chopped basil, cilantro, chives, or tarragon

3 tablespoons olive oil

To prepare the vinaigrettes/dressing, either puree all the ingredients together in a small food processor or follow the directions on page 302 for making a classic vinaigrette by hand.

warm vegetable salad with bacon bits and mustard-sherry vinaigrette

You can make this salad with asparagus, string beans, or small potatoes. Because the recipe proceeds slightly differently depending on the vegetable you choose, be sure to follow the directions below carefully.

{
½ pound fresh asparagus or string beans, trimmed, or 1 pound small Yukon Gold or red potatoes, scrubbed and parboiled (see page 304)

6 slices bacon
Mustard-Sherry Vinaigrette (recipe follows)
}

Note: For a main-dish salad, top each serving with Sarah's Olive Oil Fried Egg (page 36).

1. For asparagus or beans: Bring a large pot of salted water to a boil. Add the string beans or asparagus and cook until bright green and barely tender, about 2 minutes. Be careful not to overcook.
   For potatoes: Fill a pot with salted water and bring it to a boil over high heat. Quarter the potatoes, add them to the boiling water, and cover with a lid. Once the water is boiling again, remove the lid and cook until the potatoes are tender, 15 to 20 minutes (pierce them with a fork to test).
2. Transfer the vegetables to a colander, drain, and rinse under cold water to stop the cooking.
3. Place a large nonstick skillet over medium-high heat and lay the bacon slices flat in the pan. Cook, flipping the bacon once or twice, until it is brown and crispy, 3 to 4 minutes. Transfer the bacon to a paper towel to drain. Once it has cooled, crumble it with your fingers to create bacon bits. Use a paper towel to wipe up the bacon fat in the pan.

4. Add the vinaigrette to the cleaned skillet, and whisk it over low heat for 1 to 2 minutes. Add the vegetables and toss to coat. Top with the bacon bits. Serve warm.

{mustard-sherry vinaigrette}

Makes ½ cup

1 tablespoon Dijon mustard

1½ teaspoons whole-grain mustard

1 tablespoon sherry vinegar or red wine vinegar

½ teaspoon salt

¼ cup extra-virgin olive oil

Combine all the ingredients in a small food processor and blend until smooth.

To blend by hand, whisk the mustards, vinegar, and salt together in a small bowl. Add the olive oil in a thin stream, whisking continuously until emulsified.

dinner party desserts

Cara, Spring 2008

It's possible to host a dinner and not serve dessert, but in my opinion ending with something sweet makes an ordinary dinner feel like a party. One night in June, Phoebe was making pasta. The main event of the night was a lamb Bolognese, but she was making a mushroom sauce for Jordana and me. Knowing Phoebe doesn't usually undertake the hassle of making a cake or tart or pudding, a few days before the pasta night, I volunteered to bring dessert.

We were all sitting around the coffee table, and after we cleaned our plates of tagliatelle, I gave everyone about thirty minutes before I brought over chocolate mousse and shortbread cookies. I'm not entirely sure our friends *saved* room for it, but they definitely *made* some when I set the treats down in front of them.

Phoebe and I love cohosting. If she's serving the main course, I can concentrate completely on the sweets without worrying about overspending or making a mess right before dinner. Admittedly, when I'm having people at my place, I still don't like to give up serving dessert. I design dinner party desserts to be impressive but not fussy. Most important, I make them far, far in advance, so my apartment is cool and clean when guests arrive.

A final note: The chocolate mousse and cookies I served after Phoebe's pasta dinner is a riff on what might be the best minimalist dessert you can serve to guests: good-quality store-bought ice cream with a cookie in each bowl. Try it with any of the cookies from Tins of Treats (page 172), baked at least a day before the dinner party.

chocolate-flecked clafoutis

Makes 6 servings

A clafoutis is a simple baked dessert, a bit like a firm custard, traditionally made with cherries or other fruit. Its simplicity means that you should buy good-quality ingredients, and because this recipe uses one entire chocolate bar, you can play around with any of your favorites.

Bring the clafoutis straight to the table in a presentable baking dish or a cast-iron skillet. If you put it in the oven when you sit down to dinner, you'll have an impressive, puffed-up dessert right when you finish those last few bites of savory food.

3 large eggs

¼ cup granulated sugar, plus 1 tablespoon for topping

2 tablespoons light brown sugar

½ teaspoon salt

⅓ cup all-purpose flour

1 cup heavy cream

1 teaspoon vanilla extract

One 3.5-ounce semisweet chocolate bar, finely chopped, or ½ cup semisweet chocolate chips

1 tablespoon unsalted butter

Whipped cream, for serving (see page 305; optional)

1. Preheat the oven to 325°F.
2. In a medium bowl, beat the eggs, both sugars, and the salt until blended. Whisk in the flour until it's combined. Add the cream and vanilla, and whisk until smooth. Finally, stir in most of the chocolate pieces, reserving 1 to 2 tablespoons for garnish.
3. Place the butter in an 8- or 9-inch cast-iron skillet or a cake pan. Put the pan in the oven for 1 minute. Take it out—the butter should be melted—and brush the melted butter all around the bottom and sides. Be careful! The pan will already be hot to the touch.

4. Pour the batter into the prepared pan. Sprinkle the remaining 1 tablespoon granulated sugar over the top.

5. Bake until the clafoutis is set in the center and golden around the edges, about 35 minutes. It will have puffed up, but it will deflate as it cools. Let it cool for at least 10 minutes before serving.

6. Top the clafoutis with whipped cream, if desired, and scatter the reserved chocolate on top. Serve the clafoutis warm or at room temperature.

blueberry crisp tart

Makes 6 to 8 servings

The crust of this tart is more like a shortbread than a typical pie pastry, which means no rolling and no fuss. When peaches are in season, you can substitute 2 small peaches, chopped, for ½ cup of the blueberries.

FOR THE CRUST

8 tablespoons (1 stick) unsalted butter, melted

¼ cup sugar

⅛ teaspoon salt

¾ teaspoon vanilla extract

1 cup all-purpose flour

FOR THE FILLING

2 ½ cups (1¼ pints) fresh blueberries, picked over and washed

Juice of 1 lemon

1 tablespoon sugar

FOR THE CRISP TOPPING

¼ cup all-purpose flour

¼ cup rolled oats

¼ cup sugar

Pinch of ground cinnamon

Pinch of salt

2 tablespoons unsalted butter, at room temperature

Vanilla ice cream, for serving (optional)

1. Preheat the oven to 350°F.
2. In a bowl, mix all the crust ingredients together with a spoon or spatula. Press the dough into a 9-inch fluted tart pan with a removable bottom. Use your fingers to spread the dough evenly, and be sure to press it up the sides. Place the tart pan on a baking sheet and bake the crust for 10 to 12 minutes, until it is golden.
3. Let the crust cool to room temperature, 15 to 20 minutes. (Leave the oven on.)
4. Meanwhile, prepare the filling: In a bowl, toss the blueberries with the lemon juice and sugar; set aside.

5. Make the crisp topping: In a bowl, combine the flour, oats, sugar, cinnamon, and salt. Work in the butter, using your fingers, until you have a very dry dough that clumps together when you press it.

6. When the crust is cool, spread the fruit evenly over it. Sprinkle the crisp topping over the fruit, and return the tart to the oven. Bake for 45 to 50 minutes, just until the crust is lightly browned, the blueberries are slightly melted, and the topping is crisp. Cool slightly. Serve with vanilla ice cream if you like.

pumpkin cake with chai cream

For the Cake: Follow the variation for Pumpkin Bread on page 186. Grease a 9-inch round springform cake pan and cut a circle of parchment for the bottom. Pour the batter into the pan and bake at 350°F for 30 minutes, until a toothpick inserted in the center comes out clean. You can ice this with Cream Cheese Frosting (page 187) if you're not making the Chai Cream below.

For the Chai Cream: Combine 1 cup heavy cream with 2 tablespoons confectioners' sugar, ¾ teaspoon cinnamon, ¼ teaspoon cardamom, ¼ teaspoon ground cloves, and a grind of black pepper. Beat with a whisk or electric mixer until soft peaks are formed. Serve immediately or keep refrigerated until ready to eat.

chocolate torte

Follow the directions for Brownies with no add-ins on page 174, making 1½ times the recipe. Bake the brownie mixture in a 9-inch round springform cake pan for 30 minutes in a 325°F oven. Follow the directions for cooling brownies. To serve: Cut into wedges, sprinkle with confectioners' sugar, and serve with homemade whipped cream (see page 305) or Chai Cream (above).

LEFTOVERS

There are two types of people in this world: those who like leftovers and those who don't. Even if we once fell into the disgusted or apathetic camp, we've learned to care a lot about leftovers. While sometimes using them up is a pain, most of the time it's an exercise in creativity, a chance to re-form something from its original state into something new and exciting. It's a different kind of cooking than going to the grocery store and starting from scratch, and it's sort of a private affair. Our effort to use up leftovers is often the time when we play around the most in the kitchen.

sauces from scratch

Cara, Spring 2009

I don't get bored that much, but as the winter of 2008–09 drizzled to a close, I found myself as close to boredom as a daily condition as I ever had. The cold wouldn't break, except for icy rain. I lost interest in reading the manuscripts I was supposed to be devouring at my job. I still loved my Brooklyn apartment, but in this weather the long commute home was making me feel isolated from my friends. I guess I'd say I was malcontent—tired of the city, weary of the scene, ready to leave my office for good. My default was to dream of the new cities I could move to. I thought about Richmond, Virginia; Portland, Oregon; Burlington, Vermont; Memphis, Tennessee. I figured the work of moving and settling in would snap me out of this malaise. I even made Jordana—a born-and-bred New Yorker in love with the city—discuss this extra–New York future with me. I'd read enough novels to know that you take your problems with you when you run away, but I still liked to imagine that the temporary fix might engender a permanent one.

It was in such a spirit that I was milling around my apartment early on a Sunday morning. My friend Roshni and her boyfriend, Chris, were coming to Brooklyn for brunch. While I waited for them, I pieced together my menu, figuring out what I'd cook and how to time and prep it. I still had hours to spare when I was finished planning. Roshni's arrival seemed distant, and that feeling of boredom arose and began to bear down on me.

I needed a project.

Ketchup, from scratch, is what I settled on. I wanted a condiment to accompany the hash browns, and I thought my attempt at homemade ketchup would bring through a savoriness and a freshness that the big-batch stuff just can't deliver. The urge to make ketchup wasn't motivated only

by taste. There was a lot more to it than that: entertainment, creativity, craft.

I know how offbeat it can seem to want to labor over something that is readily available in a bottle. When you like to cook, though, and when you have time, focusing on the minutiae can be fun, exactly the thing to draw a dispirited twenty-four-year-old out of a slump. I'm not the first to say that chopping, stirring, measuring, pouring—even cleaning—can be therapeutic. Manual tasks seem to ground the mind in a very concrete way. This holds true for the process behind homemade pasta, mayonnaise, salsa, and pesto as well as ketchup. These foods give me the challenge of creating something from nothing. It's not a bad challenge on rainy Sundays or during a patch of quarter-life doldrums.

At the same time, if you're going to cook for the hell of it, it had better be something you don't mind having in the fridge—an intentional leftover—or something you'll eat all of before it gets to the fridge, like a batch of brownies. Condiments are great intentional leftovers because they're building blocks for lunchbox fare or for dinner later in the week.

On this particular Sunday, my ketchup was simmering on the stove and smelling a lot like actual ketchup. It had cooled by the time Roshni and Chris arrived, and I served it with the hash browns and eggs. It was delicious, though they did think it was weird that I had spent the morning overcomplicating something that simple. Then I kept it in my fridge for a couple of weeks, using it in even more copious amounts than I allowed myself to use the bottled stuff.

homemade ketchup

Makes 2 cups

1 tablespoon olive oil

1 yellow onion, chopped

2 cloves garlic, minced

One 28-ounce can whole tomatoes, preferably fire-roasted

½ cup sugar

1 tablespoon molasses

½ cup red wine vinegar

⅛ teaspoon ground cinnamon

⅛ teaspoon dry mustard

⅛ teaspoon dried oregano

⅛ teaspoon ground coriander

⅛ teaspoon cayenne pepper

⅛ teaspoon ground ginger

1 tablespoon raisins or dried currants

2 tablespoons tomato paste

¾ teaspoon kosher salt

Several grinds of black pepper

1. In a large pot or Dutch oven, heat the oil over medium heat. Add the onion and garlic, and sauté until softened and slightly browned, 5 to 8 minutes. Add all the rest of the ingredients, bring to a simmer, and cook, partially covered, for about 1 hour, until reduced and thickened. Let the ketchup cool to room temperature.

2. Transfer the ketchup to a food processor or blender, and process until it is completely smooth. (Or use an immersion blender to puree it right in the pot.)

3. Chill the ketchup in the refrigerator for about 1 hour before using. Then go ahead and smother your grilled cheese sandwiches and sweet potato fries. It will keep for 2 weeks in the fridge.

mayonnaise

Makes 1 cup

{
1 large egg yolk
1 teaspoon Dijon mustard
Juice of ½ lemon

1 cup vegetable oil
Salt, to taste
}

1. In a bowl, whisk (you can use a fork) the egg yolk with the mustard and lemon juice.
2. Slowly and steadily pour in the oil in a thin stream—especially slowly at first—while whisking constantly. The mixture should thicken up and emulsify quickly. When you've finished pouring in the oil, season with salt. Store, covered, in the fridge for about a week.

Herb Mayonnaise: Whisk in 2 tablespoons finely chopped fresh chives, dill, basil, parsley, or tarragon.

Spicy Chipotle Mayonnaise: Add 1 finely chopped canned chipotle chile, and substitute 1 tablespoon lime juice for the lemon juice.

basil pesto

Makes about 1 cup

If you are making the pesto in advance, leave out the lemon juice until you are ready to serve—it will turn the basil brown.

1 clove garlic

¼ cup pine nuts, toasted (see page 305)

2 cups tightly packed fresh basil leaves

Juice of ½ lemon, or more if needed

¼ cup olive oil, or more if needed

¼ cup grated Parmesan cheese

¼ teaspoon salt, or more if needed

1. In a small food processor, pulse the garlic and pine nuts together with the salt until finely chopped.
2. Add the basil leaves and lemon juice, and blend until the basil has begun to break down. Add the olive oil, and puree until the mixture is smooth and has the desired consistency, adding more oil if needed to break down the nuts and herbs.
3. Fold in the Parmesan and taste for seasoning. Add more salt and extra lemon juice as needed.

Basil-Parsley Pesto: Substitute 1 cup parsley leaves for 1 cup of the basil.

Arugula Pesto: Omit the Parmesan, and substitute 2 cups arugula for the basil.

Sun-Dried Tomato Pesto: Substitute ½ cup sun-dried tomatoes for the basil.

the takeout lover's dilemma

Cara, Fall 2009

Even though our cabinets are fully stocked and we know in our hearts that we could make our own *pad see ew* (me) or *pad thai* (Phoebe), sometimes we food bloggers get takeout. The institution of paper menus, deliverymen on bikes, and disposable plastic containers is so utterly New York City that even as a home cook, it feels way too austere not to take advantage of it at all. We just try to be careful with the menu and exercise some form of self-control.

I have an obsession with Chinese and Thai takeout. And I'm happy that I've got a stellar provider of each in my neighborhood. For about $10, I can have a delicious and thoroughly un-homemade meal. Two dishes—sesame noodles and broccoli in brown sauce, plus the rice—can sometimes even last me four days when I'm good, though the final meal will be based on a couple sad spears of broccoli floating in sauce. However, after a three-meal-long takeout fest, I'm usually aching to cook again anyway. Then I take advantage of the nicely dried-out brown rice and the remaining broccoli and sauce to make an excellent main-dish fried rice.

Fried rice was a standard in my family's dinner repertoire. It's one of those leftover dishes that doesn't quite feel like leftovers, since it really is different from what it started out as. A case of the sum transcending its parts? For the record, it is also possible to make fried rice when you haven't ordered takeout, as long as you cook the rice in advance and give it a chance to cool and dry out a bit.

basic fried rice

Makes 2 servings

{
2 tablespoons vegetable oil

1 yellow onion, diced

1 carrot, diced

2 cloves garlic, minced

1 tablespoon minced peeled fresh
ginger

2 cups cooked white rice, cooled

½ teaspoon salt

1 tablespoon soy sauce

2 eggs, beaten

1 scallion (white and light green
parts), chopped
}

1. Heat the oil in a nonstick wok or large pan over medium-high heat. Add the onion and carrot and stir-fry for about 1 minute, until softened. Then add the garlic and ginger, and stir-fry for another minute or two, until fragrant.
2. Add the rice and toss it around so it all gets lightly browned and parts even get crispy. Add the salt and the soy sauce, and mix to distribute.
3. Push the whole mixture over to the side and pour in the eggs. Scramble them around with a silicone spatula until they are fully cooked; then toss the whole thing together. Divide between two bowls, garnish with the chopped scallion, and eat.

Pineapple-Cashew Fried Rice: Omit the carrot, and add ½ cup chopped fresh pineapple after you've scrambled the egg into the rice. Cook for a minute or two to warm it through. Stir in ½ cup chopped roasted cashews at the end. Divide between two bowls, top with a few more cashews, and eat.

Broccoli-in-Garlic-Sauce Fried Rice: Instead of the soy sauce and salt, add any leftover takeout broccoli (cut into bite-size pieces) and a few spoonfuls of the sauce.

the global kitchen

Our takeout dilemma begins with an insatiable craving for a variety of different cuisines. When it becomes too embarrassing to have the woman at your favorite Chinese restaurant recognize your voice on the phone, there's only one solution to preventing leftover takeout sesame noodles in the first place: make them yourself. Part of this is learning to round out your pantry with staples from your favorite cuisine.

In New York, Chinatown is a gold mine of ingredients. There you'll find not only the soy and hoisin sauces of Chinese cuisine, but also Indian spice blends, Japanese miso, and a variety of Thai curry and chili pastes. The pantry ingredients needed to branch out a bit really aren't so wild or obscure as you might imagine. We're not talking about restaurant-quality pickled ginger, bulbs of lemongrass, or tubs of wasabi.

When tackling some of our favorite dishes, there are certain components that we leave out, which might make the end result taste less authentic. For instance, for frequent Thai pantry cooking, we use Sriracha as a viable substitute for fresh Thai chile peppers or more obscure chili pastes (such as *nam phrik*). Shrimp paste, an ingredient in Thai papaya salad, is something we wouldn't necessarily buy, and the lack of it probably makes our version less nuanced than a restaurant's. The flip side is that we always have these components on hand, making a global feast fast, fresh, and easy pretty much all the time.

thai/vietnamese

Fish sauce (*nam pla*)

Coconut milk

Chile pastes (*nam phrik*) or Sriracha

Oyster sauce

Peanuts

Fresh: lime, cilantro, Thai basil, mint
Recipes: Vietnamese Fisherman's Stew (page 205), Coconut Peanut Sauce (page 264)

japanese

Soy sauce

Rice vinegar

Toasted sesame oil

Mirin

Miso

Nori

Fresh: ginger, scallions
Recipe: Soy-Honey Baked Tofu (page 76)

chinese

Soy sauce

Rice vinegar

Toasted sesame oil

Five spice powder

Hoisin sauce

Cornstarch

Fresh: scallions, garlic, ginger
Recipe: Basic Fried Rice (page 257)

moroccan

Ground cumin

Ground ginger

Ground coriander

Dried fruit (apricots, dates, raisins)

Preserved lemon (optional)

Harissa (optional)

Chickpeas

Fresh: cilantro
Recipe: Chicken Tagine with Sweet Potatoes and Golden Raisins (page 210)

spanish

Smoked paprika

Saffron

White wine

Tomato paste

Fresh: tomatoes, red bell pepper
Recipe: Scallop, Chorizo, and Artichoke Paella (page 215)

middle eastern

Ground cumin

Ground turmeric

Za'atar spice blend

Fresh: mint, cilantro, lemon, yogurt
Recipes: Mediterranean Lamb Burgers (page 220) and Chickpea and Walnut Burgers (pages 218); Classic Hummus (page 110)

indian

Garam masala

Curry powder

Ground cumin

Ground turmeric

Mustard seeds

Fresh: ginger, cilantro, yogurt
Recipe: Chana Bateta (page 262)

mexican

Chili powder

Ground cumin

Dark beer

Dried ancho chiles

Chipotles in adobo sauce

Fresh: jalapeño or other fresh chiles, cilantro, sour cream, queso fresco
Recipes: Enchiladas (page 223); Smoky Chipotle Vegetarian Chili (page 200); Black Bean Bites (page 266)

the tomato can challenge

Cara

Nothing makes me feel more like a crazy chemist than opening up my refrigerator to the sight of a dozen plastic containers storing foods of different textures, colors, and ages. I know that this is not a feeling everyone likes, and perhaps it doesn't sound very appetizing, either. There is a pressure, once food has been stored in the fridge, to use it—that is, eat it—before it goes bad. Though I've never yet been so desperate as to drink sour milk, I have used it in cornbread. We are all about being resourceful, if not quite to the point of grossness.

It is very resourceful, albeit in a slightly apocalyptic, neurotic way, to keep cans of beans, tomatoes, tuna, sardines, and coconut milk in your pantry. Many of these cans can become meals on their own (white bean and tuna salad, anyone?); others require just an onion, some oil, and a package of noodles. That versatility is easy to see. Unfortunately, once the can is opened, the contents become just as perishable as those stalks of celery wilting next to the parsley in your vegetable drawer.

Phoebe is absolutely diligent about using all of a can at one time. I am less so—partly because I'm a stickler for proportion and partly because I *like* to feel like a crazy-chemist-meets-depression-era penny-pincher who hates to waste a drop. I think it really is the impending threat of rotten food that instills in me such a surge of creativity when, upon opening the fridge, I'm confronted with the partially used contents of my cans. The recipes that follow represent a semi-mathematical account of a couple of meals that were created from leftover ounces.

I like to make Coconut Peanut Sauce with leftover coconut milk after cooking Coconut Banana Pancakes (page 144) or Vietnamese Fisherman's Stew (page 205), and Chana Bateta with the tomatoes remaining after a batch of Smoked Mozzarella Tartlettes (page 74) or Saucy Tomato Orecchiette (page 56) has been devoured.

In someone else's hands, these leftovers could have been a thousand other dishes. It's about being resourceful and creating your own new meals from the remnants in your cans.

chana bateta

I ended up with this dish as a result of trying to use up some leftovers, only to discover that it is very close to an actual Indian dish, though I wouldn't go so far as to say my Chana Bateta is authentic.

1 ½ tablespoons vegetable oil

2 shallots, thinly sliced

3 large cloves garlic, minced

1 tablespoon minced peeled fresh ginger

1 teaspoon ground cumin

1½ teaspoons ground coriander

¼ teaspoon cayenne pepper, or more to taste

½ cup canned crushed tomatoes

½ cup coconut milk

1 teaspoon sugar

1 teaspoon salt

2 large Yukon Gold potatoes (about 7 ounces total), cut into approximately 1½-inch dice

One 15-ounce can chickpeas (do not drain)

2 tablespoons finely chopped fresh cilantro, plus extra for garnish

1 teaspoon white wine vinegar

Cooked basmati rice (see page 298), for serving

Note: This dish tastes best when made ahead, so if you have time, let it cool and then refrigerate it until ready to eat. Reheat in the microwave or in a saucepan over medium heat, stirring occasionally.

1. Heat the oil in a large Dutch oven over medium heat. Add the shallots, garlic, and ginger. Cook for about 5 minutes, stirring nearly constantly, until the shallots are quite golden—but be careful not to burn the garlic. Add the cumin, coriander, and cayenne, and cook for another minute or so to toast the spices; they will be fragrant.
2. Pour in the crushed tomatoes and cook down for 3 to 4 minutes, until the mixture is reduced to an almost pastelike consistency.

3. Add ½ cup water, the coconut milk, salt, and sugar. Bring to a boil. Add the potatoes and return to a boil. Then reduce the heat to low and cover the pan. Cook until the potatoes are soft—they should be easily pierced with a knife—10 to 15 minutes.

4. Uncover the pan and add the chickpeas with their liquid. Stir until combined. Cook for 5 to 10 minutes, until heated through. Add the cilantro and cook for a minute more.

5. Add the vinegar and stir to distribute. Serve, garnished with fresh cilantro, with basmati rice alongside.

coconut peanut sauce

Makes about ½ cup

Drizzled over white rice or tossed with a bowlful of noodles, this sauce is almost as high up on my comfort list as the classic grilled cheese on page 41. It also makes a great dipping sauce for chicken or tofu satay.

1 teaspoon vegetable oil

1 clove garlic, minced

2 teaspoons minced peeled fresh ginger

1 cup light coconut milk

3 tablespoons smooth peanut butter, preferably natural and unsweetened

1½ teaspoons sugar

1½ teaspoons soy sauce

½ teaspoon chili-garlic paste, or ¼ teaspoon Sriracha sauce

1 teaspoon Worcestershire sauce

2 teaspoons fish sauce

1 tablespoon lime juice

1. Warm the oil in a small saucepan over medium-low heat. Add the garlic and ginger and sauté until golden, 3 minutes.

2. Add the coconut milk and bring to a simmer. Add the peanut butter (you may need to use a fork or a whisk to break it up and help dissolve it into the coconut milk). Then add the sugar, soy sauce, chili paste or Sriracha, Worcestershire sauce, and fish sauce.

3. Simmer for about 3 minutes to let the flavors meld. Stir in the lime juice, and taste for seasoning.

a leftover's journey into croquettes

While we're all for forcing our guests to have seconds or thirds, we also know that some-times we have to call it quits. People can't always get to the bottom of a cast-iron pan of mac 'n cheese. What remains goes back into the fridge.

One of the best ways to repurpose is to fry leftover mashed potatoes, roasted squash, bean dip, or risotto and call the results cakes, croquettes, or patties. These bites are good for appetizers, cocktail parties, and, if you size them a bit bigger, for classy dinners too.

Phoebe is known for bringing Black Bean Cakes to Mag Club the day after hosting a dip party. Sure, it's a little like regifting, but when the repurposed leftovers are delicious in their own right, no one tends to care.

risotto cakes

Makes 4 cakes

You can easily make these cakes from scratch by following the instructions for making risotto on page 121.

1 cup leftover risotto

¼ cup freshly grated Parmesan cheese

¼ cup chopped fresh chives, parsley, or basil

½ cup fresh breadcrumbs

½ cup panko

2 to 3 tablespoons olive oil

1. Combine the risotto, Parmesan, herbs, and fresh breadcrumbs in a mixing bowl. Form the mixture into four 2-inch cakes.
2. Pour the panko onto a plate. Dredge each cake in the panko so it is coated on both sides.
3. Pour enough olive oil into a nonstick skillet to coat it, and heat over medium-high heat. Fry the cakes until they are golden brown on both sides, 3 to 4 minutes. Serve immediately.

black bean bites

If making the cakes from scratch, follow the Black Bean Dip recipe, which yields about 2 cups, and double the amounts for the breadcrumbs and cilantro.

{
Vegetable or olive oil
1 cup Black Bean Dip (page 111)
½ cup fresh breadcrumbs

¼ cup chopped fresh cilantro, plus more for garnish
Sour cream, for garnish
}

1. Preheat the oven to 400°F. Line a baking sheet with parchment paper, and lightly oil the paper.
2. In a bowl, combine the black bean dip, breadcrumbs, and cilantro. Roll the mixture into eight 1-inch balls, and arrange them on the prepared baking sheet.
3. Bake the bites for 20 minutes, until crisped on the outside. The texture will resemble falafel.
4. Arrange the bites on a plate or platter, and top each one with a dollop of sour cream and some cilantro.

mashed potato croquettes

Makes 10 to 12 croquettes

1 cup Semi-Sweet Potato Mash
    (page 137) or prepared mashed
    potatoes (page 303)

Salt, to taste

Freshly ground black pepper

¼ cup grated cheddar cheese
    (optional)

1 egg, lightly beaten

About ¼ cup olive oil

Herb Mayonnaise (page 253),
    for serving

1. Taste the leftover mashed potatoes for salt, and add more if needed. Stir in a generous grind of black pepper, and mix in the cheese if you're using it. Add the egg and stir to distribute it evenly in the potato mixture.

2. Pour olive oil into a nonstick or cast-iron pan to a depth of about ⅓ inch. Heat it over medium-high heat until flicking water across the surface makes it sizzle loudly.

3. Drop large spoonfuls of the potato batter (about 2 tablespoons' worth) into the pan. Don't overcrowd it; you want 2 to 3 inches of space around each croquette. Fry for 2 to 3 minutes per side, letting the croquettes develop a dark golden crust. Transfer the croquettes to a plate lined with paper towels to drain.

4. Repeat until you've used up all the potatoes. If the olive oil in the pan has gotten low, add a bit more before frying the next batch.

5. Serve immediately, with a dollop of Herb Mayonnaise.

winter squash patties

Makes 10 to 12 patties

{ 1 cup leftover Roasted Butternut
   Squash (page 102)

Salt, to taste

1/8 teaspoon ground nutmeg

1 egg, lightly beaten

About 1/4 cup olive oil

1/4 cup sour cream, for serving }

1. In a bowl, mash the leftover squash cubes with a fork, a spoon, or a potato masher. You want a relatively smooth consistency, but it doesn't have to resemble a puree. Taste for salt, and correct as necessary. Mix in the nutmeg. Add the egg and beat to distribute it evenly.

2. Pour olive oil into a nonstick or cast-iron pan to a depth of about 1/3 inch. Heat it over medium-high heat until flicking water across the surface makes it sizzle loudly.

3. Drop large spoonfuls of the squash batter (about 2 tablespoons' worth) into the pan. Don't overcrowd it; you want 2 to 3 inches of space around each patty. Fry for 2 to 3 minutes per side, letting the patties develop a dark golden crust. Transfer the patties to a plate lined with paper towels to drain.

4. Repeat until you've used up all the squash mixture. If the olive oil in the pan has gotten low, add a bit more before frying the next batch.

5. Serve immediately, topped with sour cream.

ONE YEAR CLOSER
TO THIRTY

In years, we're not that much older now than we were when we began this project, but a lot has changed. We're not the newbies we were when we set out to start first days at first jobs, moved into first apartments, hosted first dinner parties on our floors, and fried Manchurian Cauliflower in Jordana's kitchen. We're more practiced cooks now. We entertain more often. We play around with our tried-and-true recipes; we *have* tried-and-true recipes. We don't sweat it when our experiments don't turn out perfectly. We like to think we have the maturity to look back on this year as a learning experience. And it's possible that these days we have more fun in the kitchen than ever before.

the official quarter-life cook

Cara, Fall 2009

The first Saturday in October was drizzly, then torrential, then drizzly again. I remained optimistic, though, pulling out the grill and rearranging the lawn furniture. An hour before my twenty-fifth-birthday party was supposed to start, the sky seemed to clear—but the rain returned with the first guest, Claire, my college roommate, and it poured for most of the afternoon. People came anyway, and we heated up the countertop grill and made the best of it.

I had lots of help preparing for the big day. Alex came early and went with my older sister, Jill, to pick up the keg. He was also there for moral support when I concluded that it had been dumb to hold the party at my mom's house in Riverdale and that absolutely no one was going to show up. ("Of course they will," he said. "No one minds a little rain.") Jill helped me plan the menu, and she did the bulk of the shopping. There were chicken sausages and hot dogs with toasted buns, and from-scratch onion dip served with crinkly potato chips. I made loads of mozzarella, tomato, and basil sandwiches on baguettes. Jill had bought containers of peanut M&M's and Bazooka bubble gum, and we put those out in huge bowls around the house. Last but not least, I baked my favorite cake: simple, buttery white cake layers, with the rich chocolate icing my mom always used to make.

The theme, in spite of my twenty-odd years, was retro nostalgia. I wanted to evoke a barbecue straight out of the '90s. And homemade or not, onion dip and vanilla cake with chocolate icing are kid food.

The party went on from the afternoon into the early evening, and people dropped by throughout the day. There were high school friends, college buddies, the girls from Mag Club, my colleagues at the publishing house, and a bunch of friends from my writing group—some mingling, all eating. Late in the day, I looked outside to see two stragglers, Nathan and Lydia, who had biked all the way from lower Manhattan. I watched as they got off their bikes and squeezed water from their pant legs. They waddled to the front door.

"Where can I change?" Nathan asked.

Once dry, they joined the party. Much to the bikers'—and everyone else's—delight, the sky soon cleared for good. We pulled the chairs back out and brought chips and onion dip to a table on the lawn, settling close to the keg. Jill brought the cake from the house and lit the candles, and people sang.

After dark, we moved back inside. My college friends JoJo, Joe, Zach, and Zach's little dog, Topsy, sat in the living room, nursing beers (well, not Topsy).

"Good party?" JoJo asked.

"Yeah, it was good," I pronounced.

Alex went outside for a moment. He came back looking stern. "You guys, there's a lot of beer left in the keg." Obediently, we all went down for refills.

I think we must have sat there for hours, watching Topsy trying to get at the food, picking at the savory leftovers and the last few slices of cake ourselves. Even I, up until a few weeks ago a vegetarian purist, had a sausage—it was some of the first meat I'd eaten in years, and I could feel I was ready to change my ways. I don't remember what we talked about, but I do remember what was on my mind: (1) I was still mad that it had rained. (2) I was glad that people hadn't minded the trek out to Riverdale; and a couple of my friends told me they thought more people should have parties at houses, rather than at the usual bars. (3) I was twenty-five. Old. (4) I had given my boss two weeks' notice the day before and told my work friends that afternoon at the party that I'd be moving on.

It was a Saturday night, but after everyone left, I went to sleep in my childhood bed at about 10:30 p.m. Twenty-five going on ten, maybe, consistent with the party's theme. But I felt mature, very different from how I'd felt when I graduated college or started my job. I had decided to create my own path, which took a while for me to work up the motivation to do, since I had never minded the path I had found myself on by default. I may have thought I had direction before, but it turned out that two and a half years out of college, and about to be out of a job, I was closer to finding the place I wanted to be. Or at least the place I wanted to head. And that place had nothing to do with age twenty-six, even though it hit me that night that I was heading there, too.

three-onion dip

Makes 2 cups

Serve this with kettle-cooked potato chips or crudités.

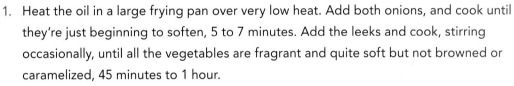

{
1 tablespoon safflower or canola oil

1 large yellow onion, diced

1 small red onion, diced

1 leek, white and light green parts, cut in half vertically, sliced into half-moons, and washed well (see page 298)

1 clove garlic, minced

½ teaspoon salt

½ cup mayonnaise

1½ cups sour cream

Freshly ground black pepper
}

1. Heat the oil in a large frying pan over very low heat. Add both onions, and cook until they're just beginning to soften, 5 to 7 minutes. Add the leeks and cook, stirring occasionally, until all the vegetables are fragrant and quite soft but not browned or caramelized, 45 minutes to 1 hour.
2. Stir in the minced garlic and the salt, and cook for another 1 to 2 minutes to incorporate the flavor. Let the mixture cool to room temperature.
3. Combine the cooled sautéed onions with the mayonnaise, sour cream, and several grinds of black pepper. Refrigerate, covered, for at least 2 hours and preferably overnight.
4. Before serving, taste for salt and flavor, adding a little more sour cream if the mixture has thickened in the fridge.

vanilla-chocolate layer cake

Makes one 2-layer cake

This cake features my mom's chocolate icing, but I've updated it by using two vanilla cake layers. In my mind, vanilla cake lets chocolate frosting stand out, and this frosting deserves your attention.

{
10 tablespoons (1¼ sticks) unsalted butter, at room temperature, plus more for greasing the pans

3 large eggs, at room temperature

¾ cup sour cream

1½ teaspoons vanilla extract

1¾ cups all-purpose flour

1 cup sugar

1 teaspoon baking powder

½ teaspoon baking soda

½ teaspoon salt

Rich Chocolate Frosting (recipe follows)
}

Note: If you have only one springform pan, measure 2 cups of the batter into the pan, bake it, cool it slightly, and then remove it from the pan. Bake the remaining 2 cups the same way.

1. Preheat the oven to 350°F. Grease two 9-inch springform cake pans with softened butter, and line the bottom of each one with a round of parchment paper. Grease the parchment paper, too.
2. In a bowl, whisk together the eggs, ¼ cup of the sour cream, and the vanilla.
3. In a separate bowl (the bowl of a stand mixer, if you have one), whisk together the flour, sugar, baking powder, baking soda, and salt. Add the butter and the remaining ½ cup sour cream. Using a handheld mixer, stand mixer, or your very strong arm, beat this together for nearly 2 minutes. At first it will be quite crumbly, but after a minute or so, it will become creamy.
4. Pour in the egg mixture in two additions, beating for nearly a minute after each.
5. Divide the batter between the prepared cake pans. Bake for 20 to 22 minutes, until the cakes are golden and the edges are pulling away from the sides of the pans. (Test

for doneness by sticking a toothpick or skewer into the cake; if it comes out clean, they're done.) Let the cake layers cool in the pans for 10 minutes before loosening and removing the sides and bottom. Cool completely on a rack or baking sheet.

6. Place one cake layer, top side down, on your cake plate. Using an offset or regular spatula, frost the top with about 2 cups of the chocolate frosting—you want the frosting to be about 1 inch thick.

7. Place the second cake layer, top side up, on top of the frosting. Frost the top and sides generously—you want at least ½ inch of icing on top. Smooth the icing with an offset spatula, or decorate it any way you please.

8. Decorate with candles, sing "Happy Birthday," and serve.

{rich chocolate frosting}

Makes 3½ cups

6 ounces unsweetened baking chocolate

10 tablespoons unsalted butter

3½ cups sifted confectioners' sugar

5 tablespoons strong brewed coffee

2 eggs

1½ teaspoons vanilla extract

¼ teaspoon salt

> *Note: To make the icing in a double boiler: soften the chocolate and butter in a heatproof bowl set over a pan of hot, not quite boiling, water. Stir occasionally. When they have melted, stir in the confectioners' sugar and coffee, and cook for 1 minute more. Remove the bowl from the heat, and continue at step 3.*

1. Combine the chocolate and butter in a microwave-safe bowl that can hold at least 2 quarts. Melt them in 30-second spurts in the microwave until smooth, stirring each time you check on the chocolate.
2. Stir the confectioners' sugar and the coffee into the melted mixture, and microwave for 30 seconds. (This partially cooks the confectioners' sugar, reducing the starchy taste.)
3. Add the eggs, vanilla, and salt, and stir to incorporate fully.
4. Refrigerate the icing for at least 1 hour and up to 1 day. It will be quite firm.
5. Beat the cooled icing with an electric mixer for 5 to 10 minutes. It will lighten dramatically in the first minute or so, but keep mixing until it's light, fluffy, and much bulkier than when you started. Its consistency will be easy to spread.

phoebe's retro birthday bash

Phoebe, Fall 2009

Birthdays are always kind of stressful. Every year I face the approaching day with a laid-back attitude, but then 6 p.m. rolls around and I realize that I still have eight pounds of cheese to grate, countless embarrassing framed pictures to remove from my parents' living room, and absolutely nothing to wear when I've finished. At least, that's what happened on the evening of my twenty-fourth birthday.

I decided to copy Cara and trash my parents' place instead of my own. My rationale was that if I held the party uptown, I could invite a larger group and assume that only half the guest list would end up making the trek on a Saturday night. That is, until the week of, when I started to freak out that only half the people I invited would show up and I decided to invite another thirty. Perhaps I was compensating for the one person who wouldn't be there, the only person I would have let help me with the three enormous trays of mac 'n cheese I was planning on making: Cara.

The morning of, I accepted one offer of assistance and let Will help me carry ice over to my parents' place. They didn't know about the new man in my life, so when we showed up at 11 a.m. and surprised my mother in her nightgown, there were more than a few reasons for confusion. I showed Will the apartment, even the embarrassing pictures on full display in my childhood bedroom. Then my mother put on some clothes and launched into full inter-rogation mode.

By 3 p.m. I was just returning from the grocery store, two hours behind schedule, carry-ing four heavy bags and cursing myself for not inviting everyone to a bar and calling it a birthday. Sensing my paranoia and knowing that I was probably freaking out that there wouldn't be enough food, or enough time to prepare everything, Cara sent me a text mes-sage of encouragement from Pittsburgh, where she was spending the weekend with Alex's best friend from home (his Phoebe, if you will).

The week before, I had made Cara pay for her absence by harassing her on a long subway ride about the menu I was planning. It was a page out of her book, anyway, a retro-themed night of mac 'n cheese, Adam's Big Kid Hot Chocolate on tap, and the potential for a round or two of Jenga. For at least an hour, I obsessed over the perfect combination of cheese type and pasta shape for each of the three variations I was making—one with butternut squash, one with pesto, and one classic. Usually, given Cara's nonattendance, I would have also been stressing over what I would do for dessert, since I draw the line at baking my own birthday cake. Luckily, Salima had already come to the rescue with the promise of fifty homemade red velvet cupcakes.

Even with Cara's insistence that I was overdoing it with so much mac, I worried that there wouldn't be anything to satiate the carnivores in the crowd. I needed something straight-up savory, meaty, and delicious. I landed on mini meatball subs: spicy, saucy, and just small enough to be self-served inside a dinner roll. Cara gave me her seal of approval, and then told me I was also moderately insane.

By 8 p.m., when my third guest had arrived (the first two happened to live in the next room), I had managed to pull myself together emotionally (with a glass of wine) and physically (makeup, frilly dress). I set the meatballs down on the dining room table, which had been pulled to the side to make room for the crowd. Then, fulfilling all my birthday hopes and fears, the meatballs proceeded to disappear. The first few guys who walked in the door and tasted a sub exhaled mumbled expressions of glee. They then proceeded to inhale the rest. Forty-eight meatballs later, the pot was empty and the first twenty guests were congratulating themselves on being the luckiest diners at the party.

All things considered, by midnight I was happy with how the evening turned out. Will had moved on to being interrogated by my father while eating a meatball sub I had hidden for him. My biceps hurt from the grocery bags, my stomach from too much of Salima's cream cheese icing. My face still burned red from the Happy Birthday singing, and from being made fun of for the embarrassing pictures I'd forgotten to hide. But I was having fun, as I always do on nights like these. I love stressing about feeding people. And on my birthday, I love it even more, because it distracts me from stressing about getting old.

mini meatball subs

Makes 24 sandwiches

I've made these balls with many different meat combos. You can use any type of ground beef (it doesn't have to be particularly lean) and either ground veal or pork. Veal is leaner, but may be harder to find than ground pork, which is a little fattier and cheaper. If you like a less fatty meatball, use lean beef and the veal.

To serve, place the meatballs alongside a bowl of small dinner rolls, sliced halfway down the middle. (If you can't find these in the bakery department of your grocery store, use hot dog buns and cut them in half.) Allow guests to serve themselves, and place toothpicks on the side for those modern ladies who want to skip the bread.

FOR THE MEATBALLS

1 small yellow onion

5 cloves garlic

½ cup flat-leaf (Italian) parsley leaves, finely chopped

1 cup grated Parmesan cheese

⅔ cup fresh breadcrumbs (see Note)

⅓ cup dried breadcrumbs

2 large eggs, beaten

2½ tablespoons ketchup

½ teaspoon crushed red pepper flakes

2 teaspoons salt

1 pound ground beef

1 pound ground veal or pork

FOR THE SAUCE

1 tablespoon olive oil

1 large yellow onion, diced

4 cloves garlic, minced

One 28-ounce can crushed tomatoes

2 teaspoons kosher salt

½ teaspoon crushed red pepper flakes

3 tablespoons flat-leaf (Italian) parsley leaves, chopped

¼ cup grated Parmesan cheese

24 dinner rolls, halved

Notes: To make fresh bread crumbs, remove the crusts from 2 slices of white sandwich bread, and pulse the bread in a food processor.

The meatballs and sauce can be made up to 2 days in advance. Simply combine in a large pot and reheat over a medium-low flame.

1. Preheat the oven to 400°F. Line a cookie sheet with parchment paper or aluminum foil, and set it aside.
2. Make the meatballs: In a small food processor, pulse the onion and garlic together until finely chopped (or grate the onion and mince the garlic by hand).
3. Transfer the onion-garlic mixture to a large mixing bowl. Add the parsley, cheese, both breadcrumbs, the eggs, ketchup, red pepper flakes, salt, and meat. Fold the ingredients together with your hands, making sure not to overly break apart or mush the meat.
4. Roll the meat mixture into 1½-inch balls, and place them on the prepared cookie sheet. They can be fairly close together, as they will not expand like cookies.
5. Bake the meatballs in the oven for 25 to 30 minutes, until the tops have browned and they are cooked through.
6. Meanwhile, make the sauce: Heat the olive oil in a large Dutch oven or saucepan over medium heat. Add the onion and cook until translucent and soft, about 8 minutes. Add the garlic and cook for an additional 2 minutes. Carefully pour in the tomatoes, add the salt and red pepper flakes, and stir to combine. Simmer over medium heat for 15 minutes, until the mixture has thickened and the flavors have incorporated.
7. Stir 2 tablespoons of the parsley into the sauce. Cover the pot and keep the sauce warm over low heat while the meatballs are finishing cooking in the oven.
8. Gently stir the meatballs into the sauce. Garnish with the remaining 1 tablespoon parsley and the grated Parmesan. Set alongside a bowl of dinner rolls.

white cheddar mac and cheese

Makes 6 servings

I like to use two types of cheese in most variations of my mac. You can easily go with all one cheese, but I like to cut the sharp cheddar with a cup of something a little milder, like Jack.

{

4 tablespoons (½ stick) unsalted butter, plus extra for the baking dish

1 quart whole milk

1 pound conchiglie pasta (medium shells)

¼ cup all-purpose flour

1½ teaspoons salt

½ teaspoon freshly ground black pepper

2 teaspoons Dijon mustard

1 pound sharp white cheddar cheese, grated (4 cups)

¼ pound Monterey Jack cheese, grated (1 cup)

}

1. Preheat the oven to 400°F. Butter a large cast-iron skillet or a 9 × 13-inch baking dish, and set it aside.
2. Warm the milk in the microwave or in a saucepan set over medium-low heat.
3. Bring a large pot of salted water to a boil. Add the pasta and cook, following the package directions, until 3 minutes shy of al dente. The pasta should still have a bite to it. Drain, and shake out all the water.
4. In a large pot or Dutch oven, melt the butter over medium-high heat. Whisk in the flour and cook until it is fully incorporated, 1 to 2 minutes. Add the warm milk and whisk gently over medium heat until the mixture has bubbled and thickened enough to coat the back of a spoon, about 10 minutes.
5. Stir in the salt, pepper, mustard, and most of the grated cheese, reserving about 1 cup. Add the pasta and toss to combine. Distribute the mixture evenly in the prepared skillet or baking dish, and sprinkle the remaining cheese over the top. Bake for 20 to 25 minutes, until bubbling and browned. Serve hot.

the mid-twenties

A year has gone by, and we are now "juniors" in the real world. Twelve months closer to our thirtieth birthdays and official, no-joke adulthood. We have a blog. We have boyfriends. We no longer have nine-to-five jobs that involve going to the office. But we do still have the same very small kitchens, and every morning we wake up ready to go to work in them.

We also have this book.

But this little feat, we assure you, in no way brings us closer to being professional chefs. Our expertise is strange and quirky. We continue to cook from need, desire, and request, and we are still developing new methods and recipes for feeding our friends and ourselves in the best way we know—casually, comfortably, and thoughtfully.

We hope we've been able to pass some of this know-how on to all of you, our readers, who have been with us through countless finger food parties, nerdy theme nights, quiet dinners in front of the tube, oven experiments, and all manner of disasters. We hope you've enjoyed your time in our kitchens, at our coffee tables, and on our journey to figuring out what kind of cooks and what kind of people we are. More important, we hope you will continue to share in our meals to come, in new kitchens, maybe in different cities, and certainly beyond quarter-life.

As we celebrate many milestones, we celebrate a year in the life of our food-blogging selves with edible treats: cupcakes filled with raspberries and topped with too much peanut butter frosting.

peanut butter and raspberry cupcakes

Makes 16 cupcakes

We made these cupcakes for the first time the night of Jordana's twenty-fifth birthday. And we made them again at our next party: to celebrate the birth of this book.

{
2 large eggs, at room temperature

²/₃ cup sour cream

1 teaspoon vanilla extract

1³/₄ cups all-purpose flour

½ cup packed light brown sugar

½ cup granulated sugar

½ teaspoon baking powder

½ teaspoon baking soda

½ teaspoon salt

10 tablespoons (1¼ sticks) unsalted butter, at room temperature, cut into rough 1-tablespoon chunks

1 cup frozen organic raspberries

Peanut Butter Frosting (recipe follows)

1 pint fresh raspberries
}

1. Preheat the oven to 350°F. Coat two cupcake (muffin) pans with cooking spray and place liners in 16 cups.
2. In a bowl, whisk the eggs with ⅓ cup of the sour cream and the vanilla.
3. In a separate bowl (the bowl of a stand mixer, if you have one), whisk together the flour, both sugars, the baking powder, baking soda, and salt. Add the butter and the remaining ⅓ cup sour cream. Using a handheld mixer, stand mixer, or your very strong arm, beat this together for nearly 2 minutes. It will be quite creamy. Pour in the egg mixture in two additions, beating for nearly a minute after each. Gently fold in the frozen raspberries.
4. Spoon 3 tablespoons of the batter into each cupcake liner. Bake for 20 to 25 minutes, until the cupcakes bounce back when pressed lightly. Let them cool for 10 minutes in the pans, then transfer to a plate to cool completely. Ice each cupcake with a little more than a tablespoon of the frosting. Garnish each cupcake with a fresh raspberry.

{peanut butter frosting}

Makes 2 cups

½ cup smooth peanut butter, at room temperature

½ cup cream cheese, at room temperature

4 tablespoons (½ stick) unsalted butter, at room temperature

¾ cup confectioners' sugar

1 teaspoon vanilla extract

2 to 3 teaspoons heavy cream or sour cream, if needed

1. In a food processor, combine the peanut butter, cream cheese, butter, confectioners' sugar, and vanilla. Puree until very smooth and uniform in color. If the frosting seems very thick, add the cream or sour cream, 1 teaspoon at a time.
2. Store the frosting in the fridge for up to 3 days. Use it at room temperature. It goes on very smoothly with a knife if, like me, you're not into piping.

ACKNOWLEDGMENTS

Our warmest and most heartfelt thanks are due to the following people:

To Heather Schroder, our agent, who believed in us from the moment she loaded our url on her browser and who has gone to bat and hit homers for us when we were sure we would strike out. We owe thanks to her assistant, Nicole Tourtelot, for her patience and organization.

To Katie Salisbury, our faithful editor, who befriended us at the first meeting we had with her in spite of our failure to bring her a cookie. Thanks go to those who worked on our book at HarperCollins and William Morrow: Cassie Jones, Megan Swartz, Debbie Stier, Mary Schuck, Kathie Ness, Lorie Young, Tavia Kowalchuk, Shawn Nicholls, Christine Maddelena, and Ashley Halsey.

To Josh Shaub, who thought he was getting a cup of coffee at the Ace Hotel when he found himself spending several days at several locations, shooting most of the pictures for this book. We owe him thanks not just for his photos but also for his insights on styling, lighting, business, and more.

To Allison Badea, whose cheer and sweetness motivated us through days of shooting beautiful lifestyle shots, and to Sarah Lederman, who styled us for the photos. We owe thanks to Jonathan Meter, for shooting Magazine Club, and to Alexander Solounias, for capturing our sweets on (digital) film.

We are indebted to Adelaide Mueller for testing our recipes. She carefully and thoroughly went through our ingredient lists and directions and edited them until they were set to go out into the world.

For reading the book and the proposal, for brainstorming titles, and for various words of wisdom, thanks to Stephanie Dishart, Caitlyn Fox, Robert and Aaron Gibralter, JoJo Glick, Lisa Goodrich, Jenny Steingart, Andrew Puschel, Christina Rodriguez, Susan Toepfer, David Warmflash, and Wendy Wecksell.

To Amelia Durand, for getting the book into the hands of so many tastemakers.

To Ina Garten, for writing the remarkable foreword, and for believing in our ability to follow in her footsteps enough so that she wrote, on the eve of an exhausting book tour, that we should be careful what we wished for.

To our friends, for eating our cooking and cooking our food, for coming to potlucks and inviting us to parties, for spreading the BGSK word and asking our advice, and for encouraging us along our way.

To our families, of course—the Eisenpresses and the Blums, the Lapines and the Kernochans—for their love, generosity, and constant enthusiasm.

From Cara: Thanks to Jill, for backseat-driving the best meals; to Kate, for cooking BGSK's recipes (and reading a draft of the book); and to Mom, for encouraging me to cook, write, and always do what I loved. For his appetite, support, and daily entertainment, thanks go to Alex.

From Phoebe: A special thank-you to Sarna, for without her intolerance for unproductive complaining the blog might never have been born; to Mom, for teaching me how to live life creatively through the contents of my pantry and beyond; and to Dad, who always believes I am capable of anything, even when I overcook the rice.

MEALS, MENUS, AND A YEAR'S WORTH OF OCCASIONS

stormy weeknight weather
Yogurt "Carbonara"   34
Peas with White Wine and Butter   27

bollywood movie night
Chana Bateta   262
White basmati rice
Pumpkin Cake with Chai Cream   246

at-home dinner date
Pasta Primavera   133
Mixed Greens with Avocado, Corn, and
    Lemon-Herb Vinaigrette   236
Resignation Brownies   174

weekend fiesta
Dump and Stir Mexican Dip   79
Chicken Enchiladas with Creamy Green
    Chile Sauce   223
Thin and Snappy Ginger Cookies   176

breakup lunch for one
White basmati rice
Coconut Peanut Sauce   264
Steamed or roasted vegetables left over
    from better times (optional)

april showers dinner party
Sweet Pea Crostini   95
Shrimp Risotto with Sweet Peas and
    Leeks   121
Warm Asparagus Salad with Bacon Bits
    and Mustard-Sherry Vinaigrette   238
Chocolate-Flecked Clafloutis   242

mezze finger food party
Classic Hummus   110
White Bean and Rosemary Dip   111
Eggplant Caponata Crostini   97
Pita chips

takeout at home
Vietnamese Fisherman's Stew   205
Basic Fried Rice   257
Baby Arugula Salad with Radishes, Mango,
    and Creamy Ginger Dressing   236

mother's day brunch
Swiss Chard Frittata   32
Corn and Barley Salad with Lemon-Chive
    Vinaigrette   73
Yogurt Cake with Raspberries   187

bff catch-up dinner
Risotto Cakes   265
Warm String Bean Salad with Bacon Bits
    and Mustard-Sherry Vinaigrette   238
Lotus Blondies   173

outlaw theme party
Smoky Chipotle Vegetarian Chili   200
Cornbread   191

hangover brunch for one
Spinach Pie Quesadilla   30
Spiked Lemonade   115

tapas party
Mashed Potato Croquettes   268
Scallop, Chorizo, and Artichoke Paella   215
Pretzel-Toffee Chocolate Bark   45

hangover brunch for ten
Breakfast Burrito Buffet   167
Cherry Tomato Pico de Gallo   169
Guacamole   168
Mexican Hot Chocolate   113

vegetarian cinco de mayo dinner
Spiced Corn Quesadillas   103
Black Bean–Zucchini Enchiladas, with
     Creamy Green Chile Sauce   223

healthful lunch
Green Goddess Soup   50
Roasted Cauliflower and Quinoa Salad   59
Apple Bread   187

ladies' brunch
Baked French Toast   157
Bacon
Baby Spinach with Toasted Pecans, Dried
     Cranberries, and Balsamic
     Vinaigrette   236

why did i invite my boss to dinner?
Butternut Squash and Leek Confit
     Crostini   103
Polenta Steaks with Asparagus Pesto,
     Cherry Tomatoes, and Burrata   203
Blueberry Crisp Tart   242

vegetarian burger party
Chickpea and Walnut Burgers   218
     with Mint Raita   221
Warm Potato Salad (omit the Bacon Bits)
     with Mustard-Sherry Vinaigrette   238
Carrot Cupcakes with Cream Cheese
     Frosting   186–187

weekend sail
Chipotle Hummus   110
Pesto Chicken Salad Sandwiches   64
Apple Bread   187
Pimm's Cup   67

fourth of july beach day
Fusilli with Pomodoro Fresco   68
Warm String Bean Salad with Bacon Bits
     and Mustard-Sherry Vinaigrette   238
Soy-Honey Baked Tofu   76
Classic Chocolate Chip Cookies   180

tropical buffet
Black Bean Dip   111
Lime-Marinated Fish Tacos   197
Cilantro-Lime Crema   198
Mango Salsa   198
Orange Loaf   186

elegant birthday
Smoked Mozzarella Tartlettes   74
Cioppino   226
Crusty bread

Baby Spinach with Toasted Pecans, Dried
    Cranberries, and Balsamic
    Vinaigrette   236
Vanilla-Chocolate Layer Cake   276

labor day mediterranean bbq
Eggplant Caponata Crostini   97
Mediterranean Lamb Burgers with Mint
    Raita   220
Roasted Cauliflower and Quinoa Salad
Cherry-Walnut Chocolate Bark   45

tv dinner
Saucy Tomato or Springy Asparagus
    Pasta   56–57
Peas with White Wine and Butter   27

back to (grad) school dinner party
Butternut Squash and Leek Confit
    Empanadas   104
Chicken Tagine with Sweet Potatoes and
    Golden Raisins   210
Butterscotch Pecan Cookies   178

pre-marathon carbo loading
Noodles with BGSK Peanut Sauce   91
Pumpkin Chocolate Chip Bread   186

big kid brunch for two
Plain Jane Pancakes   143
Apple Compote   159

make-ahead meal
Green Lasagna   212
Ratatouille for Two   129
Cherry-Walnut Chocolate Bark   45

blow-out birthday
Three-Onion Dip with Potato Chips   275
Mini Meatball Subs   281
White Cheddar Mac and Cheese   284
Boozy Cider   112
Peanut Butter and Raspberry
    Cupcakes   287

vegan feast
White Bean and Rosemary Dip   111
Barbecue Lentils with Garlicky Swiss
    Chard   147, 149
Zucchini Bread, replacing the eggs with
    ½ cup applesauce   186

fireside dinner for two
Beer Beef Stew   138
Egg noodles
Warm String Bean Salad with Bacon Bits
    and Mustard-Sherry Vinaigrette   238
Pumpkin Cake with Chai Cream   246

new year's eve dinner
Sexy-Ugly Onion Tart   80
Pork Tenderloin with Roasted Fennel and
    Cider Jus   229
Chocolate Torte   246

PREP SCHOOL

browning meat

Recipe references: *Beer Beef Stew; Chicken Tagine with Sweet Potatoes and Golden Raisins*

To get good color and a crust on your meat, it's important to dry it well with paper towels before you begin; then season the meat with salt and pepper. Coat your cast-iron skillet or Dutch oven (it's best to use a heavy pot or pan) with olive oil, and set it over high heat. Once the oil is nice and hot, add your meat in one even layer, making sure not to crowd the pan. You want each piece to get the maximum amount of heat. Cook on the first side until very well browned—do not flip before that (be patient). Turn the meat and brown on the opposite side. Don't worry if the meat sticks to the bottom of the pan; any wayward bits will only add more flavor to your dish later on. Set the meat aside in a bowl to catch all the juices—you don't want them to go to waste.

caramelizing onions

Recipe references: *Sexy-Ugly Onion Tart; Semi-Sweet Potato Mash with Spiced Caramelized Onions*

Use 2 large yellow onions to generate about 1 cup of caramelized onions. Coat a large skillet with olive oil and sauté the onions over medium heat, stirring very infrequently. Once they soften and begin to brown, reduce the heat to low and allow the onions to caramelize slowly. During this time, it is important to make sure the onions are spread as evenly as possible across the pan. Every few minutes, scrape the bottom and redistribute the onions so each gains the maximum amount of surface area. The intention is to slowly cook the onions by enticing the remaining liquids to sweat out, and for the onions to sweeten by condensing in their own juices. If you stir too often, the onions will turn to mush. This process takes about 40 minutes.

cleaning leeks

Recipe references: *Leek Confit; Shrimp Risotto with Sweet Peas and Leeks*

Trim off the root end and dark green leaves of a leek. Split the leek in half vertically with your knife. Slice each half into half-moons. Place the leeks in a large bowl and fill it to the top with lukewarm water. Use your fingers to briefly agitate the water and leeks, and then allow the leeks to sit in the water for 5 minutes. Use your fingers to gently remove the leeks from the water—do *not* strain or dump the bowl. (As the leeks sit, the sand and dirt will sink to the bottom. By grabbing the leeks with your fingers, you're leaving the dirt in the bottom of the bowl.) This is also a good method for cleaning the leaves of fresh herbs.

cleaning mushrooms

Recipe reference: *Creamy Mushroom Tartines with Chive Scrambled Eggs*

First, discard the mushroom stems. They can be either sliced off or pulled with your fingers. Place the mushrooms on a cutting board with the caps facing up. Use a moist paper towel or kitchen towel (that you don't care about) to gently wipe off any dirt or debris from the caps. Do not rinse the mushrooms, as they'll soak up the water and become rubbery.

cleaning and storing clams and mussels

Recipe reference: *Cioppino*

Clams and mussels should be bought shortly before cooking and from a reputable store with fresh seafood—they are not buy-in-advance ingredients. As soon as you bring the mussels and clams home from the store, remove them from the plastic bags or containers. Place them in a large bowl under running water. Use a paring knife, your fingers, or a sponge to scrape off any grit, beards (the ropy strand on mussels), and barnacles on the shells. If any clams or mussels are open or cracked, discard them. Place the mussels and clams in a large bowl of fresh cool water, and store it in the fridge, uncovered. When ready to cook, carefully remove the clams and mussels with your hands so that the grit and sand remain in the bottom of the bowl. If any clams or mussels remain closed after cooking, remove and discard them.

cooking white rice

Recipe references: *Vietnamese Fisherman's Stew; Chana Bateta; Coconut Peanut Sauce*

Though we love brown rice, we find white rice to be a better go-to because it's so quick to cook. To make 3 to 4 servings of long-grain white rice, combine 1 cup rice and 1½ cups water in a small saucepan and bring to a boil, watching carefully the whole time. As soon as it boils, put the lid on and reduce the heat to the lowest possible setting. Cook for about 15 minutes; then check and give it a stir. Add a little more water if there seems to be none. Cook for 5 more minutes. Then remove from the heat and let it sit with the lid on for 10 more minutes. Add a pinch of salt, fluff with a fork, and serve.

cutting and shaving chocolate

Recipe references: *Chocolate-Flecked Clafoutis*

It's easier than one might think to create restaurant- or bakery-quality chocolate curls for garnishing desserts. By lightly running a vegetable peeler against a corner of a chocolate bar, you can shave curls onto the top of your dessert. Shave the chocolate as you would a carrot or cucumber.

This is easiest if the chocolate is not ice-cold. To make chunks of chocolate for cookies or the clafoutis, use a serrated knife to cut through a large piece—you'll find this much more productive than trying to chip off pieces with a chef's knife.

defrosting and draining spinach

Recipe references: *Dump and Stir Mexican Dip; Panko-Crusted Spinach Dip*

If you've done your grocery shopping a day in advance, place the frozen spinach in a bowl and leave it in the fridge or on the counter to defrost. When ready to use, remove the spinach from the bag or box and place in your least favorite kitchen towel (or a bunch of paper towels). Fold the spinach in the towel to form a bundle and squeeze until all the water has been released. Unwrap, and use the dry greens in your recipe.

Alternatively, if you need to use the frozen spinach immediately, empty the package into a pot or Dutch oven and place it over medium heat. Cover with a lid and allow the spinach to defrost, stirring occasionally. Once almost all the frozen chunks have broken down, remove the lid and let the moisture evaporate completely. Then, if needed, use the towel method to make sure any excess moisture is removed.

deglazing the pan

Recipe reference: *Scallop, Chorizo, and Artichoke Paella*

Deglazing is a crucial step in adding flavor to a dish. After browning, sautéing, or searing, add wine and use a spatula to scrape up all the caramelized bits on the bottom of the pan (called sucs). Adding the sucs to the wine as it boils increases the flavor of a dish tremendously.

deveining shrimp

Recipe reference: *Shrimp Risotto with Sweet Peas and Leeks*

It is often much more economical to buy shrimp that haven't been deveined, or even with their shells on. If you buy shell-on, slip the shells off first. Then, holding one shrimp in one hand, use your other hand to run a sharp paring knife all along the spine of the shrimp, revealing the dark vein. With the tip of the knife, gently lift it out, then pull it firmly to remove from the shrimp. If the vein breaks, simply pull it up from elsewhere. Toss the shells and the veins, wash the shrimp, and proceed with the recipe.

handling jalapeños and other chile peppers

Recipe references: *Creamy Green Chile Sauce; Cherry Tomato Pico de Gallo*

The seeds are the hottest part of a chile pepper, and most recipes will tell you to remove them. But also deceptively spicy are the ribs—the white portions of the interior of the pepper. You'll probably want to run your knife along the pepper and remove these as well, but if you are a spice freak, then feel free to leave in the ribs and the seeds.

Make sure to wash your hands very thoroughly after handling hot peppers, and *do not* touch your eyes or any other sensitive parts of your or anyone else's body long after the prepping is done.

making bacon and bacon bits

Recipe reference: *Warm Vegetable Salad with Bacon Bits and Mustard-Sherry Vinaigrette*

As long as we're not frying bacon for millions, we do it stovetop. Place a large nonstick skillet over medium-high heat and lay the bacon slices flat in the pan. Cook until the bacon is brown and crispy, 3 to 4 minutes, flipping once or twice. Remove to a paper towel to drain. If you are cooking for a large crowd, line as many baking sheets as you need with foil. Lay the bacon out in one layer and cook in a preheated 400°F oven for about 20 minutes, flipping once, until the bacon is crispy.

To make bacon bits, crumble cooled bacon slices with your fingers until they're bite-size. After you cook bacon, you'll have a good deal of leftover fat in the pan. Either use a paper towel to wipe the oil from the pan and discard, or save it in a glass jar and use in place of olive oil to give vegetable and grain dishes an added smoky flavor.

making garlic croutons

Recipe reference: *Crispy Romaine with Cherry Tomatoes, Garlic Croutons, and Green Goddess Dressing*

A little bit of crouton makes the lettuce leaf go down, and homemade clearly trumps purchased. Cut a loaf of good country bread (crusts removed) into 1-inch cubes, enough to generate 3 cups. Toss with ¼ cup olive oil and ½ teaspoon salt. Arrange the cubes in a single layer on a parchment-lined cookie sheet, and bake at 350°F for 10 minutes. Then add 2 cloves garlic, minced, and toss to distribute. Bake for another 15 minutes, turning once, until they are evenly golden. Serve warm or at room temperature, within a few hours of baking.

making garlic paste

Recipe reference: *Provençal Baked Chicken*

To make garlic paste, crush a clove of garlic with the flat side of your knife, pressing down hard. The garlic will flatten and then you can easily peel away the skin and discard it. Sprinkle a pinch of kosher salt on top of the flattened clove. Mince the garlic as usual, using the salt to help turn the garlic into a paste. Towards the end, use the flat side of your knife to press on the minced clove, pulling the knife towards you to really grind the garlic. If needed, add an extra pinch or two of salt. When you use garlic paste, be sure to reduce the salt in your recipe.

making vinaigrettes by hand

Recipe reference: *Side-Dish Salads*

If you don't have a food processor, it is very easy to make a dressing or vinaigrette by hand. Place the vinegar and any emulsifying ingredients in the bottom of your salad bowl. (Emulsifying ingredients include mayonnaise and Dijon mustard. Lemon juice can be classified as a vinegar.) Whisk together with the seasoning (salt, ginger, etc.) until combined. Add the olive oil in a thin stream, whisking continuously until the ingredients begin to emulsify and become a dressing. Whisk in any additional ingredients, such as honey, herbs, shallots, avocados, or scallions, until combined. If the dressing begins to separate, rapidly whisk the ingredients together until re-formed. Just before serving, add the salad ingredients on top of the dressing, and toss. (Alternatively, make the dressing in a small bowl and then pour it down the side of the larger bowl filled with salad.)

mashing potatoes

Recipe references: *Semi-Sweet Potato Mash with Spiced Caramelized Onions; Mashed Potato Croquettes*

Everyone has their own personal preference when it comes to mashed potatoes, and they really are quite versatile. To make them, first place the peeled potatoes (cut into 2-inch pieces if you want the process to go faster) in a large pot of salted water and bring to a boil over high heat. Cook the potatoes until tender. (Use a fork or knife to test tenderness—if the knife or fork goes in easily, the potatoes are done. If there's resistance, the potatoes need more time.) Drain in a colander, reserving about ½ cup of the cooking liquid, and return the potatoes to the pot for mashing.

When it comes to the mashing, use whatever technique your kitchen affords you. Phoebe finds that a ricer or food mill creates the best texture, but this equipment is not a small-kitchen necessity. You can use a masher or simply a fork or spoon. If you don't have a dedicated tool, cook the potatoes a few extra minutes to make mashing easier. Add butter, milk, cream, stock, or cooking water as needed to thin the mixture to the desired consistency. The potatoes will become smoother as you add the liquids. Never puree potatoes because they can get gluey.

One pound of potatoes will leave you with just over 1 cup of mashed potatoes.

measuring flour

Recipe reference: *All the baked goods in the Giving section*

Measuring flour properly will help ensure that your baked goods consistently come out perfect. Use a large spoon to scoop flour into your measuring cup until it's overflowing (do this over a clean bowl to save the excess flour). Don't pack the flour in. Level off the top of the cup with a straight-bladed knife. Return any extra flour to the bag. If you bake a lot, you might want to purchase a large jar or canister to hold your flour—that way you can measure directly over the container.

melting chocolate

Recipe reference: *Chocolate Bark*

We most often melt chocolate in the microwave, but if you don't own one, you will need to use a double boiler on the stove. To melt chocolate in the microwave, place the chocolate in a microwave-safe bowl or container and zap it on medium-high power for 20 seconds at a time, stopping to stir between intervals. You don't want the chocolate to overheat, so stir it when it starts to look melted. The stirring motion will melt any last few solid pieces.

To use a double boiler, fill a pot with 1 inch of water and bring it to a simmer. Place the chocolate in a heatproof bowl that sits firmly atop the pot of simmering water. Make sure the bottom of the bowl does not touch the water. Stir the chocolate occasionally with a heatproof spatula until melted.

parboiling

Recipe references: *Hash Browns; Warm Vegetable Salad*

Parboiling is a way of precooking so that an ingredient can be ready to go when you need it. It works really well for tough green vegetables and potatoes. Bring a pot of salted water to a boil. Add the vegetables and cook until nearly tender but not completely cooked through (for potatoes, 5 to 10 minutes; for asparagus, 1 to 2 minutes; for string beans, 2 to 3 minutes). Drain in a colander and rinse under cold water (this is called shocking). You can parboil a day or two in advance and keep the cooked vegetables in a sealed plastic container in the fridge.

preparing butternut squash

Recipe reference: *Roasted Butternut Squash Quesadillas*

The skin on a butternut squash is tough and intimidating to remove. Make sure you have a very sharp, preferably flat-faced, peeler. Peel the skin off the vegetable so all you see is the bright orange flesh. With a large chef's knife, cut off the top and bottom. Halve the squash crosswise—one part will be the skinnier top area, the other will be fatter and contain the seeded interior. The top of the squash can be diced. Stand the bottom half upright and halve it lengthwise. With a spoon, remove the seeds and pulpy interior. Then prepare as directed.

removing fresh corn kernels from the cob

Recipe references: *Corn and Barley Salad with Lemon-Chive Vinaigrette; Spiced Corn; Cornbread; Mixed Greens with Avocado, Corn, and Lemon-Herb Vinaigrette*

To make any of these recipes using fresh corn instead of canned or frozen, shuck one ear of corn and remove all the hair from the cob. Stand the cob upright in a large mixing bowl, and run your knife along it, shaving off the kernels into the bowl. Make sure not to take off the tough pieces of the cob. Two ears of corn should yield about 1 cup of kernels.

roasting chicken breasts

Recipe references: *Pesto Chicken Salad Sandwiches; Side-Dish Salads*

Here's how to roast a standard chicken breast to top a salad, use inside an enchilada, or become part of a sandwich. Arrange 3 boneless, skinless chicken breasts (about 1½ pounds total) on a baking sheet. Brush the chicken with olive oil, season with salt and pepper, and roast in a 350°F oven for 30 minutes. Cool for 10 minutes. Then cut the chicken into chunks or shred it with your hands. Boneless, skinless chicken breasts tend to be pricier than regular halved chicken breasts with the bone in and skin on. If you choose to buy bone-in, skin on, roast them for an additional 5 to 10 minutes. Three breasts yields about 3 cups cubed chicken.

toasting nuts and sesame seeds

Recipe references: *Chickpea and Walnut Burgers; Roasted Cauliflower and Quinoa Salad; Chicken Tagine with Sweet Potatoes and Golden Raisins; Noodles with BGSK Peanut Sauce*

Two senses come into play when toasting nuts: sight and smell. Nuts can be toasted in a dry skillet over low to medium heat, or a dry baking sheet in a 350°F oven. Make sure they are in an even layer in the skillet or on the sheet, and allow them to toast slowly. Watch the nuts carefully to make sure they don't brown or burn too quickly—that's when you use your nose. Nuts are done toasting when fragrant and golden. Sesame seeds toast particularly quickly.

whipping cream

Recipe references: *Chocolate-Flecked Clafoutis; Chocolate Torte*

If a dessert appears to need a little extra something, whip some cream. Pour 1 cup heavy whipping cream into a large bowl. Add as little as 1 teaspoon confectioners' sugar and as much as 3 tablespoons, depending on your taste. Using a whisk or an electric mixer, beat the cream until its consistency has changed from liquid to solid. When you lift up your whisk or a beater, the cream should form a soft peak. You can flavor the cream with vanilla extract, espresso powder, ground cinnamon, mint extract, or grated lemon zest before whipping.

INDEX